THE NEW YANKEE WORKSHOP

kids' stuff

THE NEW YANKEE WORKSHOP

kids' stuff

Companion
to the public
television series

norm abram

Little, Brown and Company
Boston   New York   Toronto   London

FIRST EDITION

Illustrations by John Murphy and Mary Reilly
Photographs by Richard Howard
Designed by Barbara Werden

Library of Congress Cataloging-in-Publication Data
Abram, Norm.
    The New Yankee workshop kids' stuff / Norm Abram. — 1st ed.
        p.   cm.
    Includes index.
    ISBN 0-316-00493-6. — ISBN 0-316-00492-8 (pbk.)
    1. Children's furniture — Design and construction. I. New
Yankee workshop (Television program) II. Title.
TT197.5.C5A2   1998
684.1'04 — dc21   97-17889

10 9 8 7 6 5 4 3 2 1

RRD-OH

Published simultaneously in Canada by Little, Brown & Company (Canada) Limited

Printed in the United States of America

To all the kids who watch *The New Yankee Workshop*.
Soon you will be mastering tools and woodworking techniques yourselves,
and building projects such as these.

contents

acknowledgments

MY BOOKMAKING doesn't keep pace with my woodworking. In 1994, when my fourth book (*Outdoor Projects*) went to the printer, Russell Morash and I were producing the seventh season's shows. Here is my fifth book in 1998, concurrent with the broadcast of the first of the tenth season's shows. (Russ, the executive producer and director, and I certainly didn't expect when we launched the first season that *New Yankee* would be going strong a decade later.) Between these two woodworking books, however, I have published two books on other topics, *Norm Abram's New House* and *Measure Twice, Cut Once: Lessons from a Master Carpenter*.

I've taken special pleasure in preparing a book of projects that grown-ups can make for kids. Many of my past projects have been based on actual pieces that Russ and I found in museums or shops or private homes. Two of the kids' projects are inspired by museum pieces: an alphabet wagon in the Peabody-Essex Museum in Salem, Massachusetts, and a cradle at Old Sturbridge Village in Sturbridge, Massachusetts. Richard Howard showed me his antique marble roll, which inspired mine. The dollhouse is a scale model of the workshop studio where *The New Yankee Workshop* is videotaped. Otherwise, the pieces in this book are of my design.

In the ninth television season we altered our system of producing the measured drawings that are an essential component for replicating my projects in home workshops. I used to render all of the preliminary drawings myself, which saddled my busy schedule with truly difficult time demands. Then I delivered the preliminaries to John Murphy, who brought the talent of an artist and the training of a draftsman to the execution of the final drawings. Now we are relying on computer-generated drawings, which saves me valuable time. But the drawings for this book were done by John Murphy under the former system, and I thank him for years of valuable service to our projects.

Richard Howard continues to be our photographer of choice, taking process shots of the projects that I make specifically for the development of the book chapters. Richard also takes the gallery shots of the finished pieces. In this book we have introduced some extra characters, kids who are enjoying the stuff I've made for them. Kate Cohen rounded up the cheerful volunteers to be photographed, including the contented baby in the cradle who was a last-minute substitute after the original candidate was sidelined with a cold.

I delivered text and illustrations for this volume, as for all its predecessors, to William D. Phillips at Little, Brown and Company, who handed it on to these colleagues: Susan Canavan, who edited the text and captions; Stephen Lamont, who copyedited the work; Teresa LoConte, who supervised production; and Barbara Werden, who designed the volume. Professionals all, I thank you.

Finally, thanks to all of the folks at WGBH Educational Foundation in Boston, Massachusetts, who coproduce *The New Yankee Workshop* with Morash Associates. Our efforts would yield nothing without the generous support of corporations that underwrite the initial production costs.

marble roll

"Here's the New Yankee Workshop version of a classic marble roll. Made entirely of wood, it offers plenty of action and plenty of noise — more than enough to keep a child (or an adult like me) happy for hours."

2 toy chest

❝As a parent, I can appreciate the value of a good toy chest. It's a place to keep the children's playthings out of sight. Here's a toy chest that does double duty; you can store toys in it and you can also play on it. If you have a toy-totin', checker-playin' youngster in your home, you may want to build a toy chest like this one.❞

3

alphabet wagon

"Alphabet blocks have been a favorite toy for countless generations of children. It's nice to know some things never change. And what better container to store blocks in than a little wagon to pull around the house?"

4 easel

"Every child has a natural talent for art. Kids will spend hours and hours happily drawing with crayons and markers and paint. If you have a budding Rembrandt in your home, you might want to build this easel."

"Every child dreams of having his or her own playhouse. Here's one that's guaranteed to be a sure-fire hit with the children in your family. Don't wait too long to get started on this one — your kids (or your grandkids) won't be little forever."

5 playhouse

"I wanted to build a special dollhouse, one that could be enjoyed by boys as much as by girls, by adults as well as by children. I studied old dollhouses and looked at some new ones. I thought long and hard, and here's the result: a true 1/16th scale model of (you guessed it) the New Yankee Workshop!"

6 dollhouse

7 cradle

"These days, when the average American family has only one or two children, most people don't think of a cradle as an essential piece of furniture. Yet in today's age of gadgets and modern devices, there's still nothing that soothes a baby more than being rocked to sleep in a cradle."

8 **trundle bed**

"If you have a child's bedroom that's too small for twin beds, you might consider a trundle bed. They are great space savers, and kids really love them for sleepovers. If you don't need the extra bed, the trundle makes a great place for storing toys or blankets."

storage units

"Any parent can tell you that chaos is the natural state of a child's room, so this handsome storage unit is a dream come true. These three units provide plenty of room, and it's furniture your children can grow with, too, being as useful for college students as it is for preschoolers."

THE NEW YANKEE WORKSHOP

kids' stuff

Rules for Safe Woodworking

Woodworking is inherently dangerous. Failure to follow commonsense safety procedures can result in serious injury. Here are some simple, but important, rules for safe and sensible woodworking.

- Read, understand, and follow all the safety instructions that come with the tools you buy.

- Be alert and aware. Stop working if you're fatigued or distracted, and never use alcohol or other mind-altering substances when working in the shop.

- Protect your eyes and ears. Always wear safety glasses or goggles. Wear earmuffs or earplugs to protect your hearing from permanent damage by loud machinery.

- Secure your clothing. Roll up your sleeves, remove any jewelry, and make sure your shoelaces are securely tied.

- Use a push stick when feeding small pieces of stock through a table saw, jointer, or other machine.

- Keep dust levels under control by using dust-collection bags on tools and periodically cleaning your workshop. Wear a dust mask when doing extended sanding.

- Light your work area well. Good lighting is essential to safe work. Lights and power tools should run on separate circuits so a blown fuse won't leave you in the dark with a still-spinning power tool.

introduction

Children usually love simple toys best and play with them longest. This isn't because children are simple — it's because they have so much imagination.

DR. BENJAMIN SPOCK

DO YOU HAVE A SPECIAL CHILD in your life? A grandchild or two, a nephew who thinks you're the greatest — maybe a little one who's still on the way? If you are also a woodworker, chances are that you've already thought about making something special for that child. Wooden toys, playroom furniture, a dollhouse, just a simple set of blocks, may come to mind as possibilities. Of course, you can buy these things everywhere, but for that special child, you'll want to make it yourself.

Making something imaginative, unique, and fun for the precious little people in your life is the idea behind this book. In it you'll find classic wooden toys like an old-fashioned marble roll and an alphabet wagon complete with handcrafted blocks. You'll find heirloom keepsakes like a traditional hooded cradle; functional favorites like a two-sided easel and a toy chest with a built-in checkerboard; and practical furniture like storage units and a trundle bed that will help you make the most of the space in your home. There's even a playhouse complete with a front porch, window box, and Dutch door that will be the envy of every kid in the neighborhood! I've even included plans for a dollhouse that's a 1/16 scale model of the New Yankee Workshop itself!

As you can imagine, I had a lot of fun designing and making these projects for children. I know you'll enjoy making them — and giving them, too. Children appreciate having something all their own; something unique. Each project here could easily be personalized with your child's name or painted specially by a talented friend or relative. Imagine how you'll feel when your toddler proudly says, "Daddy made it!" about a favorite toy.

If your children are old enough, you might want to think about letting them help you while you work on a project or give them a little project of their own to work on. Give them a task they can do safely and successfully — hammering nails is always a favorite. Older kids can manage basic hand tools — a block plane, handsaw, or drill (with close supervision, of course). It's a good opportunity to help the child build self-confidence and whet his or her interest in making things. I think back on how much I learned from my own father, just passing him the things he needed as he worked on a project.

Playing It Safe

Safety is the most important consideration when building toys or furniture for children. Be sure that the project you're making is appropriate for the age of the child. Toys that might be perfectly safe for older children can be dangerous for toddlers and babies. Sharp edges, dangling cords, slamming lids, loose fasteners, or other small parts can all pose a significant safety hazard for small children.

Babies and toddlers tend to put things in their mouths, so it's especially important to avoid small parts that might cause a child to choke. A good rule of thumb is that any object smaller than a Ping-Pong ball can be a hazard for children three years old and younger. If you don't have a Ping-Pong ball for comparison, you can use a plastic 35mm film canister as a "go"/"no go" measuring device for small parts. If a part is small enough to fit in the film canister, it's small enough to choke on and shouldn't be used on toys for young children.

Lids on toy chests are another potential safety hazard. Lids should have "soft down" lid supports that prevent the lid from slamming on hands or heads. Chests that are large enough for kids to hide in must never have a lock or latch that might trap a child inside.

Balusters on playhouse railings and bars on bunkbeds should never be spaced more than 3½ inches apart, to prevent a small child's head from getting trapped in between.

Never use old paints on kids' toys or furniture. Old paint (or new paint in some countries outside the United States) may contain lead — a poisonous metal that can cause brain damage. I use only nontoxic, water-base finishes on toys for young children. All finishes contain some solvents and other volatile compounds when wet, but these toxic components evaporate as the finish cures, leaving behind a safe, dried finish.

That's enough talk, let's go down to the shop and start building. What are you waiting for? The kids won't be little forever!

Happy and safe woodworking.

NORM ABRAM
The New Yankee Workshop

- **Keep your shop clean.** Always clean the shop at the end of the day so that you'll return to a clean workshop.

- **Normalize the work area** after each step of the project is completed. Clean up the clutter and put away everything that isn't needed for the next step of the project.

- **Put power tools away correctly.** Unplug the cord and wind it carefully.

- **Never use a tool station,** such as a table saw, as a workbench or a piece of furniture.

- **Clamp or secure the piece you're working on.** Don't take shortcuts.

- **Don't make a tool do a job it's not meant to do.**

- **Keep your tools sharp.** A sharp tool will prevent you from "forcing" the tool to do the work.

- **Ventilate your finishing area.** Solvent fumes are toxic and flammable. Ensure adequate ventilation and wear a respirator mask if you spray on your finishes.

- **Eliminate fire hazards.** Don't use or store flammable solvents around pilot lights, heaters, or any other source of a spark or flame that could ignite the vapors. Remove oily finishing rags from the shop immediately after use — they can ignite by spontaneous combustion.

marble roll

project planner

Time: 2 days

Special hardware, tools, and materials:

- (6) 1½-in.-dia. marbles, rubber balls, or wooden balls
- (3) 6 x 1-in. screws
- (2) 8 x 1¼-in. screws
- (2) 6 x 3/4-in. screws

Wood:

(1) 10-ft. 6/4 x 3 poplar
Cut 5 pieces 24 in. long. Mill according to plan for chutes.

(1) 1-ft. 1 x 10 poplar
Cut according to plan for catcher base.

(1) 2½-ft. 1 x 4 poplar
Rip and joint 3 in. wide and cut 2 pieces 12 in. long for feet.

(1) 6-ft. 1 x 3 poplar
Cut one piece 23 in. long for top piece. Cut 2 pieces 22½ in. long for sides.

(1) 2-ft. 1 x 2 poplar
Rip and joint to 1¼ in. wide, then rip 2 pieces 1/8 in. thick and 1¼ in. wide for catcher wall. (Safety note: Use a "zero clearance" table-saw insert and a push stick for this operation, as explained in text.)

HERE'S THE NEW YANKEE WORKSHOP version of a classic marble roll. Made entirely of wood, it offers plenty of action and plenty of noise — more than enough to keep a child (or an adult like me) happy for hours. Best of all, batteries are not required. It's a wonderful gift for an old-fashioned Christmas.

I got the idea from a friend's antique marble roll, but I modified the design to make it safe for young children to play with. Toddlers can choke on a regular-size marble, so to play it safe, my design calls for extra-large, 1½-in.-dia. marbles — too large for a small child to swallow. Unfortunately, these large marbles are also expensive, so wooden or rubber balls may also be used — although the sound they make as they roll down the chutes isn't quite as appealing as the satisfying *clack* of glass marbles.

When it came to picking a wood for the marble roll, my first choice was poplar. Poplar machines nicely, is a great wood to paint, and can even be stained. But best of all, I made the entire marble roll out of bits and pieces from my scrap pile; the wood didn't cost me a dime. Frugality is a virtue for a Yankee like me.

Shaping the Chutes

The first thing to do is make the 5 troughs or chutes that the marbles will roll in. I cut 5 pieces 24 in. long from a 10-ft. length of 6/4 (1½ in.) x 3 poplar (see Project Planner). Next I joint one wide face flat on each piece and then run the

1-A Major Anatomy and Dimensions
Note: Sand to remove all sharp edges and corners.

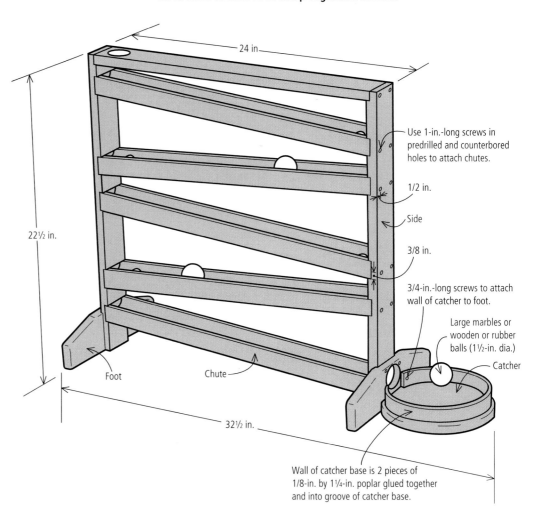

24 in.

22½ in.

Use 1-in.-long screws in predrilled and counterbored holes to attach chutes.

1/2 in.

Side

3/8 in.

3/4-in.-long screws to attach wall of catcher to foot.

Large marbles or wooden or rubber balls (1½-in. dia.)

Catcher

Foot

Chute

32½ in.

Wall of catcher base is 2 pieces of 1/8-in. by 1¼-in. poplar glued together and into groove of catcher base.

pieces through my thickness planer to take them down to a 1⅜-in. thickness. Back on the jointer, I square up one narrow edge on each piece. Then I rip and joint them to a finished width of 2½ in. (*drawing 1-B*).

Now it's time to rough out a semicircular trough down the length of each piece. I can do this on the table saw with my twin-blade wobble dado cutter. It's adjustable for different widths, and I simply turn the hub to change the setting.

On the end of one chute, I draw the profile of the trough — a half circle with a 7/8-in. radius. I hollow out this trough with a series of cuts. For the first cut, I set the dado head for a 5/16-in. width. I adjust the table-saw rip fence to position the blade in the middle of the trough and set the blade height to cut as close as possible to my pencil line (about 13/16 in. above the table). I make one pass down the middle of each piece, at the deepest point of the trough (*photo 1-1*).

Next I tilt the blade 10 degrees, lower the height a little, and move the fence a bit closer to the blade to start forming the semicircle. I make one pass, then flip the piece around and run the other end through — making a mirror-image cut on the opposite side of the chute (*photo 1-2*).

For the third pass, I tilt the blade to 25 degrees and adjust the height to cut

1-B Chutes

Note: 5 required, one does not have a hole.

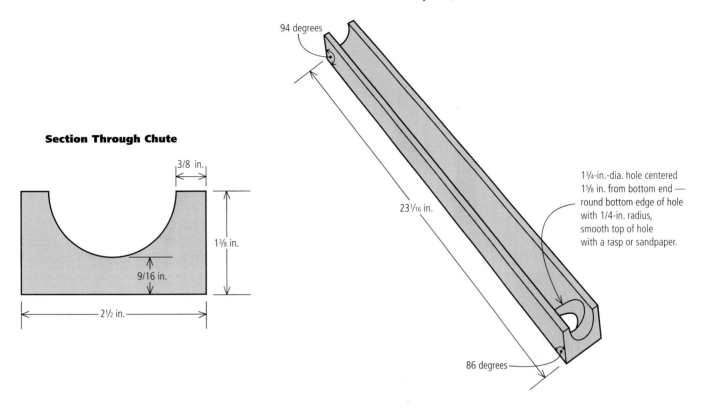

Section Through Chute

94 degrees

3/8 in.

1³/₈ in.

9/16 in.

2½ in.

23¹/₁₆ in.

1³/₄-in.-dia. hole centered
1⁵/₈ in. from bottom end —
round bottom edge of hole
with 1/4-in. radius,
smooth top of hole
with a rasp or sandpaper.

86 degrees

close to the pencil line. Here, too, I make one pass and then flip the workpiece
end for end to make a second cut on the opposite side (*photo 1-3*).

Tilting the blade to 40 degrees, I make a fourth pass, cutting on each side as
before. At this stage, the trough is almost complete — just one more pass left to
go.

Finally, I bring the blade back up to a 15-degree angle. I lower it a little bit
and make a cut along each side of the trough, cutting on the edge of the chute
that's farthest away from the rip fence (*photo 1-4*).

The saw doesn't cut a perfectly smooth trough, so now it's time for a little
elbow grease to tidy things up. First I start with some very coarse 60-grit sandpaper wrapped around a big dowel as a form (*photo 1-5*). Next I switch to 80-grit
paper and then to 120-grit. It takes time and some patience to sand all the
troughs smooth.

Milling the Sidepieces

Next up are the 2 vertical sidepieces that receive the chutes (*drawings 1-A and
1-C*). From a 6-ft. length of 1 x 3 poplar, I cut 2 pieces 3/4 in. x 2½ in. x 22½ in.
long (*drawing 1-C*). From the same piece of poplar, I also mill the top piece
(*drawing 1-E*).

The chutes fit into angled dadoes in these sidepieces. The dadoes have to
match the slope of the chutes, which is 4 degrees. I lay out the 5 angled dadoes
on each sidepiece (*drawing 1-C*). Now if I simply put a dado head in the table
saw and tilted it to 4 degrees, I'd end up with a sawtooth-bottomed dado instead

1-1
I rough out a semicircular trough down the lengh of each chute by making a series of cuts with a twin-blade wobble dado head. For the first cut, I set the dado head for a 5/16-in. width and make one pass down the middle of each chute, at the deepest point of the trough.

1-2
For the second cut, I tilt the blade 10 degrees, lower the height a little, and move the fence a bit closer to the blade to start forming the semicircle. I make one pass, then flip the piece around and run the other end through — making a mirror-image cut on the opposite side of the chute.

1-3
For the third pass, I tilt the blade to 25 degrees and adjust the height to cut close to the pencil line. Here, too, I make one pass and then flip the workpiece end for end to make a mirror-image cut on the opposite side.

1-4
After making a fourth cut with the blade at 40 degrees, I tilt the blade to a 15-degree angle and make the final cut shown here along each side of the trough, cutting on the edge of the chute that's farthest away from the fence.

1-5
I smooth up the saw cuts with some 60-grit sandpaper wrapped around a big dowel as a form. Next I switch to 80-grit paper and then to 120-grit. It takes time and patience to sand all the troughs smooth.

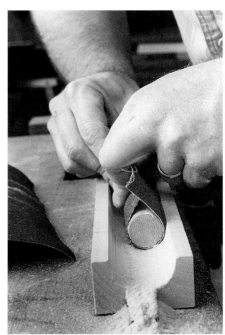

1-C Sides

Note: Dadoes for chutes are 1/4 in. deep, cut at a 4-degree angle. Arrow indicates direction of dado.

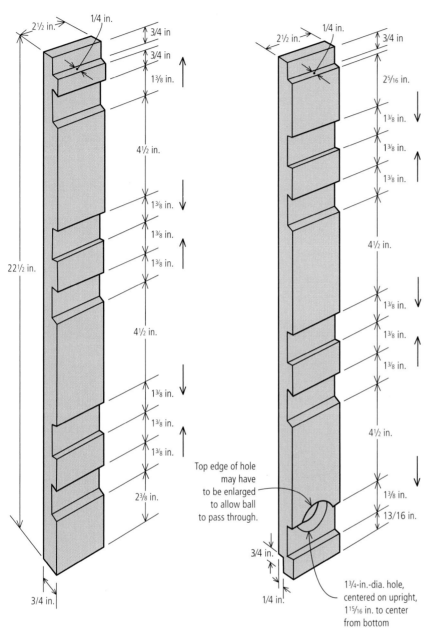

2½ in.

1/4 in.

3/4 in
3/4 in
1⅜ in.

4½ in.

22½ in.

1⅜ in.
1⅜ in.
1⅜ in.

4½ in.

1⅜ in.
1⅜ in.
1⅜ in.

2⅜ in.

3/4 in.

2½ in.

1/4 in.

3/4 in
2⁵⁄₁₆ in.

1⅜ in.
1⅜ in.
1⅜ in.

4½ in.

1⅜ in.
1⅜ in.
1⅜ in.

4½ in.

1⅜ in.
13/16 in.

Top edge of hole may have to be enlarged to allow ball to pass through.

3/4 in.

1/4 in.

1¾-in.-dia. hole, centered on upright, 1¹⁵⁄₁₆ in. to center from bottom

1-D Foot

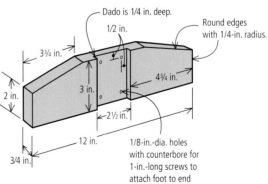

Dado is 1/4 in. deep.

1/2 in.

Round edges with 1/4-in. radius.

3¾ in.

2 in.

3 in.

4¾ in.

2½ in.

12 in.

3/4 in.

1/8-in.-dia. holes with counterbore for 1-in.-long screws to attach foot to end

1-6
The chutes fit into angled dadoes in the vertical sidepieces. To make the shoulder cuts for the dadoes, I tilt my table-saw blade to 4 degrees and adjust the blade for a 1/4-in.-deep cut. I use my miter gauge to feed the stock into the blade. Some of the dadoes angle in the opposite direction, so I have to turn the workpiece around and cut from the opposite side.

1-7
With the shoulder cuts complete, I replace the saw blade with my dado head set at 90 degrees and adjusted for a 1/4-in.-deep cut. Using the miter gauge to feed the stock, I clean out the material between the shoulder cuts.

1-8
I make the sloped cuts on the top of each foot on my power miter box with the blade pivoted about 15 degrees. To support the workpiece safely, I place a piece of plywood about 6 in. wide and a foot long on the miter-box table and position the left-hand end against a saw stop. The right-hand end of the plywood gives me a nice wide support for the workpiece.

of a flat-bottomed one. What I have to do is make the shoulder cuts first with a regular saw blade, then switch to a dado head to clean out the wood in between the shoulder cuts.

To make the shoulder cuts, I tilt my table-saw blade to 4 degrees and adjust the blade for a 1/4-in.-deep cut. I use my miter gauge to feed the stock into the blade (*photo 1-6*). Some of the dadoes angle in the opposite direction, so I have to turn the workpiece around and cut from the opposite side.

With the shoulder cuts complete, I replace the saw blade with my dado head. I return the blade to 90 degrees and adjust it for a 1/4-in.-deep cut. Using the

1-E Top

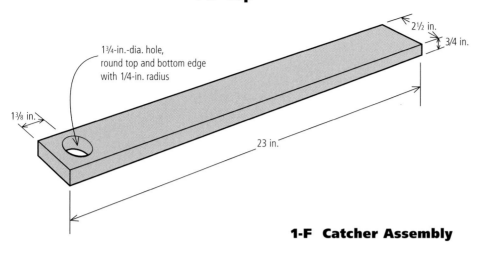

2½ in.

3/4 in.

1¾-in.-dia. hole,
round top and bottom edge
with 1/4-in. radius

1⅜ in.

23 in.

1-F Catcher Assembly

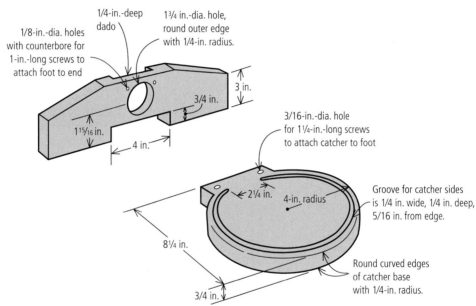

1/8-in.-dia. holes
with counterbore for
1-in.-long screws to
attach foot to end

1/4-in.-deep
dado

1¾ in.-dia. hole,
round outer edge
with 1/4-in. radius.

3 in.

3/4 in.

1¹⁵⁄₁₆ in.

4 in.

3/16-in.-dia. hole
for 1¼-in.-long screws
to attach catcher to foot

2¼ in.

4-in. radius

Groove for catcher sides
is 1/4 in. wide, 1/4 in. deep,
5/16 in. from edge.

8¼ in.

3/4 in.

Round curved edges
of catcher base
with 1/4-in. radius.

miter gauge once again to feed the stock, I clean out the material between the shoulder cuts (*photo 1-7*).

While the dado head is still in the table saw, I need to cut a rabbet along the top of each sidepiece to receive the top piece (*drawing 1-C*). I also need to mill a rabbet along the bottom of one sidepiece where the catcher will attach (*drawings 1-A and 1-C*). Both rabbets are 1/4 in. deep and 3/4 in. wide.

Making the Feet

The feet of the marble roll are 12-in. lengths of 1 x 4 poplar ripped and jointed to a 3-in. width (see Project Planner). The sidepieces fit into 1/4-in. by 2½-in. dadoes in these feet (*drawings 1-D and 1-F*). Since the table saw is already set up with the dado head adjusted for a 1/4-in.-deep cut, I might as well mill these dadoes now, before I cut the feet to shape.

With the dadoes cut, I'm ready to make the sloped cuts on the top of each

1-9
To drill the holes in the chutes, I set up my drill press with a 1¾-in.-dia. Forstner bit and a straightedge clamped across the table so each hole will be in the center of the piece. I drill from the flat underside of each chute, going gently to avoid tearout.

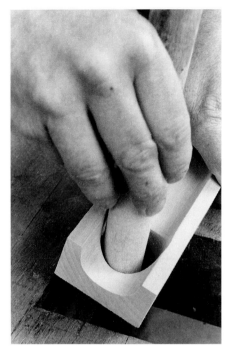

1-10
After drilling, I smooth up the sharp edges of the holes with a wood rasp and finish up with some adhesive-backed 120-grit sandpaper wrapped around a 1-in.-dia. dowel.

1-11
On the bottoms of the chutes, I ease the edges of the holes with a 1/4-in.-radius roundover bit in my router. A nonslip router pad holds the workpiece securely.

1-12
Here, I'm drilling the pilot holes and counterbores for the screws that fasten the chutes to the vertical sidepieces. To make sure the screw holes all line up neatly, I clamp a straightedge across the drill-press table so the holes are all centered 1/2 in. from the edge of the sides.

1-13
Now for a little assembly. Working on one sidepiece, I spread glue in each dado joint and put the chutes and top piece in place, fastening each with two 1-in.-long square-drive screws. With everything in place, I flip the assembly over and attach the other sidepiece with glue and screws.

foot (*drawing 1-D*). I do this on my power miter box. In order to make the cut, I need to support the end of the foot against the miter-box fence and pivot the blade about 15 degrees. But because the workpiece is only 3 in. wide, doing so would not be very stable and certainly not safe. To make the cut safely, I place a piece of plywood about 6 in. wide and a foot or two long on the miter-box table and rest the left-hand end against a saw stop (*photo 1-8*). The right-hand end of the plywood gives me a nice wide support for the workpiece as I make the angled cuts on both feet.

Next I install a 2-in.-dia. drum sander in my drill press and use it to knock off the sharp corners of the feet. I just freehand it, trying for a nice even radius by eye. After that, I ease all the edges of the feet except for the bottom with a 1/4-in.-radius roundover bit in my router. I place the feet on a nonslip router pad so I don't have to bother with clamps.

Completing the Chutes

Now it's time for me to cut the chutes to length. I need to make a 4-degree angled cut on both ends (*drawing 1-B*). It's important that all 5 chutes are exactly the same length, so I'll set a saw stop on my miter box to make sure they are. The procedure is simple.

I swing the miter-saw blade 4 degrees to the right and cut the left-hand end of one chute. Then I carefully measure 23 1/16 in. and cut the opposite end to the same angle, parallel to the first cut. Without moving the workpiece, I bring the saw stop up against the left-hand end of the chute and lock it in place. Now, after cutting an angle on one end of the other chutes, all I have to do is position the angled end of these pieces against the stop to make sure they will be exactly the same length as the first one.

Marking and Drilling the Holes

I think it's a good idea at this point to dry-fit together all the pieces to make sure they're the correct length before I put in any glue or fasteners. It also gives me an opportunity to mark the location of all the holes.

I need to drill a 1¾-in.-dia. hole at the bottom (downhill) end of 4 of the chutes. The bottom chute does not require a hole. I also need to drill a hole in the top piece (*drawing 1-E*) and a hole through the front foot and sidepiece (*drawings 1-A and 1-C*) so the balls can go into the catcher.

To drill the holes, I set up my drill press with a 1¾-in.-dia. Forstner bit and a straightedge clamped across the table so each hole will be in the center of the piece. I drill the hole in the top first. Next I drill the chutes, drilling from the flat underside of each chute and going gently to avoid tearout (*photo 1-9*).

Before I drill the hole through the front foot and sidepiece, I temporarily fasten these parts together with four 1-in.-long screws. I drill and countersink holes for the screws, attach the foot, and bore a 1¾-in.-dia. hole through both parts.

Now I need to smooth up the sharp edges of the holes I just drilled. In the troughs, I use a wood rasp to remove any tearout and finish up with some adhesive-backed 120-grit sandpaper wrapped around a 1-in.-dia. dowel (*photo 1-10*). On the bottoms of the chutes, I ease the edges of the holes with a 1/4-in.-

1-14
To cut the circular base of the catcher, I replace the base plate of my router with a homemade circle-cutting jig made of 1/4-in. plywood. This jig cuts circles up to 20 in. in diameter.

1-15
To rout the catcher base, I clamp the board between bench dogs with a couple of scrap pieces underneath to elevate the wood off the bench top. Then I attach the circle-cutting jig with a single screw in the center point of the circle. I lower the 1/2-in. straight bit into the wood and swing the jig around in a circle to rout the base.

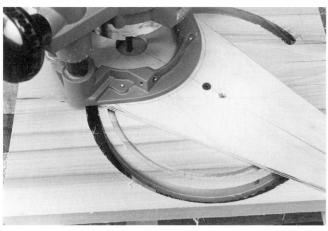

1-16
Next I unscrew the jig, replace the 1/2-in. bit with a 1/4-in. straight bit, and reattach the jig through the second pivot hole. I rout a 1/4-in.-deep groove for the catcher wall.

1-17
After routing for the catcher groove wall, I cut out the projection, or "throat," with a backsaw.

radius roundover bit in my router (*photo 1-11*). I also use the router to round over the hole in the top and the front foot.

Ready, Set, Assemble

I'm ready to drill pilot holes and counterbores for the screws that fasten the chutes to the sides. To make sure the screw holes all line up neatly, I clamp a straightedge across the drill-press table so the holes are all centered 1/2 in. from the edge of the sides (*photo 1-12 and drawing 1-A*). The screw holes are centered 3/8 in. up from the bottom edge of each dado.

A little assembly is next. Working on one sidepiece, I spread glue in each dado joint and put the chutes and top piece in place, fastening each with two 1-in.-long square-drive screws. With everything in place, I flip the assembly over and attach the other sidepiece with glue and screws (*photo 1-13*). Next I put one foot on — the one opposite the catcher.

Now for a test drive. (I just can't resist.) The marble roll works great. The only thing left to make now is the catcher.

Making the Catcher

The catcher is made from a piece of 3/4-in. poplar, cut in a circle, with a 1/4-in.-thick wall that fits into a routed groove (*drawings 1-A and 1-F*). When I built the prototype marble roll, I tried bending the wall from a single dry strip of 1/4-in. poplar. It just broke. Next I tried dry bending some thinner strips, and they broke, too. I finally hit paydirt when I tried soaking two 1/8-in.-thick poplar strips in water for a while before bending them. That approach worked fine.

The first step in making the catcher is to square up a 2-ft. length of straight-grained, 1 x 2 poplar on the jointer. Then I rip and joint it to a width of 1¼ in. Next I rip two 1/8-in. by 1¼-in. strips from this piece. To do so safely, I install a thin-kerf blade on the table saw and replace my standard metal table-saw insert with a homemade "zero clearance" wooden insert. I make this insert by raising the spinning blade through a piece of wood to create a blade slot with zero clearance on either side. This way, there's no slot for these narrow pieces to fall into. Using a thin push stick, I rip two 1/8-in. by 1¼-in. strips. I soak these strips in water while I make the catcher base.

The base is an 8-in.-dia. circle with a projection, or "throat," on the end that attaches to the front foot. I cut the circle using my router, a 1/2-in.-dia. straight bit, and a homemade circle-cutting jig made of 1/4-in. plywood (*photo 1-14*). This jig cuts circles up to 20 in. in diameter.

To mount the circle-cutting jig on my router, I remove the router's plastic base plate and attach the jig with the same screws. Then I install a 1/2-in. straight-cutting router bit and measure 4¼ in. from the center of the bit to locate the pivot point on the centerline of the circle-cutting jig. I drill a 1/8-in.-dia. hole and countersink through the top side of the jig at this point. I drill a second pivot hole 3⁹⁄₁₆ in. from the center of the bit to use later for routing the groove for the wall.

I lay out the catcher base on a 1-ft.-long piece of 1 x 10 poplar. I clamp the board in the bench dogs with a couple of scrap pieces underneath to elevate the wood off the bench top. Next I attach the circle-cutting jig with a single screw in

1-18
The throat of the catcher fits into a notch in the bottom of the front foot. I hold the foot against my table-saw miter gauge and nibble away the material to form the notch.

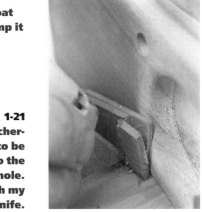

1-19
After soaking the thin catcher-wall strips in water, I place the 2 strips together and make a little notch with my utility knife at one end so the end of the wall will extend beyond the groove.

1-20
I apply glue to the throat of the catcher and clamp it in place to the foot.

1-21
The ends of the catcher-wall strips need to be trimmed a little so the marbles can clear the hole. I trim the ends with my utility knife.

the center point of the circle. I start up the router, lower the bit into the wood, and swing the jig around in a circle to rout the base (*photo 1-15*).

Now I unscrew the jig, replace the 1/2-in. bit with a 1/4-in. straight bit, and reattach the jig through the second pivot hole. I rout a 1/4-in.-deep groove for the wall (*photo 1-16*).

With the groove complete, I cut out the projection, or "throat," with a backsaw (*photo 1-17*) and trim off the excess length with my miter box. Then I ease the edges of the circle with a 1/4-in.-radius roundover bit. I don't round the edges of the throat.

The throat of the catcher fits into a notch in the bottom of the front foot (*drawing 1-F*). With a pencil and square, I lay out the notch on the foot. Then I hold the foot against my miter gauge and nibble away the material to form the notch (*photo 1-18*).

Now for some bending. I remove the wet strips from the water, place the 2 strips together, and make a little notch with my utility knife at one end so the end of the wall will extend beyond the groove (*photo 1-19*). I slip the strips into the groove, bend them around, and tap them into place with a hammer.

When I've bent the strips around the groove, I trim off the excess length with

1-22
After trimming the ends of the strips, I drill and counter-bore through the catcher wall for two 3/4-in. screws that secure the catcher wall to the foot.

1-23
I drill and install two 1¼-in. screws to secure the catcher to the foot.

my utility knife and make a mark to cut a notch at the opposite end as well. I have to remove the strips from the groove to cut this second notch.

After all that, I'm ready to glue the strips into place. First I apply glue to the mating faces of the strips. I also put glue in the groove. Now I reinstall the strips in the groove, tapping them home with a hammer. A clamp helps to hold things in place.

Next I apply glue to the throat of the catcher and clamp it in place to the foot (*photo 1-20*). At this stage, the ends of the strips need to be trimmed a little so the marbles can clear the hole. I trim the ends with my utility knife (*photo 1-21*). With the strips trimmed, I drill and counterbore through the catcher wall for two 3/4-in. screws that secure the catcher wall to the foot (*drawing 1-A and photo 1-22*).

Next I gently tilt the marble roll upward to drill and install the two 1¼-in. screws that secure the catcher to the foot (*photo 1-23*). Now I can remove the long clamps and install a few small clamps to squeeze the two laminations of the catcher wall together. I let the glue dry overnight and do the final sanding in the morning.

Putting on Paint

There's only one color that's right for this game: bright, fire-engine red. I chose a color called Regatta Red. This water-base polyurethane paint is pretty tough; what's more, it doesn't require a primer. I apply 3 coats, sanding lightly between each with some 220-grit paper. When I'm finished, my marble roll is bright and shiny and ready to roll.

2

toy chest

project planner

Time: 5 days

Special hardware and tools:

(1) 1½-in. by 48-in. polished brass piano hinge
(2) "Soft Down" lid supports (item #69732 from The Woodworkers' Store, Medina, MN)
(4) 1/2-in. rubber tack bumpers
J roller
(10) 8 x 1¼-in. screws
Dovetailing jig

Wood:

(2) 12-ft. 1 x 10 C select pine
From each length cut 2 pieces 45 in. long and 2 pieces 20 in. long. Joint edges and glue up in pairs for sides of chest.

(1) 8-ft. 1 x 6 C select pine
Rip and joint one piece 3⅝ in. wide. From that piece cut a 44-in. length and two 19-in. lengths for lid curb. Joint remaining strip to 1⅝ in. and cut 2 pieces 17¼ in. long for fillers under lid. Cut remaining piece according to plan for front of lid and tray.

(1) 6-ft. 1 x 4 C select pine
Rip and joint into 2 pieces 1⅝ in. wide for base trim.

(1) 18-in. by 60-in. piece of 3/4-in. MDO plywood
Cut one piece 17⅝ in. x 43¼ in. for lid. Cut one piece 12 in. x 12 in. for storage tray.

(1) 18-in. by 42-in. piece of 1/2-in. MDO plywood
Cut one piece 17³⁄₁₆ in. x 41³⁄₁₆ in. for bottom of chest.

A S A PARENT, I can appreciate the value of a good toy chest. It's a place to keep the children's playthings out of sight. Here's a toy chest that does double duty; you can store toys *in* it and you can also play *on* it. The chest has a wooden checkerboard inlaid into the top, and the checkers are stored in a wooden tray that slides under the lid. Special "soft down" lid supports let the lid close slowly and gently so there's no risk of fingers getting hurt. If you have a toy-totin', checker-playin' youngster in your home, you may want to build a toy chest like this one.

The sides of the chest are made from a clear grade of pine known as C select. Select softwood grades such as C select or D select cost a lot more than common No. 2 or No. 3 construction-grade pine, but the boards are practically free of knots, pitch pockets, and similar defects — so there's very little waste.

For the top and bottom of the chest, I chose MDO (medium-density overlay) plywood — a durable, paper-faced plywood that makes an excellent surface for paint.

Making Panels

A hundred years ago, woodworkers who built a chest like this one could easily find pine boards 18 in. or 24 in. wide. That's nearly impossible to do today, so I glue up narrower boards to make the 16-in.-wide sides of the chest.

When edge-gluing boards to make a panel, I try to match the grain as closely

2-A Major Anatomy and Dimensions

(1) 2½-ft. 8/4 x 3 mahogany
Plane to 1½-in. thickness. Joint both edges, then rip one 1/4-in.-thick piece from each edge. Crosscut these 2 pieces into 1½-in. squares (32 required) for dark checkerboard squares.

(1) 2½-ft. 8/4 x 3 maple
Plane to 1½-in. thickness. Joint both edges, then rip one 1/4-in.-thick piece from each edge. Crosscut these 2 pieces into 1½-in. squares (32 required) for light checkerboard squares.

(1) 1-ft. 1 x 5 mahogany
Rip and joint 2 pieces 1 in. wide for tray tracks. Rip remainder to 1⅝ in. wide to make runners for tray.

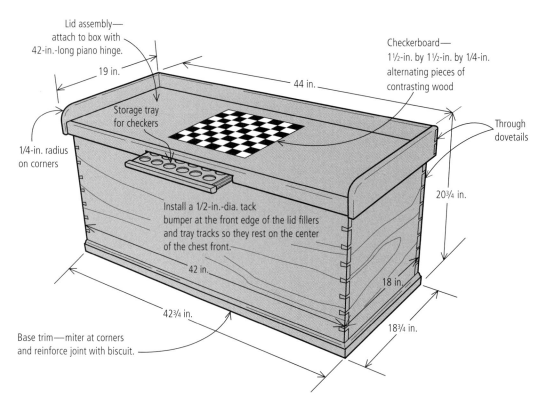

Lid assembly—attach to box with 42-in.-long piano hinge.

19 in.

44 in.

Checkerboard— 1½-in. by 1½-in. by 1/4-in. alternating pieces of contrasting wood

Storage tray for checkers

Through dovetails

1/4-in. radius on corners

20¾ in.

Install a 1/2-in.-dia. tack bumper at the front edge of the lid fillers and tray tracks so they rest on the center of the chest front.

42 in.

18 in.

42¾ in.

18¾ in.

Base trim—miter at corners and reinforce joint with biscuit.

as possible. I find that if I cut all the pieces from the same board, they usually match pretty closely. In this case, I cut all the pieces for the 4 sides of the chest from two 12-ft. 1 x 10 boards (see Project Planner). From each 12-ft. board, I cut 2 pieces 45 in. long and 2 pieces 20 in. long. Then I straighten and square the edges on my jointer.

With today's modern glues and good clamps, edge joints like these — long grain to long grain — are strong enough with just glue. But you know me . . . a little extra reinforcement doesn't hurt, so I install biscuits about every 10 in. along the edge joints, laying them out so they won't show or get cut through when I trim the panels to size. The biscuits also help align the boards so they won't slip around when I tighten the clamps. After cutting the slots, I spread on some glue, pop in the biscuits, and clamp the boards together.

When the glue is dry, I unclamp the panels and take off the excess dried glue with a scraper. Now I can sand the panels flat with my random-orbit sander and get ready to cut them to size.

The first step in truing up a panel is making one of the long edges square and straight by running it over the jointer (*photo 2-1*). The next step is to rip the panel to width. I set the table-saw rip fence 16⅛ in. away from the blade — 1/16 in. wider than the finished width. In a minute I'll remove this extra 1/16 in. of material on the jointer. Holding the jointed edge against the rip fence, I rip the panels to width (*photo 2-2*). Then, with my jointer set for a 1/16-in. cut, I joint the edge I've just sawn to make a panel that's exactly 16 in. wide.

Now I can cut the panels to length. My homemade panel cutter is the best tool for this job. I square one end of the panel, measure off the length I need (42 in. for the front and back, 18 in. for the ends), and cut (*photo 2-3*).

2-1
The first step to truing up a panel is making one of the long edges square and straight by running it over the jointer.

2-2
I rip the panels to width, holding the jointed edge against the rip fence.

2-3
My homemade panel cutter is the best tool for cutting panels to length. I square one end, measure off the length I need, and cut off the other end.

Next I cut the plywood bottom and top of the chest to size. The bottom is made of 1/2-in. MDO plywood, and the top is a piece of 3/4-in. MDO plywood. I rip these panels to width — 17¾₆ in. for the bottom, and 17⅝ in. for the top. Then I cut them to length with my panel cutter. The bottom is 41¾₆ in. long, and the top is 43¼ in. long.

Dovetails with a Router

The corners of the chest are joined with through dovetails. Dovetails take their name from the distinctive shape of the "tail," the part of the joint that resembles the fanned-out tail of a dove. (The part of the joint that interlocks with the tail is called the pin.) Through dovetails are the strongest of all corner joints. They're mechanically strong because the interlocking parts can pull apart in one direction only. And they make a very strong glue joint because there's plenty of long-grain surface contact.

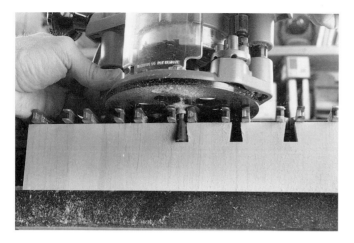

2-4
To mill the tails on the front and back of the chest, I set up my router with a guide bushing and a 1/2-in. dovetailing bit and clamp the front panel in the dovetailing jig. I adjust the bit so it extends 3/4 in. below the underside of the jig's fingers and then guide the router around the jig's fingers to cut the tails.

2-5
For the pins — the parts of the joints that interlock with the tails — I simply flip the finger assembly around and replace the dovetailing bit with a 5/16-in.-dia. straight bit. I set the bit 3/4 in. below the underside of the jig's fingers and mill the pins on the end panels of the chest.

2-B Corner Dovetail Layout

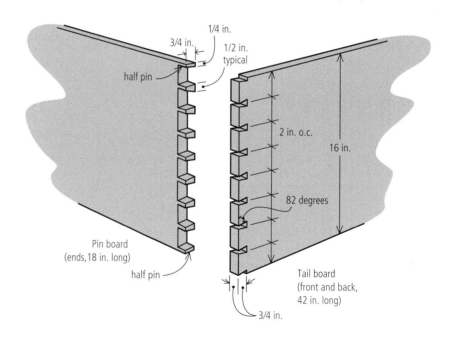

It isn't very difficult to cut through dovetails by hand with a backsaw and chisel, but it does take some practice to get nice gap-free joints. I prefer the accuracy and speed of a router and a dovetailing jig. The jig I use has adjustable fingers that allow me to vary the width and spacing of the tails and pins.

The front and back of the chest are too long to fit into my dovetailing jig unless I first raise my workbench about 6 in. higher than normal. I do this by slipping some blocks under the feet of the bench.

I want the tails of the joints to be visible on the front and back of the chest because they're more attractive than the pins. I'll start by milling the tails first. I adjust the jig's fingers to give me 8 tails spaced 2 in. o.c. (*drawing 2-B*). I set up my router with a guide bushing and a 1/2-in. dovetailing bit and clamp the front panel in the jig. I adjust the bit so it extends 3/4 in. (the stock thickness) below the underside of the jig's fingers and then rout the tails (*photo 2-4*).

With the tails cut on one end, I turn the piece around and rout the tails on the other end. Next I rout the tails on the back panel of the chest with the same jig and router settings.

Now for the pins. To cut them on my jig, I simply flip the finger assembly around and replace the dovetailing bit with a 5/16-in.-dia. straight bit. I set the bit 3/4 in. from the underside of the jig's fingers and rout the pins on a test piece to check their fit with the tails. After making any necessary adjustment to the jig to improve the fit, I mill the pins on the end panels of the chest (*photo 2-5*). Note that there's a half pin at the top and bottom edge of the panel (*drawing 2-B*). That's all there is to it.

Grooves for the Bottom

The plywood bottom of the toy chest fits into a 1/2-in.-wide groove in the 4 sides (*drawing 2-C*). I mill this groove with my plunge router, using a 1/2-in.-dia. straight bit and an edge guide.

The grooves in the front and back of the chest must stop 1/4 in. short of the end of the panels or an ugly notch will show in the dovetails. I set the depth stop on my plunge router for a 3/8-in.-deep cut and adjust the edge guide to position the groove 1/2 in. from the bottom edge of the panels (*drawing 2-C*). I plunge the bit into the wood at the start of the cut and lift the bit out at the end (*photo 2-6*). Next I rout 1/2-in. grooves on the 2 end pieces. These grooves can run the full width of the panel because the cut won't show when the chest is assembled.

Building the Box

I'm about ready to glue up the dovetails. But before I do any assembly, I finish-sand all the inside surfaces with my random-orbit sander.

Before I apply the glue, I put some masking tape along the edges of the dovetail joints on the inside of the chest (*photo 2-7*). The tape prevents excess glue from spreading on the inside of the chest, making it much easier to clean up later.

With a small brush, I spread glue on the tails and the pins, working on one corner at a time. I work as quickly as possible so the glue doesn't have time to set before the joint is put together. Now I assemble each corner, joining the 2 end pieces to the back of the chest. Then I slip the plywood bottom into its grooves and glue on the front. I tap the joints home with a mallet and then put on clamps. I check for square by measuring across diagonal corners: when the diagonals are equal, the box is square.

Before setting the box aside to dry, I carefully peel off the masking tape from the inside corners. I want to get this tape off before the glue dries. I clean up any remaining wet glue with a damp sponge.

2-C Section Through Bottom of Chest

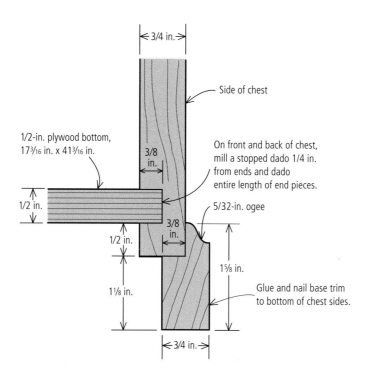

Side of chest

1/2-in. plywood bottom, 17³/₁₆ in. x 41³/₁₆ in.

3/8 in.

On front and back of chest, mill a stopped dado 1/4 in. from ends and dado entire length of end pieces.

3/4 in.

5/32-in. ogee

1/2 in.

3/8 in.

1/2 in.

1⅝ in.

1⅛ in.

Glue and nail base trim to bottom of chest sides.

3/4 in.

2-D Lid Assembly

Note: Attach lid supports to filler and sides of chest per hardware instructions.

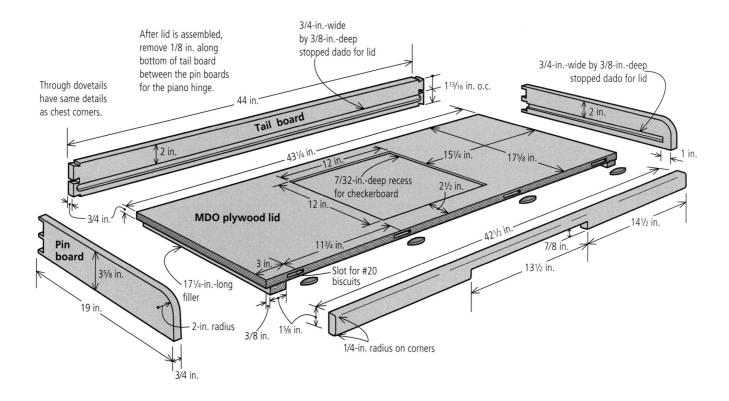

After lid is assembled, remove 1/8 in. along bottom of tail board between the pin boards for the piano hinge.

3/4-in.-wide by 3/8-in.-deep stopped dado for lid

3/4-in.-wide by 3/8-in.-deep stopped dado for lid

Through dovetails have same details as chest corners.

44 in.

Tail board

1¹³/₁₆ in. o.c.

2 in.

2 in.

43¼ in.

12 in.

15¼ in.

17⅝ in.

1 in.

7/32-in.-deep recess for checkerboard

2½ in.

MDO plywood lid

12 in.

3/4 in.

11¾ in.

42½ in.

14½ in.

Pin board

3⅝ in.

3 in.

Slot for #20 biscuits

7/8 in.

13½ in.

19 in.

17¼-in.-long filler

2-in. radius

3/8 in.

1⅝ in.

1/4-in. radius on corners

3/4 in.

2-6
To mill the stopped grooves in the front and back of the chest, I set my plunge router for a 3/8-in.-deep cut and adjust the edge guide to position the groove 1/2 in. from the bottom edge. I plunge the bit into the wood at the start of the cut and lift the bit out at the end.

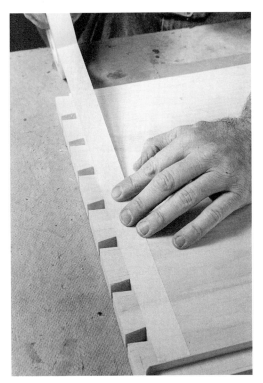

2-7
Before I apply any glue to the joints, I put some masking tape along the edge of the dovetails on the inside of the chest. The tape prevents excess glue from spreading onto the inside of the chest, making it much easier to clean up.

Making the Lid

The lid of the toy chest is made of 3/4-in. MDO plywood with a pine curb on the back and the ends to keep things from falling off (*drawings 2-A and 2-D*). In the middle of the lid is an inlaid checkerboard made of 1½-in.-square pieces of contrasting hardwood set into a routed recess.

Here's the procedure for routing the recess. With a pencil and square, I lay out the 12-in.-square recess on the plywood (*drawing 2-D*). Next I set up my plunge router with a 3/4-in.-dia. straight bit and an edge guide. I set the bit for a 7/32-in. depth. The first step is to rout along the sides of the recess. I clamp a straightedge across the plywood so that the distance from the straightedge to the layout line is equal to the distance between the edge of my router base and the near edge of the bit. When I guide the router along the straightedge, the bit cuts right to the layout line (*photo 2-8*). I use this procedure to make the right and left sides of the recess.

To rout the front and back sides of the recess, I switch to a longer straightedge clamp. Here I don't have room to position the straightedge outside the layout lines, so I have to place it inside. Now the distance from the layout line to the straightedge must equal the distance between the edge of the router base and the far side of the bit. I rout one side of the recess and reposition the straightedge to rout the last side (*photo 2-9*).

To remove the material between these cuts, I start with my router at one cor-

2-8
I rout the left and right sides of the checkerboard recess by clamping a straightedge across the plywood so the distance from the straightedge to the layout line is equal to the distance between the edge of my router base and the near edge of the bit. When I guide the router along the straightedge, the bit cuts right to the layout line.

2-9
To rout the front and back sides of the recess, I switch to a longer straightedge clamp, placing it inside the line. Now the distance from the layout line to the straightedge must equal the distance between the edge of the router base and the far side of the bit. I rout one side of the recess and reposition the straightedge to rout the last side.

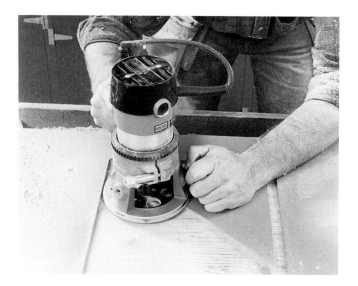

2-10
I remove the remaining material between these cuts, starting with my router at one corner and moving back and forth diagonally to the opposite corner, always leaving enough wood to support the base of the router.

ner and move back and forth diagonally to the opposite corner, always leaving enough to support the base of the router (*photo 2-10*). A little time cleaning up the corners with a sharp chisel completes the recess.

The next thing to do is make the pine curb for the back and sides of the top (*drawings 2-A and 2-D*). I rip and joint some 1 x 6 stock 3⅝ in. wide and cut 3 pieces to length (*drawing 2-D*). The back corners will be joined with through dovetails, and I cut these joints using my dovetailing jig and router. I set the jig's fingers to give me 2 tails in the back curb, spaced 1¹³⁄₁₆ in. o.c. (*drawing 2-D*).

I also need to mill 3/4-in.-wide grooves in the curb pieces to receive the plywood lid. The groove in the back curb is stopped at both ends; the side-curb grooves stop only at the front (*drawing 2-D*). I set up my plunge router with an edge guide and a 3/4-in.-dia. straight bit and use the same procedure I used to rout the stopped grooves for the bottom the chest.

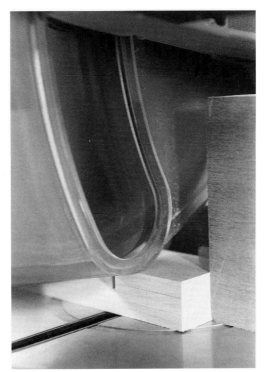

2-11
To make the checkerboard squares, I rip two 1/4-in. strips from a 1½-in.-thick piece of wood — one from each edge. To do this safely, I install a homemade "zero clearance" wooden table-saw insert so there's no slot for these narrow pieces to fall into. A push stick keeps fingers safely away from the blade.

2-12
I crosscut the 1/4-in.-thick strips into 1½-in. squares. I clamp a stop on my power miter-box fence, cut the two 1/4-in. strips in half, and stack 3 pieces together to give me 3 squares with each cut.

With the grooves completed, I band-saw a 2-in. radius on the front corners of the side-curb pieces and sand the cut smooth with the drum-sander attachment on my drill press. The last step is to ease the top edges of the rails with a 1/4-in.-radius roundover bit. On the side-curb pieces, I stop the roundover 3/4 in. from the back end.

Now for a little assembly. First I dry-assemble the parts to test the fit. Then I spread glue on the dovetails and in the grooves. I set the plywood lid in the back curb first, then put on the side curbs and clamp the assembly together.

Checkerboard Squares

The checkerboard is made of 1/4-in.-thick squares of hardwood. I chose maple for the light squares and mahogany for the dark ones because I like the contrast.

Here's how I make the squares for the checkerboard. I start with a 2½-ft. length of 8/4 x 3 mahogany and run it through my surface planer until it's 1½ in. thick. Next I joint both edges straight and square.

The next step is to rip two 1/4-in.-thick strips — one from each edge. To do so safely, I replace my standard metal table-saw insert with a homemade "zero clearance" wooden insert, which I make by raising the spinning blade through a

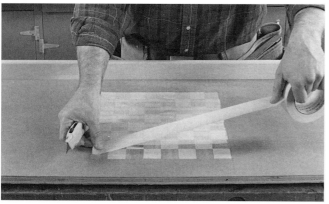

2-13
I cover the entire checkerboard with some wide masking tape. This makes it possible to pull the checkerboard out as a unit so I can apply contact cement and then reset it into the mortised area.

2-14
After taping over the entire surface, and making "witness marks" on one corner of the board and lid with a pencil so I can put it back the same way, I just lift the checkerboard out of the recess.

2-15
I apply contact cement to the back of the checkerboard and to the inside of the recess, put the checkerboard in position, and use a J roller to press the wood down and make sure the glue bond is complete.

piece of wood to create a blade slot with zero clearance on either side. This way, there's no slot for these narrow pieces to fall into. Next, with a push stick, I rip 2 pieces 1/4 in. thick by 1½ in. wide (*photo 2-11*).

Now I need to crosscut these strips into 1½-in. squares. I clamp a stop on my power miter-box fence, cut the two 1/4-in. strips in half, and stack 3 pieces together to give me 3 squares with each cut (*photo 2-12*).

I repeat this procedure to make the contrasting light-colored squares from a piece of maple (see Project Planner).

Now I'm ready to dry-fit the squares in the mortised area. I alternate the grain of the maple and mahogany squares by 90 degrees.

I could take the pieces out of the recess and glue then back in one at a time, but that would take forever. What I'm going to do instead is cover the entire checkerboard with some wide masking tape (*photo 2-13*). This makes it possible to pull out the checkerboard as a unit so I can apply some contact cement and then reset it into the mortised area. After taping over the entire surface, I make "witness marks" on one corner of the checkerboard and on the lid with a pencil so I can put the checkerboard back the same way. Now I just lift it out (*photo 2-14*).

I brush contact cement into the recess and on the back of the checkerboard. (*Fire Hazard:* Contact-cement vapors are extremely flammable. Avoid all sparks

2-E Storage Tray

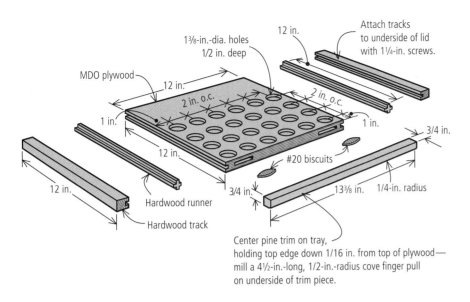

Attach tracks to underside of lid with 1¼-in. screws.

1⅜-in.-dia. holes ½ in. deep

MDO plywood

12 in.

12 in.

2 in. o.c.

2 in. o.c.

1 in.

1 in.

3/4 in.

#20 biscuits

12 in.

12 in.

3/4 in.

13⅜ in.

1/4-in. radius

Hardwood runner

Hardwood track

Center pine trim on tray, holding top edge down 1/16 in. from top of plywood— mill a 4½-in.-long, ½-in.-radius cove finger pull on underside of trim piece.

2-F Section Through Track and Runner

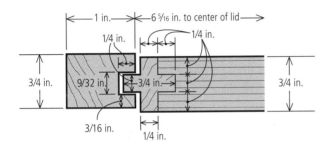

1 in.

6 5/16 in. to center of lid

1/4 in.

1/4 in.

3/4 in.

9/32 in.

3/4 in.

3/4 in.

3/16 in.

1/4 in.

or flames, including pilot lights. Use adequate ventilation and wear a respirator rated for organic solvents.) When the contact cement is dry to the touch on both surfaces, I'm ready to go. I line up the witness marks and drop the checkerboard into place. I use a J roller to press the wood down and to make sure the glue bond is complete (*photo 2-15*). Then I just peel off the tape and sand the entire surface flat with my belt sander. I finish up with my random-orbit sander, which won't show any scratch marks on the cross-grained squares.

Checker-Storage Tray

The checkers are stored in a sliding tray that fits under the lid (*drawings 2-A and 2-E*). The tray is made from a piece of 3/4-in. MDO plywood. Hardwood runners on each side of the tray ride in hardwood tracks attached to the under-side of the lid. All these pieces can be made on the table saw.

The first step is to mill a 1/4-in. groove on 2 opposite edges of this tray. I set up my dado head for a 1/4-in.-wide cut and run it down the middle of a piece of plywood scrap to test the setup. I make adjustments until the resulting groove is exactly centered. When the setup is right, I cut the grooves in the tray.

Next I mill the groove in the edges of the two 1-in.-wide hardwood tracks that support the tray (see Project Planner and *drawings 2-E and 2-F*). I set the rip

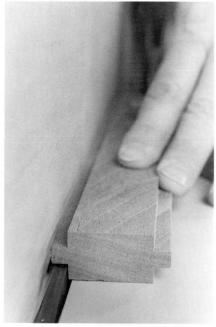

2-16
To mill the runners, I set my dado head for a 1/4-in. width, raise the blade 1/4 in. from the table, and cut a rabbet along one edge of the stock. I flip the piece upside down and make another pass on the opposite side, creating a 1/4-in.-thick tongue. Here, I'm milling an identical tongue on the opposite edge of the piece.

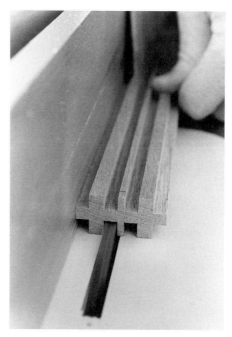

2-17
After milling the tongues on the runner, I mill two 1/4-in. grooves in the top and bottom with my dado head.

2-18
I attach the 2 storage-tray tracks to the bottom of the lid with glue and 1¼-in. screws so that the tray slides smoothly back and forth.

2-19
I drill 24 holes in the storage tray for the checkers. I lay out the holes 2 in. o.c. and drill them on my drill press with a 1³⁄₈-in.-dia. Forstner bit set for a 1/2-in.-deep hole.

fence 3/16 in. away from the blade and make one pass on each piece. Then I move the fence 1/32 in. farther away from the blade and make a second pass, being sure to keep the same edge as before against the fence. The finished groove is 9/32 in. wide and 1/4 in. deep.

Now I'll make the hardwood runners that ride in these tracks (*drawings 2-E and 2-F*). I'll mill both runners from one 1⅝-in.-wide piece of mahogany (see Project Planner) by making a series of grooves with my dado head and then ripping the piece in 2 down the middle.

To set up for the runners, I adjust my dado head for a 1/4-in.-wide cut and attach an auxiliary wooden fence on my table-saw rip fence so I can position the fence right against the blade. Now I raise the blade 1/4 in. from the table and mill a rabbet along one edge of the stock. Next I flip the piece upside down and make another pass on the opposite side, creating a tongue exactly 1/4 in. thick. I test-fit this tongue in the groove in the plywood tray and make any necessary adjustments before I proceed. When the fit is right, I mill an identical tongue on the opposite edge of the piece (*photo 2-16*).

For the next step, I move the rip fence 1/2 in. from the blade and mill a groove 1/2 in. from the edge. I flip the stock end for end and cut another groove on the same side. Turning the workpiece over, I run 2 more grooves on the opposite side (*photo 2-17*). Now I replace the dado head with a regular saw blade and rip the piece down the middle to form the 2 cross-shaped runners (*drawing 2-F*).

The next thing to do is fasten these runners to the edges of the tray (*drawing*

2-20

The pine trim piece on the front edge of the lid is notched out in the center for the checker-storage tray. The safest way to cut this notch is to clamp the piece of pine to the table-saw rip fence and raise the blade up through the workpiece. It takes 2 passes to cut the full length, so after making one cut, I lower the blade, unclamp the piece, move it forward slightly, and reclamp it in place. Then I raise the blade through the wood again to complete the rip cut.

2-21

After making the rip cut, I set the blade for a 3/4-in.-deep cut and make 2 crosscuts with my miter gauge to complete the notch.

2-F). No nails — just glue and some clamps. I also attach the 2 tracks to the bottom of the lid with glue and three 1¼-in. screws so that the tray slides smoothly in between them (*photo 2-18*).

I also attach two 1⅛-in.-wide by 17¼-in.-long pine filler strips to the bottom of the lid with glue and screws (*drawing 2-D*). These strips rest against the sides of the chest to hold the lid level when it's closed.

Back to the tray for a moment. I have to drill 24 holes for the checkers (*drawing 2-E*). I lay out the holes 2 in. o.c. and drill them on my drill press with a 1⅜-in.-dia. Forstner bit set for a 1/2-in.-deep hole (*photo 2-19*).

The front edge of the plywood lid is trimmed out with a piece of 1⅝-in.-wide pine (see Project Planner). This piece is notched out in the center for the checker-storage tray. I use the resulting cutout for the front of the tray (*drawings 2-D and 2-E*). Cutting this notch is a little tricky. The safest way is to clamp the piece of pine to the table-saw rip fence and raise the blade up through the workpiece (*photo 2-20*). It takes 2 passes to cut the full length, so after making one cut, I lower the blade, unclamp the workpiece, move it forward slightly, and reclamp it in place. Then I raise the blade through the wood again to complete the rip cut. Next I set the blade for a 3/4-in.-deep cut and make 2 crosscuts with my miter gauge to complete the notch (*photo 2-21*).

In order to be able to pull out the tray without opening the lid, I use my router and a cove bit to mill a finger pull in the bottom of the pine trim on the front of the tray (*photo 2-22*).

Now, with my biscuit joiner, I cut 4 biscuit slots in the front edge of the lid and 4 matching slots in the front trim strip. I cut a couple more biscuit slots in the front edge of the storage tray and the tray trim piece, making sure to cut slots so that the top edge of the trim piece is 1/16 in. below the top of the tray (*drawing 2-F*). A little glue and some #20 biscuits, and I clamp these pieces in place.

The next step is to create a 1/8-in.-deep mortise in the bottom edge of the rear

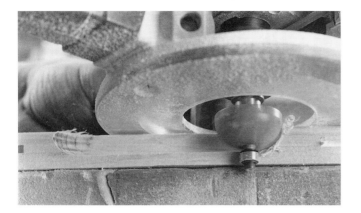

2-22
In order to be able to pull out the tray without opening the lid, I mill a finger pull in the bottom of the pine trim for the tray using a cove bit.

2-23
With a flush trim bit and my router, I mill a 1/8-in.-deep mortise in the bottom edge of the rear curb for the piano hinge. With the lid upside down on my bench, I place a 39¼-in.-long pine spacer on the plywood to guide the bit's pilot bearing. I hold the router in a horizontal position and ride the pilot bearing along the pine spacer to mill the mortise.

2-24
I mill an ogee detail on the top edge of the base molding with my router and a 5/32-in. ogee bit. I have to run the router along the narrow edge of the board, which doesn't provide a stable base for the router. To get more support, I clamp the 2 boards face-to-face to give me a 1½-in.-wide surface on which to support the router.

2-25
I have to cut a 3/8-in. by 1/2-in. rabbet in the back side of the base trim pieces to fit around the bottom of the chest. I mill this rabbet by making 2 rip cuts on the table saw.

2-26
I trim off the biscuits that join the base trim pieces with a small handsaw.

curb for the piano hinge that attaches the lid (*drawing 2-D*). I make this cut with a flush trim bit and my router. With the lid upside down on my bench, I cut a 39¼-in.-long spacer from some 1 x pine and place it on the plywood to guide the bit's pilot bearing (*photo 2-23*). I hold the router in a horizontal position and ride the pilot bearing along the pine spacer to mill the mortise. I'll install the hinge and other hardware later, after I finish the chest.

Base Molding

Around the base of the toy chest goes a decorative molding made from some 1 x 4 pine (see Project Planner and *drawings 2-A and 2-C*). This base trim has an ogee detail on the top edge, which I mill with my router and a 5/32-in. ogee bit.

I have to run the router along the narrow edge of the board, which doesn't provide a very stable base for the router. To get more support, I clamp the 2 boards face-to-face, giving me a 1½-in.-wide surface on which to support the router (*photo 2-24*).

The next step is to cut a 3/8-in. by 1/2-in. rabbet into the back side of the trim pieces to fit around the bottom of the chest (*drawing 2-C*). I mill this rabbet by making 2 rip cuts on the table saw (*photo 2-25*).

I miter the corners of the base trim on my power miter box. Then I mill a blind biscuit slot at each miter — I don't want the slot to show at the top edge of the trim.

Now for a little assembly. With the chest upside down on my bench, I put glue in the rabbets and position the base trim in place. I apply glue to the biscuits and stick them into the slots — I'll trim off the protruding ends later. Now, with my nail gun, I shoot a few 6d finish nails into the bottom of the molding to hold it in place while the glue sets. Finally, I trim off the biscuits with a small handsaw (*photo 2-26*).

Finishing Touches

After a final sanding, I remove all the dust with a vacuum and tack cloth. I'm in no hurry to install the hardware yet because it's a lot easier to finish the chest without the piano hinge and lid supports in place.

The pine parts get a couple of coats of gloss polyurethane — inside and out. When the poly is dry, I'm ready to paint the lid. I mask off the checkerboard and the pine parts of the lid with masking tape. Then I spray on a few light coats of acrylic latex paint, sanding lightly between coats with 150-grit paper. When the last coat of paint is thoroughly dry, I add a top coat of polyurethane over the paint for a durable and attractive finish.

When everything's dry, I install the piano hinge, lid, and the 2 lid supports. I also install the four 1/2-in. tack bumpers on the bottom of the lid fillers and tray tracks so the bumpers rest on the front edge of the chest when the lid is closed (*drawing 2-A*).

You know, some people say this piece looks too good to be a toy chest; maybe a blanket chest or a hope chest instead. Me? I really like the checkers. I'd just better find time for some practice.

3

alphabet wagon

Time: 2 days

Special hardware and tools:

Hot glue gun
Scroll saw
Circle cutter for drill
  press
Dovetailing jig

Wood:

1½-ft. 8/4 x 6 maple
Joint one face and one
  edge and rip 3 pieces
  1⅞ in. wide. Plane to
  1⅝ in. square. Crosscut
  24 pieces 1⅝ in. long
  to make 1⅝-in.-square
  blocks.

3½-ft. 1 x 4 mahogany
Cut one piece 18 in. long,
  then rip in half. Rip
  resulting 2 pieces in
  half along 3/4-in.
  thickness using a band
  saw (a technique
  known as "resawing").
  Plane the 4 resulting
  pieces to 1/4-in. thickness. Cut letters and
  numbers from these
  pieces, then saw them
  in half, according to
  plan, to get 2 of each
  number and letter.
Cut 4 wheels from
  remaining 2-ft. piece.

2½-ft. 1 x 3 cherry
Rip and joint 2¼ in.
  wide, then cut 2 pieces
  12 in. long for wagon
  sides.

1½-ft. 1 x 3 ash
Rip and joint 2¼ in.
  wide, then cut 2 pieces
  8½ in. long for front
  and back of wagon.

8-in. by 12-in. 1/2-in. piece
  of cabinet-grade ply-
  wood or AC plywood
Trim to 7¹¹⁄₁₆ in. x 11³⁄₁₆ in.
  for bottom of wagon.

2-ft. 3/8-in.-dia. hard-
  wood dowel
Cut 2 pieces 10½ in. long
  for axles.

ALPHABET BLOCKS HAVE BEEN a favorite educational toy for countless generations of children. Kids today still love playing with blocks, building towers and bridges, and spelling out words. (It's nice to know some things never change!) And what better container to store blocks in than a little wagon to pull around the house? When I found an antique set of blocks and a wagon in the toy collection of the Peabody Essex Museum in Salem, Massachusetts, I decided to make my own.

One of the things I like best about this project is that I didn't have to run to the lumberyard for any of the material. I built it all from scraps around the shop. I used a little bit of everything — some cherry and ash for the wagon sides, a piece of plywood for the bottom, and some mahogany for the wheels. The blocks are made from maple, with mahogany letters and numbers.

Making the Wagon

The first thing to do is make the wagon sides a uniform thickness. I do this by running the boards through my thickness planer so that they're all exactly 3/4 in. thick.

The next step is to run one edge of each board over the jointer to make sure it's straight and square. As usual, I set my jointer to remove 1/32 in. of material.

After jointing this edge, I rip the pieces to width on the table saw. I like to rip

1½-in. birch ball for knob

One set 1-in. stick-on letters and numbers

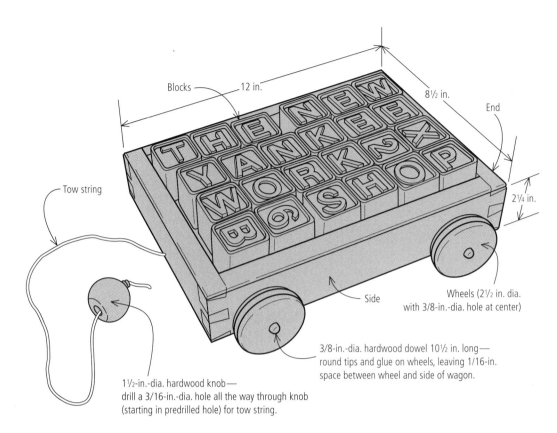

Blocks — 12 in.

8½ in.

End

2¼ in.

Tow string

Side

Wheels (2½ in. dia.
with 3/8-in.-dia. hole at center)

3/8-in.-dia. hardwood dowel 10½ in. long—
round tips and glue on wheels, leaving 1/16-in.
space between wheel and side of wagon.

1½-in.-dia. hardwood knob—
drill a 3/16-in.-dia. hole all the way through knob
(starting in predrilled hole) for tow string.

the pieces 1/32 in. wider than the final dimension I want. Then I make a single pass on the jointer to remove this extra 1/32 in. of material. This technique results in a smoother finished edge than the saw blade alone can produce. For the wagon sides, I set the rip fence for a 2⁹⁄₃₂-in. width. After ripping and joint-ing, the finished sides are 2¼ in. wide.

Now it's just a matter of cutting the pieces to length on my power miter box. The front and back of the wagon are 8½ in. long. The wagon sides are 12 in. long (*drawings 3-A and 3-B*).

I join the sides of the wagon with through dovetails (*drawings 3-A and 3-B*), but lock joints or biscuit joints would also work well. I cut the dovetails with a router and dovetailing jig. This particular dovetailing jig is different from the one I use for other projects in this book. It consists of 2 aluminum templates — one to mill the tails, one to mill the pins. The tails are cut with a dovetailing bit, and the pins are cut with a straight bit. These are special bits with a pilot bearing mounted above the cutter and came with the dovetailing jig as standard acces-sories.

To mill the tails, I clamp one of the wagon sides in the vise with one end stick-ing up. I center (by eye) 2 fingers of the dovetailing jig's tail template over the end of the board and clamp the jig in place. With the dovetailing bit in my router, I adjust the depth of cut so that when the router is placed on top of the jig, the bit cuts tails 3/4 in. long (the thickness of the workpiece). Now I just guide the bit's pilot bearing around the fingers of the jig to mill the tails (*photo 3-1*).

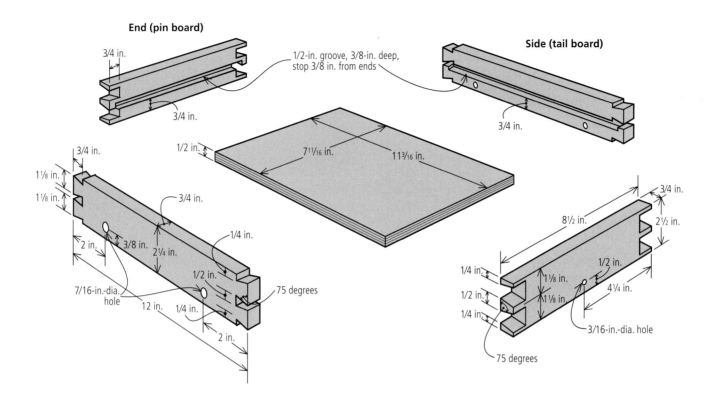

End (pin board)

3/4 in.

1/2-in. groove, 3/8-in. deep, stop 3/8 in. from ends

3/4 in.

Side (tail board)

3/4 in.

7¹¹⁄₁₆ in.

11³⁄₁₆ in.

3/4 in.

1/2 in.

3/4 in.

3/4 in.

2½ in.

1⅛ in.

1⅛ in.

8½ in.

3/4 in.

3/4 in.

1/4 in.

2 in.

3/8 in.

2¼ in.

1/4 in.

1/2 in.

7/16-in.-dia. hole

12 in.

1/4 in.

75 degrees

2 in.

1/4 in.

1/2 in.

1/4 in.

1⅛ in.

1⅛ in.

1/2 in.

4¼ in.

3/16-in.-dia. hole

75 degrees

To cut the tails on the other end of the board, I unclamp the jig, flip the board end for end, and repeat the procedure. I mill the tails on the second wagon side the same way.

The front and back of the wagon get the dovetail pins (*drawings 3-A and 3-B*). I clamp one of these pieces end up in the vise, place one of the tail pieces on top of the pin board, and flush up the edges of the 2 boards. With a pencil, I trace one edge of one tail onto the pin board (*photo 3-2*). Removing the tail piece, I align one of the fingers on the dovetailing jig's pin template so that it just covers the pencil mark. Then I clamp it in place. I replace the dovetailing bit with the straight bit, adjust it to cut 3/4 in. deep, and rout the pins (*photo 3-3*). That's all there is to it. Before cutting the other pins, I mark the matching pins and tails with a "1" so that I don't mix up the corners. I repeat this procedure to mill the other pins — always using the corresponding tails to lay them out and numbering each corner as I go.

The bottom of the wagon is a piece of 1/2-in. plywood that fits in a groove (*drawing 3-B*). I position this groove 3/4 in. from the bottom edge of the wagon sides to leave room for the axles and mill it with my plunge router, a guide fence, and a 1/2-in.-dia. straight bit. I set the depth stop on my router so the bit will make a 3/8-in.-deep cut. I don't want the ends of the groove to show through the dovetails, so I start and stop the cut just short (3/8 in.) of the ends. I mill grooves in all 4 sides of the wagon.

Next, on the drill press, I make the holes in the wagon sides for the axles using a 7/16-in.-dia. brad-point bit. The centers of these holes are located 3/8 in. from the bottom edge and 2 in. in from each end (*drawing 3-B*). To minimize

3-1

To mill the dovetail tails on the wagon sides, I guide the pilot bearing of the dovetailing bit around the fingers of the template.

3-2

To lay out the dovetail pins, I place one of the tail pieces on top of the pin board and trace one tail onto the pin board.

3-3

I align the pin template with the pencil line, clamp it in place, and rout the tails with a straight bit.

tearout when the bit exits the wood, I place the workpiece on a piece of scrap wood and drill through into the scrap.

Now I cut the plywood bottom to size on the table saw — 7¹¹⁄₁₆ in. wide and 11³⁄₁₆ in. long. I sand the bottom and the insides of the wagon sides with my random-orbit sander.

Now for a little assembly. I place the plywood bottom on my workbench and get all the sidepieces ready. I brush some glue on the mating surfaces of the pins and slip these 2 end pieces onto the plywood bottom. A little more glue on the tails and I can assemble the dovetails and tap the joints home (*photo 3-4*). I put on a couple of clamps to hold the joints together and set it aside to dry.

3-4
A mallet works well to tap the dovetails together before clamping the joints tight.

3-5
The wheels are cut from a piece of 3/4-in.-thick mahogany with a circle cutter on the drill press. A piece of scrap wood under the workpiece keeps the cutter from damaging the table. I clamp the workpiece to the table to keep it from turning.

Making the Wheels

To cut out the wheels for the wagon, I use a circle cutter. This device has a pilot drill in the middle and a sliding bar with a cutter on one end. The bar is adjustable for diameters up to 6 in. (*photo 3-5*). The circle cutter is designed to be used in a drill press only — never in a handheld drill. For safety reasons, it's very important to run it at a speed of 500 rpm or less.

The wheels are cut from a 2-ft. length of 3/4-in.-thick mahogany (see Project Planner). I place a piece of scrap wood over the drill-press table so the cutter won't cause damage when it breaks through the wood. Next I clamp the workpiece to the table so it doesn't move. I set the circle cutter to cut a 2½-in.-dia. wheel. I drill slowly, raising the cutter out of the wood frequently to clear chips and to prevent overheating. The finished wheel often sticks on the cutter, but a few taps with a hammer knocks it free.

The cutter makes circles with slightly angled sides. To square up the edges of the wheels, I mount each one on the drill press using a 1/4-in.-dia. carriage bolt as a chuck. As the wheel spins, I hold a sanding block with some 80-grit sandpaper against the edge (*photo 3-6*).

To make the wheels look more like tires, I round over the edges with a 1/4-in. beading bit in my router (*drawing 3-C*). The only safe way to rout small parts like these is to place them on one of the nonslip rubber mats available from most mail-order woodworking catalogs. Such a mat holds the wheel in place for routing the edges (*photo 3-7*).

3-6
To square up the edges of the wheels, I mount each one on the drill press using a 1/4-in.-dia. carriage bolt as a chuck and sand the edge square.

3-7
To make the wheels look more like tires, I round over the edges with a 1/4-in. beading bit in the router. A nonslip rubber mat holds the wheel safely in place.

3-C Wheel Detail

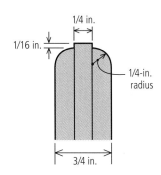

3-D Top Edge of Wagon

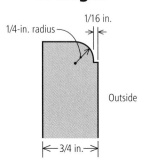

One last thing: I have to enlarge the hole in the wheel to receive the 3/8-in.-dia. axle. That's easy enough on the drill press with a 3/8-in.-dia. Forstner bit (*photo 3-8*). A little sanding, and the wheels are complete.

Completing the Wagon

Now back to the wagon for some finishing touches. After taking off the clamps, I sand the outside of the wagon with my random-orbit sander. I want to soften the top edges of the sides, so I rout a bead around the outer edge with the same 1/4-in. beading bit I used for the wheels. This makes a nice decorative edge around the top of the wagon (*drawing 3-D*). To protect little fingers, I relieve all sharp edges with some sandpaper.

It's time to install the axles and wheels. I cut two 10½-in.-long pieces of 3/8-in.-dia. hardwood dowel to make the axles. For a nice finished look, I round over the ends of these axles with the drum-sander attachment on my drill press. Just to play it safe, I slip the axles through their holes to make sure they don't bind. If they do, it may be necessary to enlarge the holes in the wagon sides slightly. The axles should turn freely in the holes.

I apply a little bit of glue to one end of an axle and in the hole of one wheel. I tap on the wheel and wipe off the excess glue. After slipping the axle through the holes, I glue another wheel on the opposite end, making sure that there's 1/16 in. of clearance between the wagon sides and the wheels. I wipe off any excess glue to make sure that the wheels don't accidentally get glued to the wagon.

All that's left is to drill two 3/16-in.-dia. holes for the tow string. One hole gets drilled in the front of the wagon, the second through the wooden ball that serves as a handle on the end of the string (*drawings 3-A and 3-B*). I'll thread the string through the holes later, after I've put on the finish.

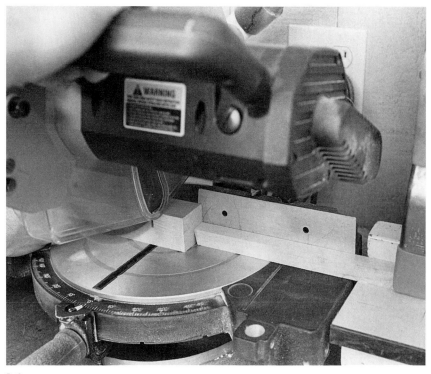

3-8
I bore out the wheel holes with a 3/8-in.-dia. Forstner bit so the holes fit the axles.

3-9
I cut off the individual blocks with my power miter saw. To make sure that each block in identical, I butt the workpiece against a stop block to get the length I want. Note that the end of the stop block is cut at an angle to prevent trapped sawdust from affecting the accuracy.

3-E Blocks
(24 required)

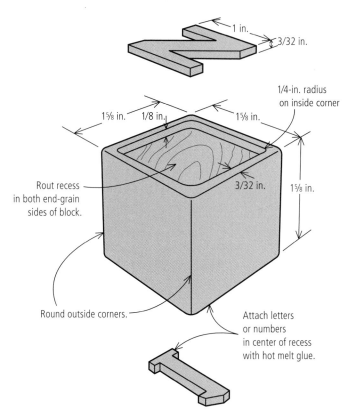

1 in.

3/32 in.

1/4-in. radius on inside corner

1⅝ in.   1/8 in.   1⅝ in.

3/32 in.

1⅝ in.

Rout recess in both end-grain sides of block.

Round outside corners.

Attach letters or numbers in center of recess with hot melt glue.

3-10
I make a special jig for routing the 1/8-in.-deep recesses in the blocks. The block fits into a 1/8-in.-deep recess in the bottom piece of plywood.

3-11
The top of the block fits into a second 1/8-in.-deep recess in the top of the jig. A smaller square hole centered in this recess goes clear through the top. Dowels in the jig sides serve to position the top.

3-12
To rout the recess, I simply guide the router bit's pilot bearing around the square hole in the top of the jig.

Building the Blocks

The best wood for making the blocks is some nice, hard maple. In my scrap pile I found a 6-in.-wide piece of 8/4 maple (called "eight-quarter," meaning 2 in. thick) about 1½ ft. long — just the right size for the job.

Each block is a 1⅜-in. cube (*drawing 3-E*). The letters and numbers are cut out with a scroll saw and glued into shallow recesses routed in the end grain of each block. The blocks are really fun to make.

The easiest way to prepare the maple cubes is to rip the lengths a little wider than the finished blocks, plane these lengths down to size on the thickness planer, and then cut the blocks off one by one.

I set the rip fence on my table saw about 1⅞ in. from the blade. I joint one face and one edge of the maple and rip three 1½-ft.-long pieces — enough to make the 24 blocks I need. Next I run these pieces through the thickness planer, planing alternately on all 4 sides until the pieces are 1⅜ in. square. Finally, I cut off the individual blocks with my power miter saw. To make sure that each block is identical, I set up a stop block so that all I have to do is butt the end of the workpiece against the stop block to get the length I want (*photo 3-9*).

Block-Routing Jig

I need to make a special jig for routing the 1/8-in.-deep recesses in the end grain of the blocks (*photos 3-10 and 3-11*). I start with some scrap 3/4-in. plywood and rip a piece 6 in. wide and about 2 ft. long. From the end of this piece,

I crosscut 2 pieces 6 in. long and 2 pieces 1⅜ in. long. In the middle of each 6-in.-square piece, I trace the outline of the block — a 1⅜-in. square. On one 6-in. piece — the one that will become the top of the jig — I trace a second 1⅜-in. square on the opposite side of the plywood. It's important that these squares — on opposite sides of the same piece — are perfectly aligned with each other; otherwise, the jig won't work properly. Next, on the drill press with a 1-in.-dia. Forstner bit, I remove the material from inside the traced outlines to a depth of 1/8 in. on one face of each piece. I clean up the corners of each recess with a chisel so a block can fit snugly inside.

Now I glue the two 1⅜-in. by 6-in. pieces of plywood to one of the plywood squares to form 2 sidepieces for supporting the top plywood square (*photo 3-10*). I place a maple cube in the bottom recess and place the other plywood square upside down on top of the block so that the block is held between the 2 recesses. Holding this sandwich together, I take it over to the drill press and bore four 3/8-in.-dia. holes through the top plywood square into the sidepieces — 2 in each side. Now I remove the top plywood piece and tap 4 short lengths of 3/8-in.-dia. dowel into the holes in the sidepieces. These dowels serve as locating pins for positioning the top of the jig.

Just one more step to completing the jig. I need to cut a square hole through the top side of the jig to guide the router bit. This hole needs to be slightly smaller than the block in order to form the 3/32-in. curb around the recess (*drawing 3-E*). To center the hole, I measure 3/32 in. from the pencil lines on the top of the jig to make a smaller 1⁷⁄₁₆-in. square centered inside the original 1⅜-in. square. I drill a couple of holes on the drill press and cut out the square with a jigsaw.

Routing the Recess

To rout the recesses in the blocks, I clamp the jig in place on my workbench and place a maple cube in the jig, end grain up (*photo 3-10*). Then I put on the jig's top piece (*photo 3-11*). I adjust a 1/2-in.-dia. flush trim bit in my plunge router to cut a 1/8-in.-deep recess. I simply guide the router bit's pilot bearing around the square hole in the top of the jig to cut the recess (*photo 3-12*). When I'm finished, I flip the block upside down and rout the other side. That's one block down and just 23 more to go!

Letters and Numbers

I'll get started on the letters and numbers by assembling the materials I need: some 1/4-in.-thick mahogany that I surfaced on my thickness planer and some 1-in. stick-on letters and numbers from the local stationery store. The stick-on letters provide a sharp outline to guide me in sawing. It's great fun to peel off the letters and numbers and stick them on the wood (*photo 3-13*). I think it looks best if the grain runs vertically on the letters. I need only 24; I'll saw them in half later to make 48 thinner letters.

It's possible to cut out these letters by hand with a coping saw or a fretsaw, but a scroll saw is much faster (*photo 3-14*). My scroll saw has an adjustable speed control, which I set to around 1,000 strokes per minute for this kind of work.

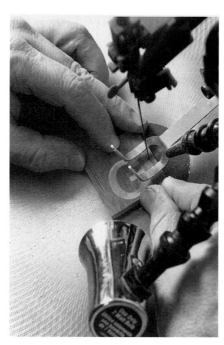

3-13
Stick-on letters and numbers provide a sharp, crisp outline for sawing out the mahogany characters for the blocks.

3-14
A scroll saw is the ideal tool for sawing out the numbers and letters.

3-15
I saw the letters in half on the band saw with a homemade jig of 3/4-in.-thick scrap wood with a 1/4-in.-wide slot cut in one end for the letters to fit into. A thin strip of wood attached to the bottom keeps the letter from getting pulled through the slot. I guide the jig against a fence to split the letter in half.

For letters that have an interior section to cut out (like a *P,* an *A,* or an *O*), I like to cut out that part first, before I do the outside. First I drill a hole near the edge big enough to hold the scroll-saw blade. Then I release the top blade clamp and insert the blade through the hole in the wood. I reclamp the blade and cut out the inside of the letter. I reverse the procedure to remove the blade.

At this point, the letters and numbers are 1/4 in. thick. I need to saw them in half so they're only 3/32 in. thick. I do this on the band saw with the help of a simple homemade jig to hold the letters safely (*photo 3-15*). This jig is nothing more than a narrow length of 3/4-in.-thick scrap wood with a 1/4-in.-wide slot cut in one end for the letters to fit into. On the bottom edge of the jig I attach a thin strip of wood to keep the letter from getting pulled through the slot by the downward force of the band-saw blade. I attach a fence to my band-saw table and position it so that when the jig rides against the fence, the blade splits the letter right down the middle (*photo 3-15*). I saw all 24 numbers and letters in half to give me 24 pairs.

When the letters and numbers are finished, I glue them in the end-grain recesses of the blocks with some hot glue and peel off the stick-on letters to reveal the mahogany.

The corners of the blocks are a little bit sharp, so I round them over on my stationary belt sander, turning the block to sand a radius on the corners (*photo*

3-16). I don't round the corners adjacent to the recesses but just relieve the sharp edges slightly with a little hand sanding.

Putting on Paint

Now for the finish. I want the blocks to be nice and bright, so I'm going to use a high-gloss, water-base paint. Because infants just love to gnaw on blocks, it's important to use a nontoxic paint. I bought 6 bright colors for a little rainbow variety. I blow off all the dust from the blocks and paint the outside surfaces — I'll finish the letters and recesses with polyurethane later. I don't worry much if a little paint gets on the top or bottom edges of the block — I'll sand it off later. It takes a couple of coats to build up a nice glossy finish, and I sand very lightly between coats with some 220-grit sandpaper.

While the blocks are drying, I can finish the wagon. I'm going with a tough, durable, nontoxic gloss polyurethane here so the wood shows through. But first I'll brush on a coat of water-base sanding sealer to give me a good base for the poly. Here, too, it takes a couple of coats to get a good-looking finish.

When the final coat of paint on the blocks is dry, I lightly sand the top and bottom clean on my stationary belt sander. Just a light touch will do it — to make a clean, crisp edge. After removing any dust, I coat the unpainted parts of the blocks with polyurethane.

All that's left is to put on the string. Now that it's finished, this little project should improve my spelling dramatically.

easel

project planner

Time: 4 days

Special hardware

(1 pair) 1½-in. by 1¼-in. brass loose-pin butt hinges

Wood:

(1) 2-ft. 6/4 x 3 ash
Surface plane to 1¼ in., then rip and joint to 2 in. wide for marker/crayon holder.

(1) 3-ft. 1 x 6 ash
Cut one piece 20 in. long. Rip and joint into 2 pieces 2⅝ in. wide, then trim to 18¼ in. long for drawer support sides. Cut remainder according to plan for inner pieces of upper leg assembly.

(1) 4½-ft. 1 x 4 ash
Cut one piece 32 in. long and rip and joint to 3 in. wide.
Cut one piece 18¾ in. long for storage tray end. Cut remaining piece according to plan for outer pieces of upper leg assembly.
Cut one piece 14 in. long and rip a 15-degree bevel according to plan. Crosscut into 4 pieces 3⅛ in. long for upper leg assembly end caps.
Rip and joint remaining piece into 2 pieces 1 in. wide, then cut 2 pieces 6½ in. long for height extensions of storage tray sides.

(1) 6-ft. 1 x 4 ash
Rip and joint 3 pieces 7/8 in. wide, then cut 4 pieces 25 in. long and 4 pieces 20 in. long for chalkboard and art-board frames.

(1) 10-ft. 1 x 3 ash
Cut one piece 16 in. long, then rip and joint to 2⅜ in. wide for back of drawer support.

EVERY CHILD HAS A natural talent for art. Kids will spend hours and hours happily drawing with crayons and markers and paint. If you have a budding Rembrandt in your home, you might want to build this easel. It has a chalkboard on one side, with plenty of storage room for chalk and erasers. On the other side there's an art board with a unique feature. Most easels use clips to hold a sheet or pad of paper. This one has a roll of paper on top. The end of the paper slips down through the frame of the art board, so kids can make one painting after another, just pulling clean paper down for a fresh start. The test of a good easel is how much kids enjoy it. The kids in my family never tire of this one.

The easel has a storage tray underneath with compartments for markers, brushes, chalk, and erasers and a drawer for storing all sorts of art supplies. Best of all, the easel folds up to about 8 in. wide for storage.

Upper Leg Assembly and Legs

I'll get started by cutting out the parts for the upper leg assembly that holds the paper roll and legs (*drawings 4-A and 4-B*). I need to make 2 of these assemblies — one for each end of the easel.

The first parts to make are the 2 inner pieces (*drawing 4-B*), which I cut from a piece of 1 x 6 ash (see Project Planner). I pivot the blade on my power miter box 15 degrees and cut one end at a 75-degree angle. Then I measure 6⅜ in.

Cut 2 pieces 30 in. long
and one piece 18¾ in.
long. Rip and joint
them to 2 in. wide for
storage tray sides and
end.

Cut one piece 16 in. long,
then rip and joint to
2⁵⁄₁₆ in. wide for drawer
front. Use remaining
scrap to make drawer
runners.

(2) 10-ft. 1 x 2 ash

Cut 4 pieces 48 in. long
for legs. Cut one piece
18¾ in. long for stor-
age tray crosspiece.
Use remainder to
make brush/pencil
trough.

(1) 24-in. by 36-in. piece
of 1/4-in.-thick chalk-
board

Cut 2 pieces 17 in. x 23 in.
for chalkboard and art
board.

(1) 12-in. by 18-in. piece of
1/2-in. cabinet-grade
plywood

Rip 4 pieces 2⁵⁄₁₆ in. wide
along 18-in. dimension.
Cut 2 pieces 17⅞ in.
long and 2 pieces
13⅞ in. long for
drawer sides.

(1) 24-in. by 48-in. piece
of 1/4-in. cabinet-grade
plywood

Cut one piece 18¾ in. x
28¼ in. for storage
tray bottom.

Cut one piece 13⅞ in. x
17⅜ in. for drawer
bottom.

(1) 2-ft. 1-in.-dia. ash or
oak dowel

Cut one piece 18¾ in.
long for paper roll
holder

(1) 3/4-in.-dia. Shaker
drawer knob

4-A Major Anatomy and Dimensions
Note: Sand or chamfer all sharp edges.

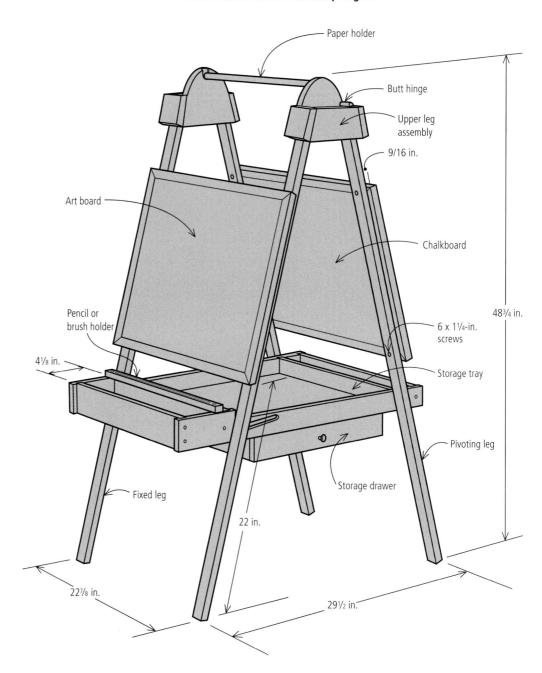

Paper holder
Butt hinge
Upper leg assembly
9/16 in.
Art board
Chalkboard
48¾ in.
6 x 1¼-in. screws
Pencil or brush holder
Storage tray
4⅛ in.
Fixed leg
Pivoting leg
Storage drawer
22 in.
22⅞ in.
29½ in.

along the bottom edge of the piece and make another 75-degree angle cut, making sure the cuts are mirror images of each other (*drawing 4-B and photo 4-1*). I
cut a second, identical piece in the same way. These angled blanks will become
the inner pieces that hold the paper roll and will be rounded over on top.

The next parts to cut are the 2 outer pieces of the upper leg assembly (*drawing
4-B*). From a length of 1 x 4 ash, I rip and joint a piece 3 in. wide. Then, using
the same 15-degree-angle setting on my power miter saw, I cut two pieces 6⅜ in.
long, measured along the bottom edge.

These inner and outer pieces join with 2 small blocks of wood I'll call "end
caps" (*drawing 4-B*). The tops of these end caps are beveled at a 15-degree

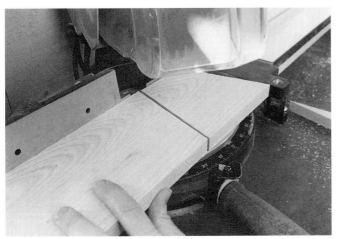

4-1
To cut the 2 inner pieces that hold the paper roll, I pivot my power miter box blade 15 degrees and cut one end at a 75-degree angle. Then I measure 6⅜ in. along the bottom edge of the piece and make a second cut at the same angle.

4-2
To complete the 2 inner pieces, I band-saw a 2⅜-in.-radius arc and then smooth up the cuts with the drum-sander attachment on my drill press.

4-3
To make the slot that holds the paper-roll dowel, I drill 2 overlapping 1-in.-dia. holes 1/4 in. deep and taper the sides of the slot with a chisel.

4-B Upper Leg Assembly

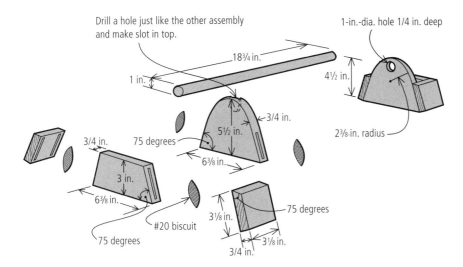

Drill a hole just like the other assembly and make slot in top.

1-in.-dia. hole 1/4 in. deep

18¾ in.

1 in.

4½ in.

3/4 in.

5½ in.

2⅜-in. radius

3/4 in.

75 degrees

6⅜ in.

3 in.

6⅜ in.

#20 biscuit

3⅛ in.

75 degrees

75 degrees

3⅛ in.

3/4 in.

angle. Starting with a 14-in. length of 1 x 4, I tilt my table-saw blade 15 degrees and rip a bevel along one edge so that the finished piece is 3⅛ in. wide along the bevel's long point. Next, on the miter box, I crosscut 4 pieces 3⅛ in. long.

To complete the 2 inner pieces of this assembly, I have to round off the tops. I draw a centerline down the middle of each piece and mark off 5½ in. from the bottom — the finished height of the piece. Next I set my compass to a 2⅜-in. radius and scribe an arc on the top of each piece. I saw out the curves on the band saw (*photo 4-2*) and smooth up the cuts with the drum-sander attachment on my drill press.

The paper roll is supported by a 1-in.-dia. dowel that mounts in the upper leg

4-4
The parts of the upper leg assemblies are fastened together with biscuits and glue. Using my biscuit joiner, I cut one biscuit slot in each joint.

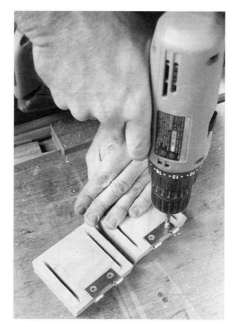

4-5
To install the hinges, I remove the pin and fasten one leaf to the inside of each end cap with screws. I line up the top of the hinge leaf so the knuckle sticks up. The hinge just lies flat on the surface — no need for a mortise.

4-6
The matching hinge leaves get secured to the angled ends of the pivoting legs.

assembly (*drawing 4-A*). To hold this dowel, I drill a hole in the inner piece of one assembly and a slot in the opposite inner piece so the dowel can be removed. With a 1-in.-dia. Forstner bit in my drill press, I drill a 1/4-in.-deep hole in both pieces, centered 4½ in. from the bottom edge (*drawing 4-B*). To make the slot, I drill a second hole overlapping the first (*photo 4-3*) and taper the sides of the slot with a chisel. The top is a little bit wider than the bottom. I then relieve the top corners of the slot with a rasp so the dowel doesn't catch on the corners.

The parts of the upper leg assemblies are fastened together with #20 biscuits and glue — I don't want any nails or screws to show. Using my biscuit joiner, I cut one biscuit slot in each joint (*drawing 4-B and photo 4-4*).

Next I have to make the legs. I cut four 48-in.-long legs from 1 x 2 ash (see Project Planner). I cut the top ends of the 2 pivoting legs to a 75-degree angle (*drawing 4-C*), but the fixed legs are square.

Before I can do any assembly, there are 2 more steps to take care of: I have to install the fixed legs and attach the butt hinges, which allow the other legs to pivot.

To install the hinge, I remove the pin and screw one leaf to the inside of the end cap, which receives the pivoting legs. I line up the top of the hinge leaf so the knuckle is above the top edge (*photo 4-5 and drawing 4-C*). The hinge just lies flat on the surface — no need for a mortise. I repeat the procedure for the other end cap. The other hinge leaves get secured to the angled end of the pivoting legs (*drawing 4-C and photo 4-6*).

Next I attach the fixed legs to the opposite end caps (*drawing 4-D*) by drilling and countersinking 2 holes through each leg and fastening the end cap with glue and 6 x 1¼-in. screws (*photo 4-7*).

4-7
I attach the fixed legs to the opposite end caps. I drill and countersink 2 holes through each leg and fasten them with glue and 6 x 1¼-in. screws.

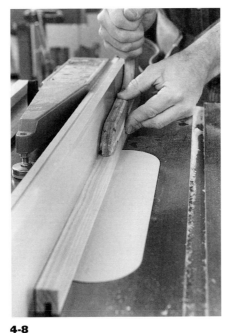

4-8
Using my stack dado head set for 1/4-in. width and a depth of 3/8 in., I mill a groove in the frame pieces to receive the chalkboard. I position the rip fence to center the groove in the frame stock.

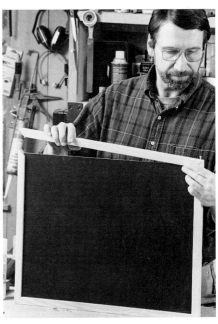

4-9
I slip the chalkboard into the frame and attach the last frame piece with glue and screws.

4-C   Pivoting Leg

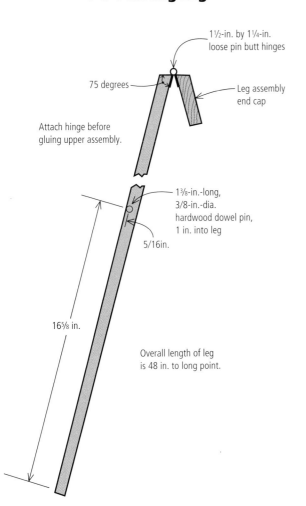

1½-in. by 1¼-in. loose pin butt hinges

75 degrees

Leg assembly end cap

Attach hinge before gluing upper assembly.

1⅜-in.-long, 3/8-in.-dia. hardwood dowel pin, 1 in. into leg

5/16in.

16⅝ in.

Overall length of leg is 48 in. to long point.

4-D   Fixed Leg

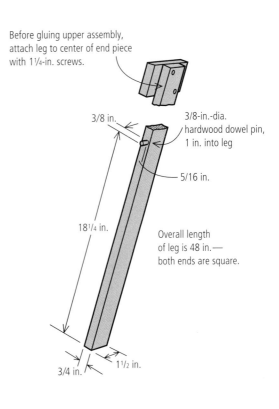

Before gluing upper assembly, attach leg to center of end piece with 1¼-in. screws.

3/8 in.

3/8-in.-dia. hardwood dowel pin, 1 in. into leg

5/16 in.

18¼ in.

Overall length of leg is 48 in.— both ends are square.

3/4 in.

1½ in.

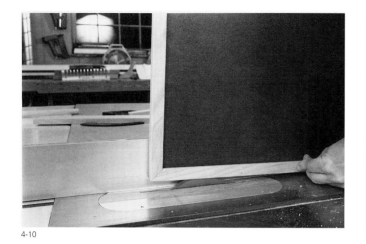

4-10

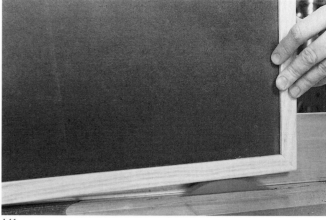

4-11

4-10, 4-11, and 4-12
I have to cut slots for the paper in the top and bottom of the art-board frame. With a thin-kerf blade on my table saw, I set the rip fence so that the blade cuts flush against the art board. Then I raise the blade about 1 in. and cut a slot by carefully pivoting the frame down onto the spinning blade (*photo 4-10*), making the cut, and then carefully pivoting the frame up off the blade at the end of the cut (*photo 4-11*). The table-saw blade leaves a radiused cut at the ends, so I square them up with a handsaw to complete the paper slots (*photo 4-12*).

4-12

Now I'm ready for a little assembly. I put glue and biscuits into the slots and put the upper leg assemblies together with a few clamps to hold things in place.

Chalkboard and Art Board

While the upper leg assemblies are drying, I'll get started on making the chalkboard and art board (*drawings 4-A and 4-E*). Both are made from a 1/4-in.-thick tempered hardboard with a factory-applied chalkboard finish. It took a bit of searching to find this stuff, but I finally tracked some down at a school supplier. I cut two 17-in. by 23-in. panels, using my homemade panel cutter to keep things nice and square.

Each board is surrounded by a mitered ash frame that starts out as a piece of 1 x 4 stock (see Project Planner). I rip and joint 3 pieces 3/4 in. thick x 7/8 in. wide and cut 4 pieces 25 in. long and 4 pieces 20 in. long for the frames.

I want to run a groove down the middle of the frame pieces to receive the chalkboard (*drawing 4-E*). I use my stack dado head, which I set up for 1/4-in. width and a depth of 3/8 in. I position the rip fence to center the groove in the frame stock (*photo 4-8*).

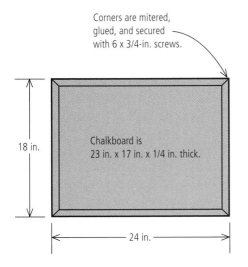

Corners are mitered, glued, and secured with 6 x 3/4-in. screws.

Chalkboard is 23 in. x 17 in. x 1/4 in. thick.

18 in.

24 in.

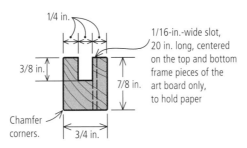

Section Through Frame

1/4 in.

1/16-in.-wide slot, 20 in. long, centered on the top and bottom frame pieces of the art board only, to hold paper

3/8 in.

7/8 in.

Chamfer corners.

3/4 in.

Now I set my power miter box blade at a 45-degree angle and cut the frame parts to length (*drawing 4-E*). The 4 long pieces measure 24 in. on the outside of the frame, and the 4 short parts are 18 in. long.

I take a lot of kidding about the number of clamps I have in the New Yankee Workshop, but it's hard to beat corner clamps for gluing up frames. I glue and clamp one long side and 2 short sides together, drill a pilot hole in each miter, and install a screw to reinforce the joint. For the opposite long side of the frame, I predrill for the screw but don't glue the piece until the chalkboard's in place. The chalkboard isn't going to go anywhere after it's in the frame, but I'm going to add a little glue in the long frame pieces just so it won't move around when you draw on it. Now I just slip in the chalkboard and attach the last frame piece with glue and screws (*photo 4-9*).

That takes care of the chalkboard. Next I'll build another frame for the art board. This frame requires one extra step: after the frame is complete, I have to cut slots for the paper in the top and bottom of the frame (*drawing 4-E*). Installing a thin-kerf blade on my table saw, I set the rip fence so that the blade cuts flush against the outside face of the chalkboard. Then I raise the blade about 1 in. and cut a stop slot by carefully pivoting the frame down onto the spinning blade (*photo 4-10*), making the cut, and then carefully pivoting the frame up off the blade at the end of the cut (*photo 4-11*). The table-saw blade leaves a radiused cut at the ends so I square the ends up with a handsaw to complete the paper slots (*photo 4-12*).

Storage Tray

While the board frames dry, I'll start working on the storage tray. The sides are the first parts to make. Each sidepiece is sort of L-shaped: wider at one end. I need to glue 2 pieces together to get this extra width (*drawing 4-F*). I rip and joint two 30-in. pieces of 3/4-in. by 2-in. ash and also cut 2 pieces 3/4 in. x 1 in. x 6½ in. long (see Project Planner). I don't want any screws or nails to show, so I

4-F Storage Tray

Note: All dadoes are 1/4 in. deep.
Assemble with 1¼-in. screws in predrilled and counterbored holes.
Plug all holes.

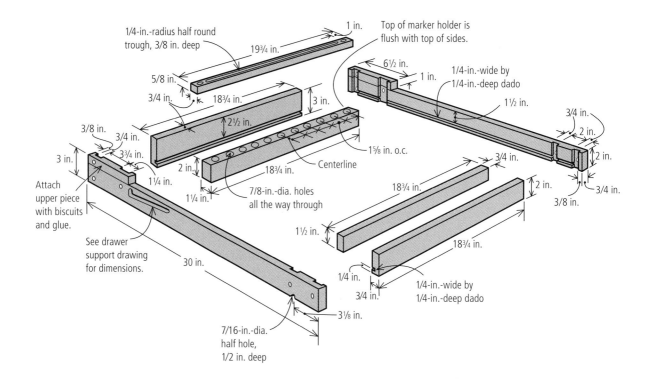

join the large and small pieces with biscuits and glue, cutting 2 biscuit slots in each joint (*photo 4-13*).

While the table saw is still set up for a 2-in.-wide rip, I rip the stock for the back of the tray and the marker/crayon holder (see Project Planner and *drawing 4-F*). I also cut the crosspiece that forms the chalk and eraser compartment, and the plywood bottom (see Project Planner).

The marker holder has a series of holes for large markers and crayons that seem to be pretty popular. I make these holes on the drill press with a 7/8-in.-dia. Forstner bit. I space the holes 1⅝ in. o.c. (*photo 4-14*).

The storage tray also has a trough to hold small brushes and pencils (*drawing 4-F*). I rip and joint this piece to the dimensions shown and rout the groove with a 1/4-in.-radius round-nose bit (also known as a core-box bit). I set up my plunge router with an edge guide to rout a 3/8-in.-deep cut. I make a pencil mark 1 in. from each end to mark the ends of the groove. Then I plunge the bit in one mark and release it at the other.

Now is a good time to do a little sanding. Whenever I build a project like this one, especially when kids are going to be using it, I like to remove all the sharp corners from the wood. I use a little chamfer plane to slightly bevel the edges (*photo 4-15*). Then, with my random-orbit sander, I sand all the parts of the storage tray (inside and out) as well as the chalkboard and art-board frames and the leg assemblies. I'm careful to knock off all the edges so children won't get any slivers or cuts.

4-13
I need to glue 2 pieces together to make the sides of the storage tray. I don't want any screws or nails to show, so I join the large and small pieces with biscuits and glue, cutting 2 biscuit slots in each joint.

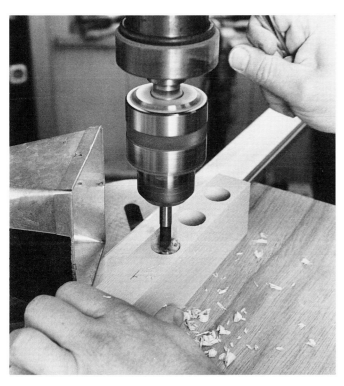

4-14
I drill the marker-holder holes on the drill press with a 7/8-in.-dia. Forstner bit. I space the holes 1⅝ in. o.c.

The storage tray is held together with dado joints; milling these joints is the next order of business. I set up my stack dado head in the table saw and adjust it for a 3/4-in.-wide dado that's 1/4 in. deep. Each sidepiece requires three 3/4-in.-wide dadoes and one 1¼-in.-wide dado for the marker holder. I lay them out as shown in the drawing, making sure that each side is a mirror image of the other (*drawing 4-F*). I use my table-saw miter gauge to feed the wood into the blade (*photo 4-16*). The 1¼-in.-wide dado requires 2 passes.

The 1/4-in. plywood bottom of the storage tray fits into 1/4-in. grooves in the sides and back- and front-end pieces (*drawing 4-F*). The groove in the back and front can run the entire length of the piece. I can't do that with the grooves in the sidepieces: the groove would show through the end — and that wouldn't look very good. It's easier and safer to cut stopped grooves on a router table than on the table saw.

I set up my router table with a 1/4-in. straight bit set for a 1/4-in. depth. I put a piece of tape on the table and make pencil lines to show the width of the bit.

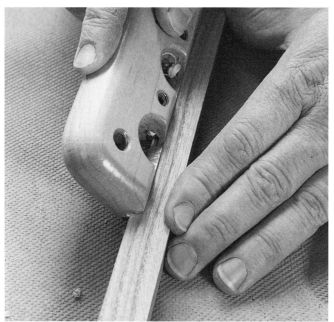

4-15
I use a little chamfer plane to slightly bevel all the edges to remove sharp corners.

4-16
I mill the storage-tray dado joints with my stack dado head set for a 3/4-in.-wide dado that's 1/4 in. deep. I use my table-saw miter gauge to feed the wood into the blade.

4-G Drawer Support

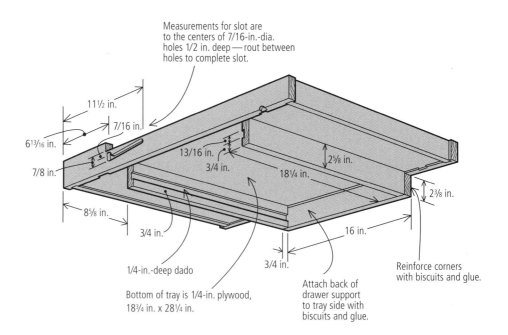

Measurements for slot are to the centers of 7/16-in.-dia. holes 1/2 in. deep — rout between holes to complete slot.

11½ in.

7/16 in.

6¹³/₁₆ in.

7/8 in.

13/16 in.

3/4 in.

18¼ in.

2⅝ in.

2³/₈ in.

8⅝ in.

3/4 in.

3/4 in.

16 in.

1/4-in.-deep dado

Bottom of tray is 1/4-in. plywood, 18¾ in. x 28¼ in.

Attach back of drawer support to tray side with biscuits and glue.

Reinforce corners with biscuits and glue.

To rout the grooves, I position the workpiece over the bit and carefully lower the left-hand dado down onto the spinning bit. I cut down to the dado at the right-hand end of the piece, and switch off the router. On the end pieces, I just run grooves the full length of the piece.

As I mentioned before, the easel folds up for storage: the storage tray slides forward about 4 inches, then pivots on dowels that are in the fixed legs and that fit into L-shaped grooves in the sides of the storage tray (*drawings 4-A, 4-D, 4-F,*

4-17
Making a groove consists of two steps: drilling holes at the end points of the slot and then routing out the material between them. I start by laying out and drilling three 7/16-in.-dia. holes, 1/2 in. deep, on the outside face of the sidepiece.

4-18
I set up my plunge router with a 5/8-in. o.d. guide collar and a 3/8-in. straight bit. I secure the work in my bench vise and clamp a straight piece of 1/4-in. plywood so that the edge of the plywood is 1/8 in. below the 2 bottom holes.

4-19
I run the guide collar against the plywood to rout a 1/2-in.-deep groove between the 2 holes, making several shallow passes to reach the full depth. So the dowel won't bind, I make it just a tiny bit wider by moving the plywood 1/16 in. closer to the holes and making another light pass.

and 4-G). When you unfold the easel to set it up, the storage tray is locked into position, partially by these 2 dowels in the L-shaped groove and partially by 2 additional dowels in the pivoting legs, which engage half-round notches in the bottom of the storage-tray sides *(drawings 4-F and 4-G).*

I'll drill the half-round notches first. I simply clamp the 2 storage tray side-pieces together — bottom edges butting, outside face up — so the ends are even. I set the depth stop on my drill press for a 1/2-in.-deep hole and then drill both pieces at once with a 7/16-in.-dia. bit.

The grooves are a little bit trickier to make. Making them consists of 2 steps: drilling holes at the end points of the groove and then routing out the material in between. I start by laying out and drilling three 7/16-in.-dia. holes, 1/2 in. deep at the ends of the groove, on the outside face *(drawing 4-G and photo 4-17).*

Next I set up my plunge router with a 5/8-in. o.d. guide collar and a 3/8-in. straight bit. I secure my work in my bench vise and clamp a straight piece of 1/4-in. plywood so that its edge is 1/8 in. below the lower edges of the two bottom holes *(photo 4-18).* I run the guide collar against the plywood to rout a 1/2-in.-deep groove between the 2 holes, making several shallow passes to reach the full depth *(photo 4-19).* Now I have a groove that's exactly 3/8 in. wide — the same width as the dowel pin. So the dowel won't bind, I make it just a tiny bit wider by moving the plywood 1/16 in. closer to the holes and taking another light pass. To complete the short leg of the L, I remove the wood between the other two holes with a chisel. Then I cut an identical groove on the other sidepiece.

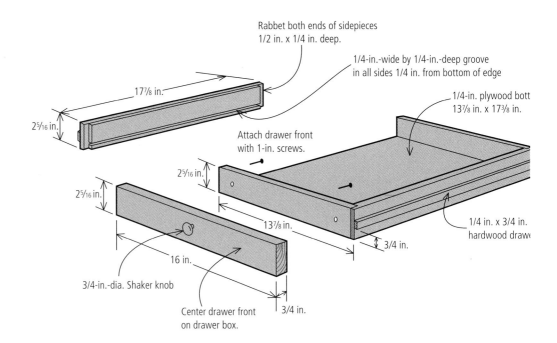

Rabbet both ends of sidepieces
1/2 in. x 1/4 in. deep.

1/4-in.-wide by 1/4-in.-deep groove
in all sides 1/4 in. from bottom of edge

1/4-in. plywood bott
13⅞ in. x 17⅜ in.

17⅞ in.

2⁵⁄₁₆ in.

Attach drawer front
with 1-in. screws.

2⁵⁄₁₆ in.

2⁵⁄₁₆ in.

13⅞ in.

1/4 in. x 3/4 in.
hardwood draw

3/4 in.

16 in.

3/4-in.-dia. Shaker knob

Center drawer front
on drawer box.

3/4 in.

Now for a little assembly. The front and back are secured to the sides with 8 x 1¼-in. screws concealed by 3/8-in.-dia. ash plugs. I drill and counterbore for these screws and plugs as I go along. I spread some glue in the dadoes and a little bit on the ends of the front and back and fasten them, with screws, to one of the sidepieces. The plywood bottom slides into its grooves next, and I put on the opposite sidepiece. The tray crosspiece that forms the chalk and eraser compartment sits right on the plywood bottom, and I fasten it with a screw in each end and a few brads through the plywood bottom for good measure.

The marker/crayon holder sits flush with the top of the sidepieces to allow for a bit of a space underneath so that anything small (like a paper clip) getting in a hole just falls out. Next I install the brush/pencil trough with a single 1¼-in. screw in each end, locating each screw off center so it won't project into a marker hole.

To plug the screw holes, I cut ash plugs with a 3/8-in.-dia. plug cutter in my drill press. I glue these plugs into the holes, trim off the excess with my dovetail saw, and sand the plugs flush when the glue is dry.

Storage Drawer and Supports

The storage drawer is suspended underneath the storage tray. Hardwood runners on the sides of the drawer slide in grooves milled in the drawer supports (*drawings 4-G and 4-H*).

I rip, joint, and crosscut the drawer supports to size (see Project Planner). The side supports are 2⅝ in. wide, and the back support is 2⅜ in. wide. Next I mill the slots in the side supports with my stack dado head set for a 3/4-in. width and a 1/4-in. depth.

The back drawer support is fastened to the storage tray with glue and

4-20

The back drawer support is fastened to the storage tray with glue and 3 biscuits. I mill matching slots in the top edge of the drawer support and in the bottom edge of the storage tray side.

4-21

To attach the drawer front, I place it face down on the bench and position the drawer box on top of it. Then I predrill and install two 6 x 1-in. screws to fasten the drawer front to the box.

biscuits — 3, to be specific. I mill matching slots in the top edge of the drawer support and the bottom edge of the storage tray side (*drawing 4-G and photo 4-20*). I also mill biscuit slots in each butt joint to connect the side supports to the back support.

To assemble the supports, I place the storage tray upside down on my bench and glue and clamp the back support to the side of the storage tray. Next I glue the side supports to the back support and the plywood bottom. I check with a framing square to make sure the sides and back are square, then I fasten the side supports with a few brads through the plywood bottom of the storage tray.

The drawer is the simplest part of the project to make. The box is made from 4 pieces of 1/2-in. cabinet-grade plywood with a rabbet joint at each corner. The front of the drawer is made of ash and attached to the drawer box with screws.

After cutting the drawer parts to size (*drawing 4-H*), I'm ready to mill the corner rabbet joints. I set up my table saw with my dado head adjusted for a 1/2-in.-wide cut and mill a 1/4-in.-deep rabbet at each end of the plywood sides. Next I set my dado head for a 1/4-in.-wide cut and mill 1/4-in.-deep grooves for the bottom in all four sides of the box.

After sanding all the parts, I assemble the drawer with glue and 1-in. brads. I put 3 sides together, slide in the plywood bottom, and glue and nail the last side.

To attach the drawer front, I place it face down on the bench and position the drawer box on top of it. Then I predrill and install two 6 x 1-in. screws to fasten the drawer front to the box (*photo 4-21*).

Finally, I glue and nail a 1/4-in. by 3/4-in. by 17⅞-in. runner to each side of the drawer with 5/8-in. brads (*photo 4-22*). The finishing touch is a 3/4-in.-dia. Shaker knob, centered in the front of the drawer.

Assembling the Easel

I'm almost ready for the grand finale — putting it all together. But there's one last step before I'm ready to go; I have to install the dowels that support the stor-

4-22
I glue and nail a 17⅞-in. 1/4-in. by 3/4-in. runner to each side of the drawer with 5/8-in. brads.

4-23
To install the dowels that support the storage tray, I made a wooden jig that allows me to drill perpendicular holes with a handheld drill. Using this jig, I drill a 3/8-in.-dia. hole in each leg, 1 in. deep.

age tray. I made a little wooden jig that allows me to drill perpendicular holes with a handheld drill (*photo 4-23*). It's just a block of wood with a groove that fits over the leg and a 3/8-in.-dia. hole bored on the drill press. The center of the hole is 5/16 in. from one edge of the groove. Using this jig, I drill a 3/8-in.-dia. hole in each leg, 1 in. deep. The holes in the pivoting legs are located 16⅝ in. from the bottom (*drawing 4-C*). The holes in the fixed legs are 18¼ in. from the bottom (*drawing 4-D*). With the holes drilled, I glue in 3/8-in. dowels and cut them off so they project 3/8 in. from the leg.

Now for a little assembly. First I attach the art board and chalkboard to the legs with a screw in each corner (*photo 4-24*). Each board is located 22 in. from the bottom end of the leg (*drawing 4-A*), and the legs are spaced 19⅞ in. apart (inside to inside). I make sure to check that the legs are parallel, or the storage tray will stick when it folds.

When the chalk- and art boards are installed, I attach the hinged legs by slipping the hinge pins into place. (If the pins are loose, I bend them slightly before installing them to keep them from falling out.) Now I can install the tray assembly by removing a screw from one bottom corner of the art board on the fixed-leg side and spread the legs apart enough to engage the dowels in the slots in the storage tray sides. Then I just reinstall the screw.

Next the paper-roll dowel drops into the slot on top. And that's all there is to it. Now I need to think about a finish.

On ash, I really like the look of a honey maple stain with a gloss polyurethane

top coat. The polyurethane will be easy to clean when it gets covered with markers and paint. I just disassemble the easel so I can get into every corner with the stain and finish. I mask off the chalkboard and art board to keep them pristine, and I brush on the stain and wipe off the excess with a rag. Finally, I add a couple of coats of polyurethane, sanding lightly between coats with some 220-grit paper.

Now, that's what I call an easel!

5

playhouse

project planner

Time: 8 days

Special hardware, tools, and materials:

(1) 8-in.-wide lead flashing, 3 ft. long
(1) 6-in.-wide lead flashing, 7 ft. long
(24) 5-in. by 7-in. aluminum step flashing
(1) 1½-in. barrel bolt
(2) pair of 6-in. galvanized T hinges
(1) thumb latch
(1) roll 15# felt paper
(5 lb.) 3d hot-dipped galvanized box nails
(3 lb.) 16d galvanized common nails
(10 lb.) 12d common nails
(6 lb.) 6d ring-shank galvanized nails
(3 lb.) 6d galvanized finish nails
(5 lb.) 6d ring-shank stainless-steel nails (for corner boards)
(5 lb.) 6d common nails
(100) 1¼-in. galvanized bugle-head or deck screws
(200) 3-in. galvanized bugle-head or deck screws
(6) concrete blocks

Wood:

Note that all dimensions given are for 1 x and 2 x lumber that is exactly 1½ in. (2 x) or 3/4 in. (1 x) thick.

(4) 8-ft. 2 x 6 pressure-treated
Cut 2 pieces 96 in. for rim joists, one piece 81 in. for a joist, 2 pieces 21¾ in. for blocking, and 2 pieces 22½ in. for blocking.

(2) 14-ft. 2 x 6 pressure-treated
Cut 4 pieces 81 in. long for joists.

(1) 8-ft. 2 x 4 pressure-treated
Cut 2 pieces 21¾ in. and 2 pieces 22½ in. for

EVERY CHILD DREAMS of having his or her own special playhouse. Here's one that's guaranteed to be a sure-fire hit with the children in your family. It has a front porch, a Dutch door, a wood-shingle roof — even a flower box! I designed it with "panelized" floor, walls, and roof so it can be built in the workshop and then taken out and assembled in the yard. The panels can even be disassembled, if necessary, should the playhouse ever need to be knocked down and moved. Don't wait too long to get started on this one — your kids (or your grandkids) won't be little forever.

I designed the playhouse on paper to work out the details and dimensions. As with all large projects, I use the dimensions on my plan as a guideline. It's always best to mark pieces and cut to fit as you go along. There's wisdom in the old carpenter's motto, "Measure twice, cut once."

Floor Platform

I get started with the floor platform, the largest element of the playhouse (*drawing 5-C*). The frame is made from 2 x 6 pressure-treated lumber. The floor itself is made of 1/2-in. CDX plywood, and I use 1 x 4 square-edge fir decking for the porch floor.

The first thing to do is cut the 2 x 6 floor joists to length with my circular saw.

5-A Major Anatomy

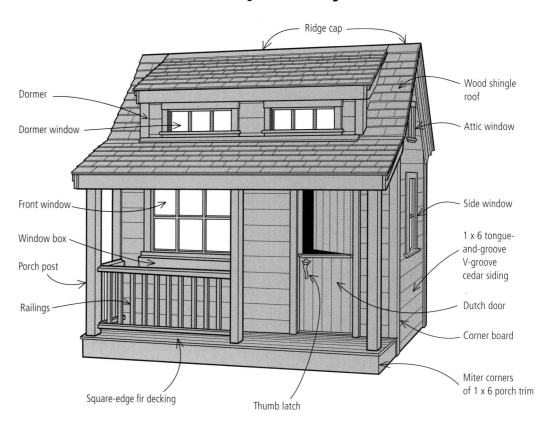

Ridge cap

Wood shingle roof

Dormer

Attic window

Dormer window

Front window

Side window

Window box

1 x 6 tongue-and-groove V-groove cedar siding

Porch post

Dutch door

Railings

Corner board

Square-edge fir decking

Miter corners of 1 x 6 porch trim

Thumb latch

(1) 14-ft. 4 x 4 fir
Cut 3 pieces 53¼ in. long for porch posts.

(1) 12-ft. 2 x 8 spruce
Rip according to plan, then cut one piece 99 in. and 2 pieces 12 in. for ridge beams for main-roof panels.

(1) 16-ft. 2 x 6 spruce
Cut one piece 99 in. and one piece 75 in., then rip according to plan for ridge for porch- and dormer-roof panels.

(5) 14-ft. 2 x 4 spruce
Cut three 14-ft. lengths into 12 main roof rafters. From two 14-ft. lengths cut 4 studs 73¹¹⁄₁₆ in. for long front-wall studs.

(3) 12-ft. 2 x 4 spruce
From each of 2 lengths cut one piece 99 in. and rip according to plan for pieces to tie bottom of porch rafters together. Cut scrap according to plan for nailers for roof flashing.
Cut one length into one piece 99 in. for plate to tie bottom of main-roof rafters together and cut one piece according to plan for a main-roof rafter.

(17) 10-ft. 2 x 4 spruce
Cut 8 lengths into 9 pieces 57 in. for front- and back-wall studs and one piece 52½ in. for stud at door. Cut 2 pieces 53 in. for sole-plates for gable walls. Cut 4 pieces 57⅞ in. to the long point of a 45-degree angle for gable-wall studs.
Cut each of 4 lengths into one piece 74⅛ in. to the long point of a 45-degree angle for gable studs and 2 pieces

I need two 8-ft. rim joists for the front and back of the floor platform and 5 joists 81 in. long (*drawing 5-C*).

When the pieces are cut, I lay them out on the shop floor and nail the frame together with 16d galvanized common nails (*photo 5-1*). In the old days, I would have driven these nails with a framing hammer, but my pneumatic nail gun sure makes the job go faster and easier.

Next I need to install some blocking to support the front wall of the play-house and the joint in the plywood floor (*drawing 5-C*). From pressure-treated 2 x 6, I cut 2 pieces 22½ in. long and 2 pieces 21¾ in. long. From pressure-treated 2 x 4, I cut 2 pieces 22½ long and 2 pieces 21¾ in. long. I measure 60 in. from the outer edge of the back rim joist and snap a chalkline across the joists to locate the 2 x 6 blocks that will support the front edge of the floor sheathing. I snap a second line 9¾ in. from the inside face of the back rim joist to locate the 2 x 4 blocks. I nail the 2 x 6 blocking on the back side of the line; the 2 x 4 blocking is nailed to the front side of the line.

With the floor frame complete, I'm ready to install the floor. First I check to make sure the frame is square by measuring across the diagonals. If the measure-ments are equal, the frame is square. Now I nail a 4-ft. by 8-ft. sheet of plywood to the frame with some 6d ring-shank galvanized nails, holding the front edge of the sheet flush with the front edge of the 2 x 6 blocking (*drawing 5-C*). From a second sheet of plywood I rip a 12-in.-wide piece 8 ft. long. I butt this piece up against the other sheet and nail it in place (*photo 5-2*).

The porch floor comes next. I cut 7 pieces of 1 x 4 square-edge fir 98½ in. long. I space the first board 3/4 in. from the edge of the plywood and position it

5-B Section Through Frame and Trim

Note: Use 15# felt paper under roof shingles.
Secure all trim with 6d galvanized box nails or stainless-steel nails.

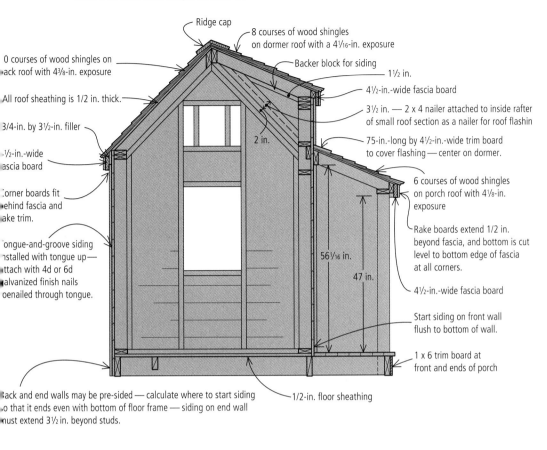

Ridge cap

8 courses of wood shingles on dormer roof with a 4¹/₁₆-in. exposure

Backer block for siding

1½ in.

4½-in.-wide fascia board

3½ in. — 2 x 4 nailer attached to inside rafter of small roof section as a nailer for roof flashin

75-in.-long by 4½-in.-wide trim board to cover flashing — center on dormer.

6 courses of wood shingles on porch roof with 4⅛-in. exposure

Rake boards extend ½ in. beyond fascia, and bottom is cut level to bottom edge of fascia at all corners.

4½-in.-wide fascia board

Start siding on front wall flush to bottom of wall.

1 x 6 trim board at front and ends of porch

½-in. floor sheathing

0 courses of wood shingles on ack roof with 4⅜-in. exposure

All roof sheathing is 1/2 in. thick.

3/4-in. by 3½-in. filler

½-in.-wide ascia board

orner boards fit ehind fascia and ake trim.

ongue-and-groove siding nstalled with tongue up— ttach with 4d or 6d alvanized finish nails oenailed through tongue.

2 in.

56¹/₁₆ in.

47 in.

ack and end walls may be pre-sided — calculate where to start siding o that it ends even with bottom of floor frame — siding on end wall must extend 3½ in. beyond studs.

5-C Floor Frame

Note: Framing is pressure-treated 2 x 6, except as noted.
Assemble with 16d galvanized common nails.
Set floor on a minimum of six 8-in. concrete blocks, 3 at front and 3 at back.

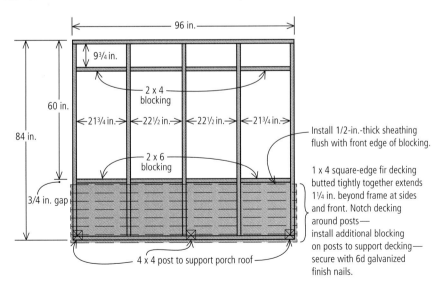

96 in.

9¾ in.

60 in.

84 in.

2 x 4 blocking

21¾ in.   22½ in.   22½ in.   21¾ in.

2 x 6 blocking

3/4 in. gap

Install ½-in.-thick sheathing flush with front edge of blocking.

1 x 4 square-edge fir decking butted tightly together extends 1¼ in. beyond frame at sides and front. Notch decking around posts — install additional blocking on posts to support decking — secure with 6d galvanized finish nails.

4 x 4 post to support porch roof

17½ in. for gable-window and attic-window sills and headers.

Cut one length into 3 pieces 24½ in. for header sill and flat block for dormer window above large front window and one piece 24¹⁵/₁₆ in. for window stud.

From each of 3 lengths cut 2 rafters according to plan for dormer roof and 2 rafters according to plan for porch roof.

Cut one length into one piece 78 in. and rip according to plan for piece to tie bottom of dormer rafters together and one piece according to plan for a porch rafter.

(8) 8-ft. 2 x 4 spruce

Cut 4 lengths into 3 pieces 96 in., one piece 75 in., and 2 pieces 10½ in. for sole- and top plates for front and back walls.

Cut 2 lengths into 4 pieces 37½ in. from the short point to the long point of a 45-degree angle for top plates for gable walls.

Cut one length into 3 pieces 24½ in. for header sill and flat block for dormer window above door and one piece 19¹¹/₁₆ in. for window stud.

Cut one length into 3 pieces 30 in. long for headers and sill for front door and window.

From remaining scrap 2 x 4s cut 4 pieces 12 in. for studs for sides of attic-window opening and any backers and fillers according to plan.

(7) 10-ft. 1 x 4 square-edge fir decking

Cut 7 pieces 98½ in. long for porch decking and

one piece 18⅜ in. for door threshold.

(1) 10-ft. 1 x 4 No. 2 common pine
Cut one piece 97½ in. for filler behind back fascia and 4 pieces 5 in. for spacers over dormer windows.

(4) 4-ft. by 8-ft. ½-in. CDX plywood
For floor and roof sheathing.

(25) 8-ft. 1 x 6 V-groove tongue-and-groove red cedar siding
For siding for front and back walls.

(16) 10-ft. 1 x 6 V-groove tongue-and-groove red cedar siding
For siding for gable end walls.

(4) 12-ft. 1 x 4 V-groove tongue-and-groove red cedar siding
Cut each of 3 lengths into 2 pieces 27¾ in., 2 pieces 24 in., and 2 pieces 19½ in.
From remaining length cut one piece 27¾ in., one piece 24 in., and 2 pieces 26 in. for boards, shelf, and Z-brace for Dutch door. Rip and joint 19½-in. and 26-in. pieces to 2½ in. wide for shelf and Z-brace.

(4) 14-ft. 1 x 6 No. 1 common pine
Cut 2 lengths to fit for rake boards.
Rip one length into one piece 3 in. wide and one piece 2¼ in. wide and cut to fit for corner boards for front and dormer.
Cut one length to fit for porch trim to cover joists.

(2) 12-ft. 1 x 6 No. 1 common pine
Rip one length into one piece 3 in. wide and

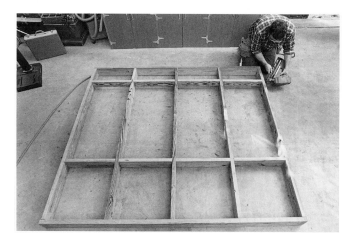

5-1
When the pieces of the floor-platform frame are cut, I lay them out on the shop floor and nail them together with 16d galvanized common nails.

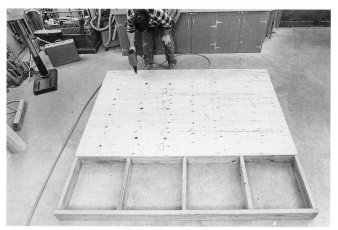

5-2
To complete the interior floor, I cut a 12-in.-wide piece 8 ft. long. I butt this piece up against the other sheet and nail it in place.

so that the ends extend 1¼ in. beyond each side of the frame. I nail it in place with some 6d galvanized finish nails, driving the nails through the face of the board (*photo 5-3*). I install 4 more boards, butting the edges together before I nail them in place. I install only 5 boards now — I'll put on the last 2 later.

Gable Walls

Before I build any walls, I snap lines on the plywood floor 3½ in. from the outside face of the joists and 3½ in. from the front blocks. These lines indicate the inside faces of all the walls.

The 2 gable walls of the playhouse are identical. Each wall has a 2 x 4 frame made of 13 pieces. There are some angle cuts required, but they're all simple 45-degree cuts — easy to make on my power miter box. I measure and cut all the frame parts to length according to the dimensions in the plan (*drawing 5-D*) and the Project Planner. When cutting duplicate parts of the same length, I set a saw stop on my miter-box fence so that the pieces are all exactly the same length.

With the frame pieces cut, I lay each frame out on the floor platform (a convenient place to work) to mark the location of the joints and make sure everything fits as it should (*photo 5-4*). Then I nail together the frame with 12d common nails (16d common nails are also acceptable). Next I temporarily tack the sole-plate along one of the chalklines I snapped on the plywood floor and measure across the diagonals to make sure the frame is square. I rack the frame as neces-

5-3
I install 1 x 4 square-edged fir boards for the porch floor. I nail the boards in place with some 6d galvanized finish nails.

5-4
I lay out the parts for the gable wall frame on the floor to mark the location of the joints and to make sure everything fits. Then I nail together the frame with 12d common nails.

5-D Gable Wall (2 required)

Note: Frame with 2 x 4s.
All angle cuts are 45 degrees.

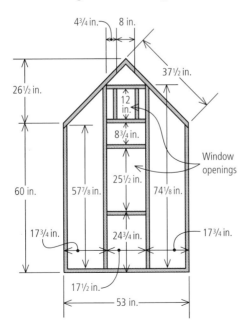

4³⁄₄ in. 8 in.

37¹⁄₂ in.

26¹⁄₂ in.

12 in.

8³⁄₄ in.

Window openings

60 in.   57⁷⁄₈ in.   25¹⁄₂ in.   74¹⁄₈ in.

17³⁄₄ in.   24³⁄₄ in.   17³⁄₄ in.

17¹⁄₂ in.

53 in.

one piece 2¼ in. wide and cut to fit for corner boards for back. Rip one length into one piece 2¾ in. wide and one piece 2 in. wide. Cut according to plan for door jamb and door casings.

(2) 10-ft. 1 x 6 No. 1 common pine
Rip to 4½ in. wide and cut to fit for porch and back fascia.

(1) 8-ft. 1 x 6 No. 1 common pine
Rip 4½ in. wide and cut to fit for dormer fascia.

(1) 14-ft. 1 x 4 No. 1 common pine
Cut 2 pieces 30 in. and rip one piece 2⁷⁄₈ in. wide and one piece 1/2 in. wide from each. Rip remainder into one piece 2 in. wide and one piece 1¼ in. wide, then cut according to plan for sill, trim, casings, and jamb for dormer windows.

(1) 12-ft. 1 x 4 No. 1 common pine
Rip and joint into 2 pieces 7/8 in. wide and cut according to plan for window muntins.

(1) 10-ft. 1 x 4 No. 1 common pine
Cut one piece 36 in. From it, rip one piece 2⁷⁄₈ in. wide and one piece 1/2 in. wide. Rip remainder into one piece 2 in. wide and one piece 1¼ in. wide, then cut according to plan for sill, trim, casings, and jamb for front window.

(3) 8-ft. 1 x 4 No. 1 common pine
From each of 2 lengths cut one piece 23 in. and from it rip one piece 2⁷⁄₈ in. wide and one piece 1/2 in. wide. Rip remainder into one

piece 2 in. wide and one piece 1¼ in. wide, then cut according to plan for sill, trim, casings, and jamb for side windows.
From one length cut 2 pieces 13 in.; rip one piece 2⅞ in. wide and one piece 1/2 in. wide from each. Rip remainder into one piece 2 in. wide and one piece 1¼ in. wide, then cut according to plan for sill, trim, casings, and jamb for attic windows.

(2) 14-ft. 1 x 2 No. 1 common pine
Cut to fit for shingle cleats on rake boards.

(5 bundles) No. 1 Blue Label cedar shingles
For roofing.

(1) 12-ft. 1 x 10 western red cedar
Cut one piece 108 in., then cut to fit for ridge cap.
Cut one piece 33 in., then rip according to plan for front of window box.

(1) 14-ft. 1 x 6 western red cedar
Cut one piece 75 in. and rip to 4½ in. wide for trim to cover lead flashing on porch roof.
Cut 2 pieces 33 in. and 2 pieces 6 in. for back, bottom, and ends of window box.

(1) 14-ft. 2 x 6 vertical-grain redwood
Cut one piece 46 in. and one piece 20 in., then rip and joint each into 2 pieces 2½ in. wide for top and bottom porch rails.
From remaining piece rip and joint 2 pieces 3/8 in. x 1 in. for lattice strips and 3 pieces 1 in. square for balusters for railings.

5-5
I fasten the siding to the frame by angling a 6d finish nail right through the tongue into each stud. This way the nails won't show.

5-6
I set the nail heads below the surface of the wood with a hammer and a nail set.

sary until the diagonals are equal and then temporarily tack the frame to the floor to make sure it stays square while I put on the siding.

Now I'm ready to install the siding. I've chosen nice 1 x 6 V-groove red cedar tongue-and-groove siding — a weather-resistant wood that will last for years. I install this siding horizontally. On the gable walls, the ends of the siding boards must extend 3½ in. beyond the frame on both sides of the wall so that the siding will overlap the studs of the front and back walls when I assemble them later. For each wall I cut 9 pieces of siding 60 in. long and 8 pieces 21½ in. long. I also need to cut a few more pieces to fill in at the top around the little attic window, but I'll cut these to fit as I go by using the offcuts left from the longer pieces.

Let's get started. I position a long piece of siding — tongue facing up — at the bottom of the wall, making sure that the ends extend 3½ in. beyond the frame on each side. I hold the bottom edge of the first board 1½ in. below the bottom edge of the wall. I do this because later, after the wall is in place, I'll add another siding board below this one in order to extend the siding down to the bottom edge of the floor-platform joists (*drawing 5-B*).

I fasten the siding to the frame by angling a 6d galvanized finish nail right through the tongue into each stud (*photo 5-5*). This way the nails won't show. I also face-nail this first board to the studs and soleplate. I set the nail head below the surface of the wood with a hammer and a nail set (*photo 5-6*). The next board goes on over the tongue. I tap it in place to close up the gap and nail it through the tongue. A scrap piece of siding works well to tap the pieces together so you don't damage the tongue. Six boards takes me just above the bottom of the window opening. At this point, I switch to the 21½-in.-long pieces and

5-7

5-7 and 5-8
I trim off the excess siding along the pitch of the roof and around the window openings with my router and a flush trim bit.

5-8

5-E Back Wall

Note: Frame with 2 x 4s.

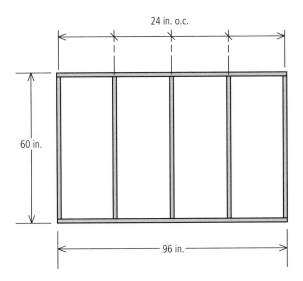

install them on either side of the window opening. I flush up the outer ends with the longer boards — the inner ends extend into the window opening slightly, but I'll trim that off later. Three more long boards go over the top of the window. Now I cut shorter boards and finish installing the siding around the attic window and roof pitch. I want the ends to extend beyond the roof pitch and into the window opening slightly — I'll trim off the overhanging material later. The last little piece at the peak of the roof has to be face-nailed to the frame.

Now I'm ready to trim off the excess material. I set up my router with a flush trim bit and remove the excess around the window openings and along the pitch of the roof (*photo 5-7*). Next, on each side of the wall, I measure 60 in. up from the soleplate and make a 3½-in.-long cut with my circular saw, parallel to the bottom of the wall. That takes care of one gable wall — now I'll do the other one.

Back Wall

The back wall is the simplest of all walls to frame — just 5 studs and 2 plates (*drawing 5-E*). I cut five 2 x 4s 57 in. long for the studs, and two 2 x 4 plates 8 ft. long. I lay out the pieces on the floor platform, mark the studs on 2-ft. centers, and nail up the frame with 12d common nails.

The back wall has no windows in it, so it's also very easy to put on the siding.

5-F Front Wall
(viewed from inside)

Note: Frame with 2 x 4s.
Assemble wall and roof framing with 12d or 16d common nails.

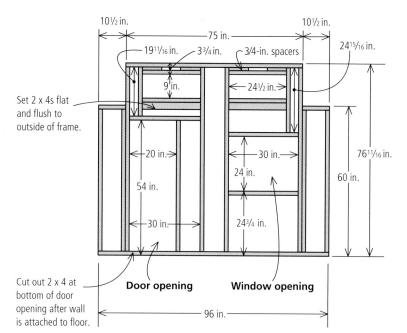

Set 2 x 4s flat
and flush to
outside of frame.

10½ in.

75 in.

10½ in.

19¹¹⁄₁₆ in.   3¾ in.   ¾-in. spacers

24¹⁵⁄₁₆ in.

9 in.

24½ in.

20 in.   30 in.

76¹¹⁄₁₆ in.

24 in.

54 in.

60 in.

30 in.   24¾ in.

Door opening   Window opening

Cut out 2 x 4 at
bottom of door
opening after wall
is attached to floor.

96 in.

5-9
**The floor platform rests on concrete
block piers.**

I check the frame for square and tack it to the floor so it won't move. Next I cut twelve 8-ft. lengths of 1 x 6 tongue-and-groove siding. On this wall, the ends of the siding are flush with the studs. I hold the edge of the first board 1½ in. below the bottom of the soleplate, just as I did with the gable walls. Once I attach this first piece of siding, I nail on the others with 6d galvanized finish nails. I stop the siding 3/4 in. above the top of the wall.

Front Wall

The front wall comes next. Since it's bigger than the floor platform, I build it on the shop floor. The front wall is framed up with 2 x 4s, and there are 24 pieces required. I lay out and cut the pieces according to the plan (*drawing 5-F* and Project Planner). Nothing fancy about the cuts on this wall — they're all 90-degree cuts.

For the bottom of each dormer window, I need to fasten two 24½-in. lengths of 2 x 4 together to make an L-shaped piece (*drawing 5-F*). One 2 x 4 of this L forms the bottom of the dormer-window opening. The other piece makes a nailing area for the porch-roof panel. I nail together these pieces with 12d common nails.

Before I can assemble the wall, I also need to cut four 5-in. spacers from 1 x 4. These spacers go between the top plate of the wall and the headers for the dormer windows (*drawing 5-F*).

I lay out all the pieces on the shop floor and mark the locations of all the parts. I fasten the frame together with 12d common nails, making sure to hold the lower 2 x 4 of the L-shaped window pieces flush with the *outside* of the front-wall frame.

With the frame complete, I cut and install the siding, first making sure that the frame is square. The long pieces are 96 in. long (no overhang on the ends for this wall), and I fill in around the window and door with short pieces as I did for the gable walls. For the front wall, I hold the bottom edge of the first piece of siding flush with the bottom of the soleplate. I extend the siding up the wall to 3/4 in. above the lower top plates (*drawing 5-F*). When I'm finished, I trim around the insides of the door and window openings with my router (*photo 5-8*).

Leveling the Floor Platform

The floor platform rests on 6 concrete blocks — 3 in the front and 3 in the back (*photo 5-9*). I locate a block at the lowest corner of the site. I remove the topsoil and replace it with gravel. Then I put the block in position and level it. I use the height of this block as a baseline for leveling the other corner blocks with a straightedge and level. I excavate underneath the other concrete blocks and vary the amount of gravel as necessary to level them with the first one. When the corner blocks are all level, I put the other 2 blocks in place and level them. Different sites may require a different foundation treatment. You could even pour concrete piers to support the playhouse.

Now I can put the floor platform on the blocks. I check the platform to make sure it's level and fine-tune, if necessary, with shim shingles.

Putting Up the Walls

With the floor platform leveled and ready to go, it's time to assemble the walls. I start with the front wall. I position it up against the edge of the porch

5-10
I slip the gable wall into place against the front wall so the siding overhangs the front wall's corner stud and align the soleplate with a chalk line snapped on the plywood floor platform. I attach the gable wall to the floor platform and the front wall with screws, making sure the screws penetrate the floor frame.

5-G Main Roof

**Note: 12:12 roof pitch —
roof frame extends 1½ in. beyond end walls.**

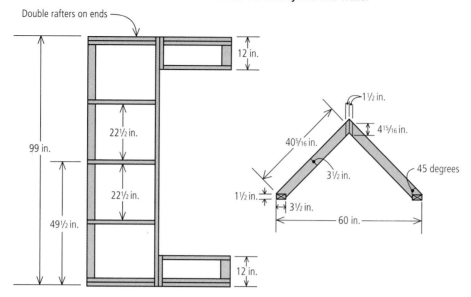

5-H Dormer Roof

**Note: 5:12 roof pitch — front of roof frame
extends 1½ in. beyond top of front wall.**

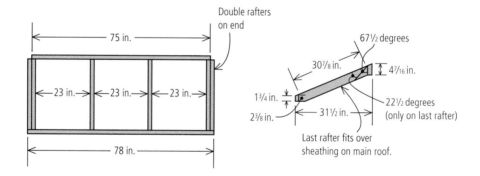

5-I Porch Roof

**Note: 5:12 roof pitch — roof frame
extends 1½ in. beyond 4 x 4 posts.**

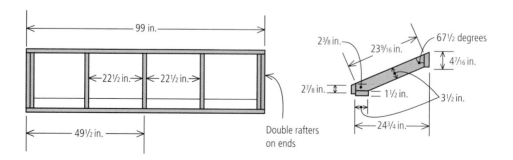

flooring and attach it to the floor platform with 3-in. screws through the sole-plate and into the joists. I use screws instead of nails so I can disassemble the playhouse later in case I ever need to move it or store it.

One of the gable walls goes on next (*photo 5-10*). I slip it into place against the front wall so the siding overhangs the front wall's corner stud and so the siding at the bottom of the wall fits up against the edge of the floor platform. Then I attach the gable wall to the front wall and floor platform with 3-in. screws, being sure the screws go into the floor frame. The other gable wall goes up the same way. And finally the back wall gets fastened to the floor platform and gable walls.

With the walls in place, I install the additional siding boards to cover the floor-platform joists at the back and sides of the house. I also install 2 courses of siding on the front wall, starting from the top down.

Roof Panels

The roof of the playhouse consists of 5 separate panels. The main roof has 3; the large section at the back of the house and two 12-in.-wide sections at the front on either side of the shed dormer (*drawing 5-G*). The shed-dormer roof is a separate panel (*drawing 5-H*), as is the porch roof (*drawing 5-I*).

I'm going to prefabricate the roof panels in the shop, just as I did with the walls and floor. Before I start cutting the pieces, I need to make some patterns so that I get the right shapes and angles for the rafters and ridge beams.

I start with the 12-in.-wide sections of the main roof (*drawing 5-G*). First I cut a piece of 2 x 4 12 in. long. This piece ties the bottom ends of the rafters to-gether, but for now I'm just using it to make the rafter pattern. I place this 2 x 4 on top of the front wall's top plate, next to the dormer window. The bottom end of the rafters will be notched to fit over this piece (*drawing 5-G*).

At the top end of the rafter, I need a double-beveled piece that will form half of the ridge beam (*drawing 5-G*). I cut a 12-in. piece of 2 x 8 to use as a pattern. On the table saw I rip a 45-degree bevel on each edge so that the piece, in cross-section, has a parallelogram shape measuring $4\frac{15}{16}$ in. from bevel to bevel (*drawing 5-G*).

Now I make a sample rafter. I cut a 42-in. length of 2 x 4 and make a 45-degree cut at one end on my miter box. At the other end, I need to cut a notch that fits over the 2 x 4 sitting on the front wall. In Massachusetts, where I come from, this notch at the bottom end of a rafter is called a "crow's foot." I measure $40\frac{5}{16}$ in. from the long point of the 45-degree cut I just made and lay out the crow's foot with my square as shown in the plan (*drawing 5-G*). I cut the crow's foot with my circular saw (*photo 5-11*), finishing up the corner cut with a hand-saw (*photo 5-12*).

I'll take these sample pieces out to the playhouse and see how they fit on the walls. With the 12-in. 2 x 4 on top of the front wall, I hold the sample rafter in position with the ridge board at the top. I make any necessary adjustments to the length and angles of my sample pieces and then use these as patterns to cut the roof parts.

First I'm going to rip the ridge beams for the main roof. I tilt the table-saw blade to 45 degrees. If the angle of my sample piece is slightly more or less than 45 degrees, I go with the angle on the sample. Then I rip a bevel on one edge of a

5-11

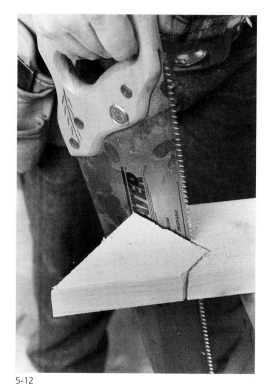

5-12

5-11 and 5-12
I cut a notch called a "crow's foot" at the bottom ends of the rafters to fit over the 2 x 4 that will sit on the top plate of the wall. I make 2 cuts with my circular saw and finish the corner with a handsaw.

99-in. length of 2 x 8 for the rear ridge beam and another 12-in. piece of 2 x 8 for the remaining ridge beam for the narrow roof panels (*drawing 5-G*). Using my sample piece, I position the rip fence to determine the width of my ridge beam and rip a second bevel on the opposite edge of each piece (*photo 5-13*).

Using my rafter pattern, I lay out and cut 12 rafters for the main roof — all with a 45-degree angle on one end and a crow's foot at the other. Note that there are double rafters on each end of the back roof panel and double rafters on the outside edge of the narrow roof panels (*drawing 5-G*).

Now I'm ready to make the large main-roof panel for the back of the playhouse. I need to cut a 99-in.-long 2 x 4 to tie the bottom ends of the rafters together. On my sawhorses, I lay out the ridge beam and this long bottom piece. I make 2 double rafters by nailing rafters together with 12d nails. Now I nail these double rafters to each end of the ridge beam and attach the other 3 rafters in between, spacing them as shown in the plan (*drawing 5-G*). Now I can nail on the long piece that connects the bottoms of the rafters together (*photo 5-14*).

With the frame complete, I'm ready to put on the plywood sheathing. First I check the frame for square and rack it as necessary until the diagonals are equal. I install a full sheet of 1/2-in. CDX plywood flush with the top of the ridge beam and centered on the length of the roof. I attach it with 1½-in. staples or 6d common nails. The sheet is 3 in. shorter than the roof panel, so I add a 1½-in.-wide strip of plywood to each end to complete the sheathing. Then I trim off the excess along the bottom edge of the panel with my circular saw. I use the same procedure to make the two 12-in. roof panels.

5-13
I rip a 45-degree bevel on one edge of the ridge beam. I position the rip fence to give me the 4^{15}/$_{16}$-in. width of my ridge beam and rip a second bevel on the opposite edge.

5-14
I assemble the large roof panel on sawhorses. I nail the double rafters to each end of the ridge beam and attach the other 3 rafters in between. Now I nail on the long piece that connects the bottoms of the rafters together.

5-15
The outer rafter of the dormer roof has to be cut to conform to the pitch of the small roof panels. I make a 22½-degree angle cut before nailing the double rafters together.

Installing the main-roof panels is easy. With a helper to assist me, I hoist the large back panel into position and align it so that the ends overhang the gable wall siding by 3/4 in. Then I attach it to the gable walls and back wall with 3-in. screws from the inside. The two 12-in. panels go on the same way, and I fasten them to the walls and to the ridge beam of the back roof panel with screws.

The dormer roof is the next thing to make. Here, too, I cut sample pieces as patterns to make sure that everything fits. Then I use the patterns to lay out the parts (see *drawing 5-H* and Project Planner). The ridge board for this roof is a 75-in.-long 2 x 6 ripped to a 22½-degree bevel along the top edge. The piece that ties together the bottom ends of the rafters is a 78-in.-long 2 x 4 with a 22½-degree bevel on the top edge. The rafters have a 67½-degree angle cut at the top end and a 2⅜-in. plumb cut at the bottom end, with a level cut underneath. The rafters measure 30⅞ in. along the top edge.

Just as with the other roof sections, the dormer-roof end rafters are double rafters, but the outer rafter has to be cut to conform to the pitch of the small roof panels I've already installed. I make a 22½-degree angle cut as shown (*drawing 5-H*) before nailing the double rafters together (*photo 5-15*).

I frame up the dormer-roof panel just as I did with the others — nail the ridge beam to the rafters and then attach the long piece at the bottom. I sheath the panel with plywood and trim off the excess with my circular saw. At the top corners, I trim the plywood out of the notches formed by the ridge beam and outer rafters (*drawing 5-H*). Now all I need to do is to install the dormer roof on the playhouse and attach it to the main ridge beam and front wall with screws.

I use the same techniques to make the porch-roof panel (*drawing 5-I* and Project Planner), but before I actually build it, I mill and install the 3 porch posts. This way, I can make any necessary adjustments to fit the structure.

Porch Posts

The 3 posts that support the porch roof are the next thing to make (*drawings 5-A, 5-B, and 5-J*). They're 53¼-in. lengths of 4 x 4 fir notched to fit into the floor frame. The 2 end posts are notched on 2 sides, while the center post is notched on only one side (*drawing 5-J*).

I lay out the end-post notches with my combination square. I measure up 5½ in. from one end and square a line around the post. Then I use my square as a guide to mark layout lines, parallel to the length of the post, 1½ in. from the edge on 2 opposite faces. Then I turn the post 90 degrees and draw another pair of lines on 2 opposite faces. When I connect these layout lines by drawing pencil lines across the end of the post, I should have a 2 in. square in one corner of the post (*drawing 5-J*). I want to remove all the material except this 2-in.-square section. It's easy to make a wrong cut, so I shade in the area I want to remove with a pencil, just to be safe.

I set my circular saw for a 1½-in. depth of cut and make a crosscut, 5½ in. from the end, on adjacent faces of the post, cutting down to my 1½-in. layout lines (*photo 5-16*). Next, with the saw set at full depth, I make 2 rip cuts along the layout lines, cutting on the waste side of the lines. Then I make 2 more rip cuts along the remaining 2 layout lines, making sure to cut on the waste side of the line (*photo 5-17*). I finish up with a handsaw to remove the scrap material (*photo 5-18*).

5-16
To notch the end posts, I make a 1½-in.-deep crosscut, 5½ in. from the end of the post, on 2 adjacent sides.

5-17
Now I set my saw to full depth and make 2 more rip cuts along the remaining 2 layout lines, being sure to cut on the waste side of the line.

5-J Porch Posts

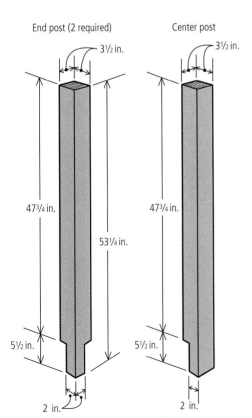

End post (2 required)   Center post

3½ in.   3½ in.

47¾ in.   47¾ in.

53¼ in.

5½ in.   5½ in.

2 in.   2 in.

5-18
I finish up the notches with a handsaw to remove the scrap material.

5-K Roof Details

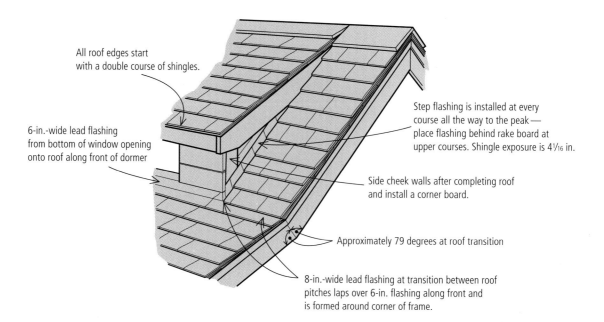

All roof edges start with a double course of shingles.

6-in.-wide lead flashing from bottom of window opening onto roof along front of dormer

Step flashing is installed at every course all the way to the peak — place flashing behind rake board at upper courses. Shingle exposure is 4 1/16 in.

Side cheek walls after completing roof and install a corner board.

Approximately 79 degrees at roof transition

8-in.-wide lead flashing at transition between roof pitches laps over 6-in. flashing along front and is formed around corner of frame.

5-L Rake Board Details

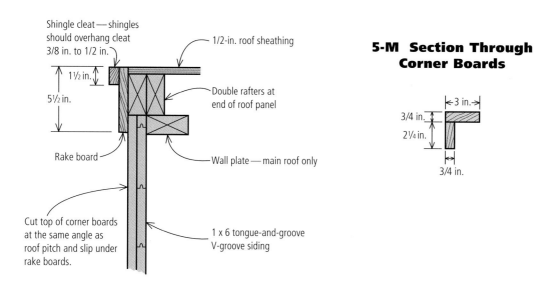

Shingle cleat — shingles should overhang cleat 3/8 in. to 1/2 in.

1/2-in. roof sheathing

1 1/2 in.

5 1/2 in.

Double rafters at end of roof panel

Rake board

Wall plate — main roof only

Cut top of corner boards at the same angle as roof pitch and slip under rake boards.

1 x 6 tongue-and-groove V-groove siding

5-M Section Through Corner Boards

3 in.

3/4 in.

2 1/4 in.

3/4 in.

The center post is easier. I square a line around 3 sides of the post 5½ in. from the end. I mark lines 1½ in. from the edge on 2 opposite sides of the post. With my circular saw set for a 1½-in.-deep cut, I make a crosscut, 5½ in. from the end, on one face of the post. Then I set my saw to full depth and make a rip cut along each of my layout lines. I finish up with the handsaw, leaving a 2-in.-wide section the full width of the post (*drawing 5-J*).

Before I install the posts, I ease the corners with a 1/4-in.-radius roundover bit in my router. Now I can put the posts into position on the playhouse (*drawings 5-B and 5-C*) and attach them to the floor-platform rim joists with 3-in. screws.

With the posts in place, I cut some short blocks of 3/4-in. scrap and attach them to the posts to support the remaining porch floorboards. With these blocks in place, I install the remaining 2 porch floorboards, marking out where I need to notch them around the porch posts and cutting these notches out with my jigsaw. I nail the boards into position to complete the porch floor.

Now that the posts are in place, I can make the porch-roof panel as explained above (*drawing 5-I*) and attach it with screws to the studs, the L-shaped nailers under the dormer windows in the front wall, and the porch posts. The edge of the roof frame extends 1½ in. beyond the posts.

Dormer Wall Nailers

I need to install some 2 x 4s along the sides of the dormer wall to give me a nailing surface for the flashing and the siding on the sides of the dormers (*drawing 5-B*). At the bottom, I mark and cut a 2 x 4 nailer for the flashing. This piece gets cut to a 45-degree angle at each end. I attach it to the inside face of the outer dormer rafter with screws. At the top, I mark and install a nailer for the siding, cutting a 67½-degree bevel at the bottom end and a 22½-degree bevel at the top end. Both sides of the dormer get the same treatment.

Installing the Trim

The next thing to do is make and install the trim for the playhouse (*drawings 5-A, 5-K, 5-L, and 5-M*). Here's a quick rundown of the items I need: the pressure-treated floor platform underneath the porch is covered by 1 x 6 trim boards, mitered at the corners (*drawings 5-A and 5-B*). Corner boards (*drawings 5-A, 5-B, 5-L, and 5-M*) cover the corners of the playhouse where the siding meets. The gable ends are trimmed out with a 1 x 6 rake board and a 1½-in.-wide shingle cleat (*drawings 5-K and 5-L*). A 4½-in.-wide fascia board trims out the front of the porch roof and dormer roof as well as the lower edge of the back roof (*drawings 5-A and 5-B*).

Rake Boards and Fascia

Let's start by trimming out the roof. For the rake boards on the gable ends I start with two 1 x 6 pine boards approximately 50 in. long. I make a 45-degree-angle cut on one end of each board. Next, with 6d galvanized finish nails, I fasten the back rake board in position on the gable, flush to the roof surface and with the 45-degree end centered at the top. The lower end of the front rake board (the one going toward the front of the house) must be cut at an angle where it meets the rake board on the porch roof (*drawing 5-K*). I tack the front rake board in place and mark where the planes of the main roof and porch roof meet, using my adjustable sliding bevel to lay out the angle (approximately 79 degrees). I remove the rake board, make the cut, and install it.

Now I cut a 32-in. piece of 1 x 6 and fit the lower rake board that trims the sides of the porch roof. I mark the angle where it meets the upper rake board (approximately 79 degrees), cut the end for a tight joint, and install it. I'll trim the bottom end later.

I need to make 2 other rake boards for the dormer roof (*drawing 5-K*). At the upper end I mark and cut the angle where the dormer rake boards meet the main roof. When installing these, I hold the upper ends 1½ in. above the plywood on the lower roof to leave room for the step flashing and shingles.

5-19
It's important to make sure that the top front edge of the fascia board is in line with the pitch of the roof.

5-20
I install a shingle cleat along the top edge of the rake boards. This gives me an additional shadow line for visual interest. I cut these to fit from 1 x 2 pine and nail them in place.

With the rake boards installed, I'm ready to put on the fascia boards along the porch roof, back roof, and dormer roof (*drawings 5-A and 5-B*). First I rip some 1 x 6 pine to a width of 4½ in. I mark and cut these to fit and install them with 6d stainless-steel ring-shank nails. The important thing here is to make sure that the top front edge of the fascia board is in line with the pitch of the roof (*photo 5-19*). The fascia board at the back of the playhouse needs a 3/4-in. by 3½-in. pine filler board underneath to space the fascia away from the siding so the corner boards can slip underneath (*drawing 5-B*). This filler board is approximately 97½ in. long.

Now I'm ready to trim the ends of the rake boards. The rake board sloping toward the back of the house gets a plumb cut and a level cut on the bottom end. I lay out the plumb cut so that the rake board extends 1/2 in. beyond the 3/4-in.-thick fascia board and I locate the level cut at the bottom edge of the fascia board. I make these cuts with my circular saw.

I like to add a 1½-in. shingle cleat along the top edge of the rake boards (*photo 5-20*). This gives me an additional shadow line, so it's more for architectural interest than anything else. I cut these cleats to fit from 1 x 2 pine and nail them in place with 6d ring-shank nails.

Porch Trim Boards

Now for the trim boards underneath the porch (*drawings 5-A and 5-B*). I need 3 pieces. I miter one end of the long front piece, hold it in position on the frame, and mark and cut the opposite miter. I attach this piece to the floor-frame joists with screws in predrilled holes. Next I miter one end of each side board and cut the other end at 90 degrees to fit. Then I attach these pieces to the floor frame with screws.

5-21
Starting at the left side of the roof, I place a shingle with the butt end against a string stretched across the ends of the rake boards. The edge of the shingle should overhang the shingle cleat by 3/8 in. to 1/2 in. I fasten the shingle with two 3d nails.

Corner Boards

I want to make corner boards to cover the corners of the playhouse where the siding meets (*drawings 5-A, 5-B, 5-L, and 5-M*). I start by ripping some 3-in.-wide lengths and some 2¼-in.-wide lengths from 1 x 6 (see Project Planner). When fastened together with stainless-steel finish nails at the corner, I end up with a 3-in. by 3-in. corner board (*drawing 5-M*).

Installing the corner boards is a mark-and-cut-to-fit procedure. The top ends of the corner boards at the wall corners get cut to match the angle of the roof pitch. They just slip up underneath the rake boards, and at the back, the top ends also slip underneath the fascia board. The front corner boards must be notched to fit around the porch floor and the porch roof. I attach the corner boards with screws. The short corner boards at the shed dormer get cut and installed later, after the roof shingles are on.

Shingles

I'm ready to shingle the roof but first, to give the plywood some additional protection from moisture, I install a layer of 15# felt paper, attaching it to the roof with 1/4-in. staples. I extend the felt paper up to the bottom of the siding on the vertical dormer wall.

Cedar shingles are a lot of fun to install. The first course of shingles, at the edge of each roof section, is a double layer; a "starter course," with a second layer on top. I begin by shingling the porch roof.

First I have to establish a line for the starter course. I drive a nail into the ends of each rake board and stretch a chalkline between the 2 rake boards to act as a guide for the butt ends of the shingles, giving me the correct overhang (*photo 5-21*). Starting at the left side of the roof, I place a shingle in position with the butt end (the thick end) against the string. I want the edge of the shingle to over-hang the shingle cleat on the rake board by 3/8 in. to 1/2 in. I fasten the shingles with 3d hot-dipped galvanized box nails. For the starter course, I'm only nailing through one thin layer of shingles, so the nails will protrude through the plywood. For this first course, I trim off the points of the nails with lineman's pliers.

5-22

I snap a chalkline 4⅛ in. from the ends of the shingles and tack a long piece of strapping along the line as a guide. The strapping serves as a ledge on which to position the butt ends of the next course of shingles.

5-23

Using a 2 x 4 block as a form, I tap the upper edge of the 6-in. lead flashing against the dormer wall, under the siding and the window openings.

This way, no nails stick through where children might bump into them. I nail the first shingle in place with 2 trimmed 3d box nails (*photo 5-21*).

Now I install a second shingle on the opposite end of the roof, aligning the butt with the string. I start adding additional shingles in between these 2, spacing the shingles a minimum of 1/8 in. and a maximum of 1/4 in. apart to allow for expansion when they get wet. Two nails in each shingle, 1/2 in. from the edge and 1 in. above the butt of the next course line — that's the rule. I trim the last shingle to fit, if necessary.

With the starter course of shingles installed, I now cover it with another layer of shingles. This time I start at each end with a shingle that's the right width to be 1 in. to 1½ in. away from the joint, and fill in between them. I like to extend the butt ends of this course about 1/16 in. beyond the starter course to let the water drip off. It's important to stagger the joints. The shingles must bridge the joints in the course underneath by 1 in. to 1½ in., or water will find its way into the roof.

On the porch roof, I want the bottom 4⅛ in. of the shingles exposed. I measure up 4⅛ in. from the bottom ends of the starter course on each side of the roof and snap a line across the shingles I've already installed. I tack a long strip of strapping or 3/4-in. plywood along this line as a guide, making sure the nails don't penetrate completely through the shingles (*photo 5-22*). The guide serves as a ledge on which to position the butt ends of the next course of shingles. I start this course with a shingle at each end so that I can bridge over the joints of the course underneath. I repeat the procedure for additional courses. Counting the first double course as one, it takes 6 courses of shingles to cover the porch roof up to the dormer. I trim the thin ends of the last 3 courses to fit against the face of the dormer wall.

Flashing

At the intersection where the roof pitch changes and where the porch roof intersects with the vertical dormer wall, I want to install some flashing to keep

5-24
I want the 8-in. lead flashing to extend a little bit up the side of the dormer, so, using my 2 x 4 block, I tap the flashing into the corner against the dormer stud.

5-25
I install aluminum step flashing over each course of shingles along the sides of the dormer. I hold the bottom edge of the flashing a little above the exposure line and fasten it to the dormer with aluminum nails.

out the rain. Where the porch roof meets the dormer wall, I install 6-in.-wide lead flashing (*drawing 5-K*). I unroll the flashing and align the top edge with the bottom of the dormer-window openings. Using a 2 x 4 block as a form, I tap the upper edge of the lead against the dormer wall, under the siding and the window openings (*photo 5-23*). I extend the flashing about 4 in. beyond the dormer wall on each side and trim off the excess with my utility knife. I tack it to the wall with a couple of nails. I'll cover it over later with a piece of cedar trim.

Where the roof pitch changes, I need to install a wider piece of 8-in. lead flashing, but first I install a layer of tar paper on this roof section. Now I hold the bottom edge of the 8-in. lead flashing flush with the bottom edge of the 6-in. flashing and tack it in place along the top edge with a couple of nails. I want the flashing to extend a little bit up the side of the dormer, so, using my 2 x 4 block, I tap the flashing into the corner against the dormer stud (*photo 5-24*). I notch this corner of the flashing with my utility knife and bend the flashing around the corner underneath the siding at the front of the dormer. I repeat this procedure with another piece of 8-in. flashing on the opposite side of the dormer.

With the flashing in place, now I can start running the shingles up the little roof panels on either side of the dormer. For the starter course, I hold the butt ends about level with the bottom edge of the siding on the dormer wall.

Before I put on the double starter course, I need to install a piece of aluminum step flashing against the dormer wall. I start out with a piece of 5-in. by 7-in. aluminum step flashing, which I bought at the lumberyard, and make a 90-degree bend along the long dimension. I place this on top of the shingle, holding it slightly above the butt end, and against the 2 x 4 nailer on the side of the dormer. I fasten the flashing to the dormer with a single 3d shingle nail.

Now I can install the next course of shingles. I extend the butt end of this course as far down as possible over the starter course to hide as much of the lead flashing as possible. As on the porch roof, it's important to stagger the joints 1 in. to 1½ in. apart.

A second piece of step flashing goes on over this course. I snap a line 4¹⁄₁₆ in. above the butt ends and hold the bottom edge of the flashing a little above this

5-26

I hold the diagonal door brace flush with the edges of the bottom and top cleats to mark the length. I use my sliding bevel gauge to set the angle I need to cut.

5-27

I attach the diagonal brace to the door with screws and repeat the procedure for the other door section.

to length for the top and bottom sections (see Project Planner). The boards for the top section are 27¾ in. long. The bottom boards are 24 in. long (*drawing 5-N*).

On the back of each door section I need to install 2 cleats to hold the boards together. I rip these 2½-in.-wide cleats from some 1 x 4 tongue-and-groove cedar siding (removing the tongues and grooves) and attach them with some 1¼-in. galvanized bugle-head screws in predrilled and countersunk holes. I install the screws in a zigzag pattern with 2 screws in each board (*drawing 5-N*). I don't use any glue here because I have a cross-grain situation. I install the top cleat on the bottom door section flush with its top to support a small shelf.

The cleats alone are not enough to support the door. I also need to install a diagonal piece which forms a Z brace on each door section to prevent racking (*drawing 5-N*). To lay out the brace, I hold a 2½-in.-wide piece of cedar flush with the edges of the bottom and top cleats to mark the length. I like to position the upper end of the brace at the upper corner away from the hinges and the bottom end of the brace right next to the lower hinge. I use my sliding bevel gauge to set the angle I need (*photo 5-26*) and then I cut the ends of the brace to length on my miter box. I attach the brace to the door with screws, repeating the procedure for the other door section (*photo 5-27*).

Now I chamfer all the edges of the cleats and braces with my router and a chamfering bit.

On the top edge of the lower door section I want to install a little shelf (*drawing 5-N*). I rip and joint a piece of 1 x 4 cedar siding 2½ in. wide and cut it 19½ in. long. On my band saw, I cut a 1-in.-wide notch in each end so the shelf can clear the door jambs. To make sure there are no sharp corners, I lay out a 1-in. radius on the front corners with my compass and cut it on my band saw. I chamfer the edges of the shelf and install it on the door with screws in predrilled and countersunk holes. The back edge of the shelf is flush with the edge of the top cleat. After sanding all the corners and edges smooth, I'm ready to hang the door.

The door swings on galvanized T hinges — one pair for each door section. I install the hinges on the door, attaching them to the cleats with screws. Now I'm ready to install the lower section of the door. I place it in the door opening and slip two 1⅛-in.-thick spacer blocks underneath to hold the door off the floor. I center the door in the opening and attach the hinges to the stud with screws.

To install the upper section, I put some shim shingles between the upper and lower door sections to give me a 1/8-in. gap between them. Then I fasten the upper hinges to the stud.

Now I install a little barrel bolt on the upper door to secure the 2 sections together (*drawing 5-N*). I have to drill a 3/8-in.-dia. hole in the top of the shelf for the bolt to slip into.

Door Frame

The door frame consists of jambs and casings (*drawing 5-N*) made from 1 x 6 pine. The door jambs are 2¾ in. wide and function as door stops. The door casings are 2 in. wide. I rip these pieces to size from 1 x 6 boards (see Project Planner) and cut them according to the plan (*drawing 5-N*).

To assemble the door jamb, I first nail the head jamb (the top of the door opening) to the side jambs with 6d finish nails. Next I attach the long 2-in.-wide side casings to the side jambs with 4d finish nails, leaving a 1/4-in. reveal between the inside edge of the casing and the inside edge of the door jamb. I hold the bottom ends of the casing up 1/4 in. from the bottom of the side jambs (*drawing 5-N*). Now I install the top piece of 2-in.-wide casing, fastening it with nails to the head jamb, leaving a 1/4-in. reveal underneath. The ends of this top piece extend 3/8 in. beyond the side casings on both sides.

Now I install the door-frame assembly in the door opening of the playhouse. I nail the casing to the siding, and the jambs to the 2 x 4 frame of the opening with 6d finish nails.

For a threshold, I rip two 3/4-in.-wide bevels on one side of a piece of 1 x 4 square-edge fir (*drawing 5-N*). I set my table-saw fence to the left of the blade, tilt the blade 15 degrees, and position the fence about 15/32 in. from the blade (measured at the table surface). I make a rip cut on 2 edges. To clean up the saw marks, I tilt my jointer fence to 15 degrees and make one pass on each bevel. I mark and cut the threshold to fit and fasten it to the floor with 6d galvanized finish nails.

One last thing to do to finish the door. I need to install a thumb latch to secure the door. The latch gets installed on the door, and the catch goes on the stud. I just follow the instructions that come with the latch.

Windows

There are 4 different windows on the playhouse, but they all have the same basic construction — only the dimensions are different (*drawings 5-A, 5-O, 5-P, 5-Q, 5-R, 5-S, and 5-T*). I'll explain the procedure for making them.

I start by ripping and crosscutting the parts for the window frame from 1 x 4 pine (*drawing 5-O* and Project Planner). I need a 2⅞-in.-wide piece for the sill, three 1¼-in.-wide pieces for the side and head jambs, and three 2-in.-wide pieces for the side and top casing (*drawing 5-O*). The scrap from the sill makes a

5-O Window Details

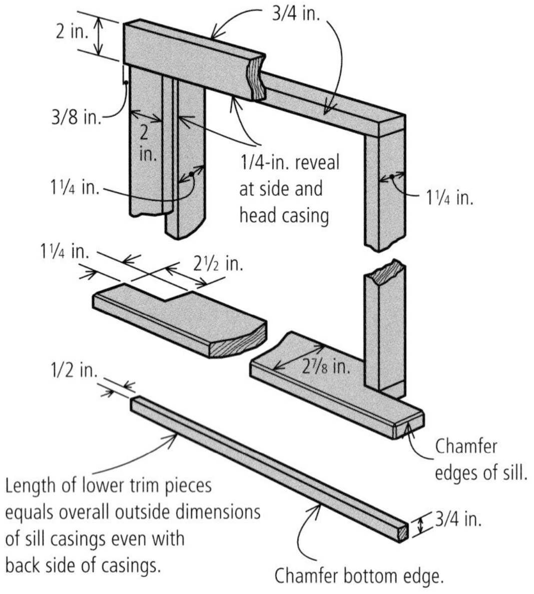
2 in.
3/4 in.
3/8 in.
2 in.
$1\frac{1}{4}$ in.
1/4-in. reveal at side and head casing
$1\frac{1}{4}$ in.
$1\frac{1}{4}$ in.
$2\frac{1}{2}$ in.
$2\frac{7}{8}$ in.
1/2 in.
Chamfer edges of sill.
Length of lower trim pieces equals overall outside dimensions of sill casings even with back side of casings.
3/4 in.
Chamfer bottom edge.

5-P Muntin Overlaps

Note: After muntin is assembled (but before it is installed in frame), chamfer inner and outer edges.

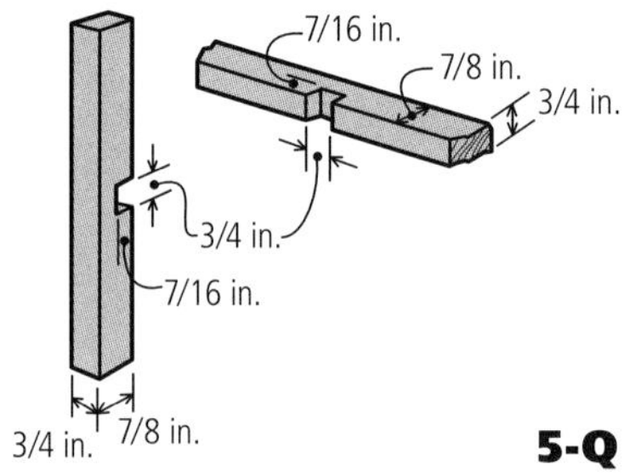
7/16 in.
7/8 in.
3/4 in.
3/4 in.
7/16 in.
3/4 in.
7/8 in.

5-Q Front Window

Note: Assemble windows with 6d galvanized finish nai or 5d galvanized box nails.

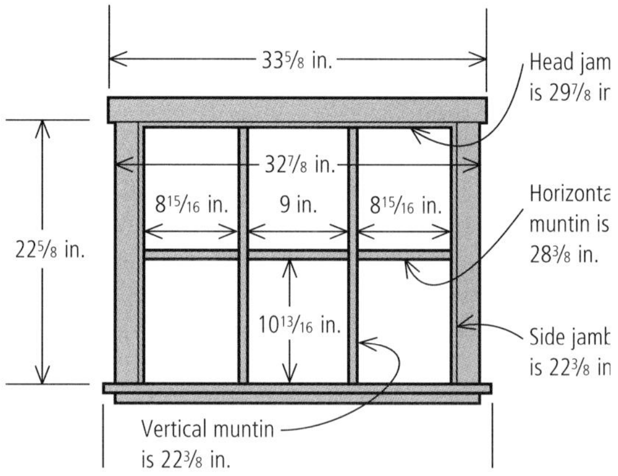
$33\frac{5}{8}$ in.
Head jam
is $29\frac{7}{8}$ ir
$32\frac{7}{8}$ in.
$8\frac{15}{16}$ in.
9 in.
$8\frac{15}{16}$ in.
$22\frac{5}{8}$ in.
Horizonta
muntin is
$28\frac{3}{8}$ in.
$10\frac{13}{16}$ in.
Side jamb
is $22\frac{3}{8}$ in
Vertical muntin is $22\frac{3}{8}$ in.

5-R Side Window
(2 required)

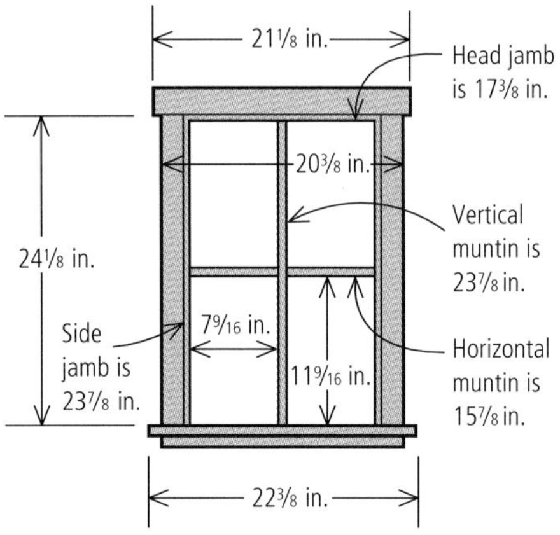
$21\frac{1}{8}$ in.
Head jamb is $17\frac{3}{8}$ in.
$20\frac{3}{8}$ in.
Vertical muntin is $23\frac{7}{8}$ in.
$24\frac{1}{8}$ in.
Side jamb is $23\frac{7}{8}$ in.
$7\frac{9}{16}$ in.
$11\frac{9}{16}$ in.
Horizontal muntin is $15\frac{7}{8}$ in.
$22\frac{3}{8}$ in.

5-S Attic Window
(2 required)

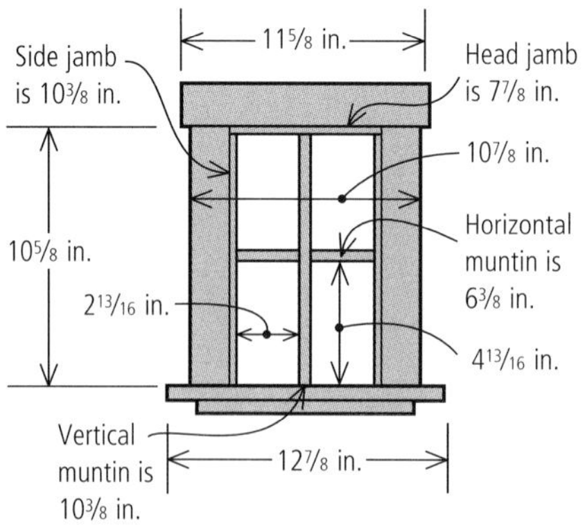
$11\frac{5}{8}$ in.
Side jamb is $10\frac{3}{8}$ in.
Head jamb is $7\frac{7}{8}$ in.
$10\frac{7}{8}$ in.
$10\frac{5}{8}$ in.
Horizontal muntin is $6\frac{3}{8}$ in.
$2\frac{13}{16}$ in.
$4\frac{13}{16}$ in.
Vertical muntin is $10\frac{3}{8}$ in.
$12\frac{7}{8}$ in.

5-T Dormer Window
(2 required)

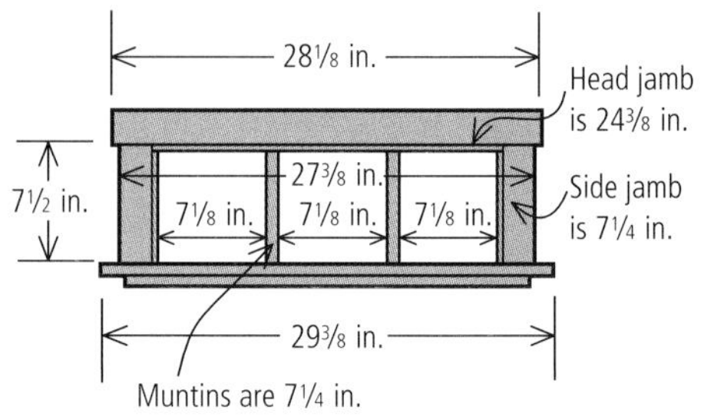
$28\frac{1}{8}$ in.
Head jamb is $24\frac{3}{8}$ in.
$27\frac{3}{8}$ in.
$7\frac{1}{2}$ in.
$7\frac{1}{8}$ in.
$7\frac{1}{8}$ in.
$7\frac{1}{8}$ in.
Side jamb is $7\frac{1}{4}$ in.
$29\frac{3}{8}$ in.
Muntins are $7\frac{1}{4}$ in.

1/2-in. by 3/4-in. molding for under the sill. I mill a chamfer on the bottom edge of this molding with a chamfering bit in my router.

With the frame parts cut to size, the first thing to do is notch the ends of the window sill so it fits into the frame opening in the wall. I lay out the 1¼-in. by 2½-in. notches and cut them on the band saw (*photo 5-28*). Next I chamfer the outside edges and the ends of the sill with a chamfering bit in my router.

Now I can attach the side jambs to the sill with 6d finish nails, nailing up through the sill into the bottoms of the side jambs (*photo 5-29*). Next I attach the head jamb across the top, nailing it to the ends of the side jambs (*photo 5-30*). The side casings go on next, leaving a 1/4-in. reveal on the jamb — just as I did with the door frame (*photo 5-31*). Now the head casing goes in place, with the ends extending 3/8 in. beyond the side casings, to match the casing detail on the door (*photo 5-32*). Finally, the little beveled molding attaches under the sill with a couple of nails to hold it in place (*photo 5-33*). That takes care of the window frame.

To make the muntin bars, I rip and joint some 7/8-in. widths of 1 x 4 pine (see Project Planner). I need to cut a notch in each piece where the muntin bars overlap, so I lay out the 3/4-in.-wide by 7/16-in.-deep notches with a pencil and square. Then I clamp the pair of muntin bars together, side by side, and cut both notches at the same time (*photo 5-34*). Here's how. I set my table-saw blade to a 7/16-in. height. I use my miter gauge to feed the bars into the blade, making a cut on each side of the notch followed by repeated cuts to nibble away the material in between.

I assemble the muntin bars with a little glue on each side of the joint, and I pin the joint together with a couple of 3/4-in. brads. I chamfer the outer edges of the muntins with my router (*photo 5-35*) before attaching them to the window frame with some 4d finish nails. I hold the muntins flush with the inside of the window frame (*photo 5-36*).

I want to prime and paint the windows before I install them in their openings and fasten them to the siding with 6d finish nails.

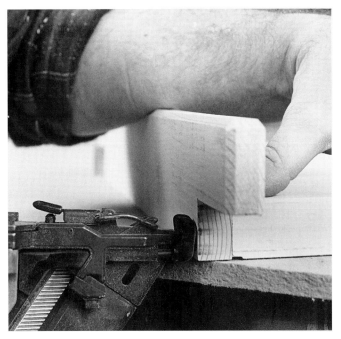

5-29
I attach the window side jambs to the window sill, nailing up through the sill into the bottom ends of the jambs.

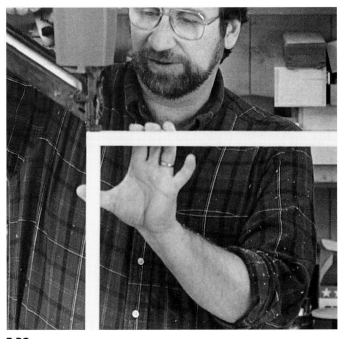

5-30
Next I attach the window head jamb across the top, nailing it to the ends of the side jambs.

5-31
The window side casings go on next, leaving a 1/4-in. reveal on the jamb — just as I did with the door frame.

5-32
The window head casing gets fastened in place with the ends extending 3/8 in. beyond the side casings.

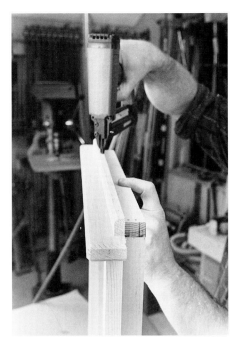

5-33
The beveled molding attaches under the window sill with a couple of nails to hold it in place.

5-34
To cut the joints for the window muntins, I clamp the pair of muntin bars together and cut both notches at the same time. I set my table-saw blade to a 7/16-in. height. I feed the bars into the blade with the miter gauge, making a cut on each side of the notch followed by repeated cuts to nibble away the material in between.

5-35
I chamfer the outer edges of the assembled muntin bars with my router before attaching them to the window frame.

5-36
I hold the muntins flush with the inside of the window frame and attach them with 4d finish nails.

Porch Railings

I need to make 2 railing assemblies for the front porch (*drawings 5-A and 5-U*). These railings are made from 2 x 6 redwood, a very beautiful and weather-resistant wood.

The first thing I do is mill up some 1-in.-square balusters. I rip and joint long pieces (see Project Planner) and then cut 14 balusters 16 in. long. Because children will be playing around these railings, I round over the edges of the balusters with a 1/4-in.-radius roundover bit in my router (*photo 5-37*).

Next I rip and joint the top and bottom rails for both sections (see Project Planner). All the rails are 2½ in. wide (*drawing 5-U*). I cut the front rails to fit

5-U Porch Railings

**Note: Verify lengths before cutting.
Bottom of rail is 2¼ in. above deck.**

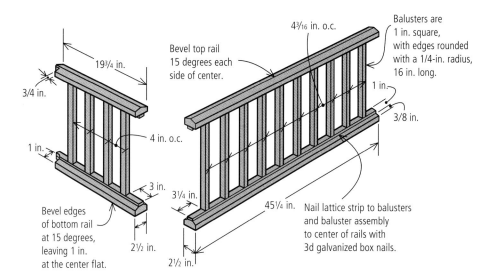

19¾ in.

3/4 in.

Bevel top rail
15 degrees each
side of center.

4³⁄₁₆ in. o.c.

Balusters are
1 in. square,
with edges rounded
with a 1/4-in. radius,
16 in. long.

1 in.

3/8 in.

4 in. o.c.

1 in.

3 in.

3¼ in.

45¼ in.

Nail lattice strip to balusters
and baluster assembly
to center of rails with
3d galvanized box nails.

Bevel edges
of bottom rail
at 15 degrees,
leaving 1 in.
at the center flat.

2½ in.

2½ in.

5-V Window Box

**Note: Assemble with 1¼-in.-long galvanized bugle-head screws.
Attach to siding under large window with 1¼-in. screws.**

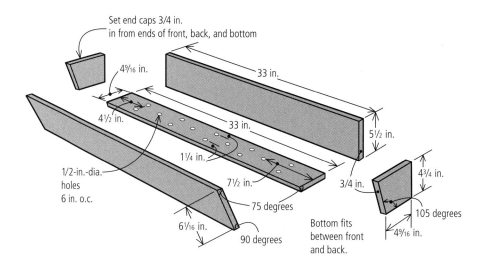

Set end caps 3/4 in.
in from ends of front, back, and bottom

4⁹⁄₁₆ in.

33 in.

4½ in.

33 in.

5½ in.

1¼ in.

4¾ in.

1/2-in.-dia.
holes
6 in. o.c.

7½ in.

3/4 in.

105 degrees

75 degrees

4⁹⁄₁₆ in.

6¹⁄₁₆ in.

90 degrees

Bottom fits
between front
and back.

between the porch posts (approximately 45¼ in.), and the side rails to fit
between the siding and the end post (approximately 19¾ in.).

I want to bevel the tops of the rails so water runs off. I set my table-saw fence
to the left of the blade and tilt the blade 15 degrees. I rip a bevel along one edge
and then turn the rail end for end and rip a second bevel on the opposite edge
(*photo 5-38*). For the top rails, I set the fence so that I end up with a flat spot
about 1/4 in. wide in the middle after making the 2 bevel cuts. To clean up the

5-37
Because children will be playing around the railings, I round over the edges of the porch railing balusters with a 1/4-in.-radius roundover bit in my router.

5-38
To bevel the tops of the porch rails, I set my table-saw fence to the left of the blade and tilt the blade 15 degrees. I rip a bevel along one edge and then turn the rail end for end and rip a second bevel on the opposite edge.

5-39
To clean up the saw marks left from ripping the bevel, I tilt my jointer fence 15 degrees and make one pass along each bevel.

saw marks, I tilt my jointer fence 15 degrees and make one pass along each bevel cut (*photo 5-39*). This eliminates the flat spot. The bevels now meet in the center of the rail.

For the bottom rails, I want to end up with a 1-in.-wide flat spot between the 2 bevels after jointing. I move the rip fence a little farther away from the blade before making the bevel cuts. I need this flat surface to attach the 1-in.-wide lattice strip that supports the balusters (*drawing 5-U*). I rip and joint the bevels on both bottom rails.

The last parts I need to mill are four 3/8-in. by 1-in. lattice strips for attaching the balusters to the rails (*drawing 5-U* and Project Planner). After ripping and jointing to thickness, I cut the lattice strips to the same lengths as the rails.

Before I can assemble the railings, I need to lay out the baluster locations on the lattice strips. On the front railing, the first baluster is spaced 3¼ in. from the end post, and the remaining balusters are spaced 4³⁄₁₆ in. o.c. (This distance meets the recommended safety standard for baluster spacing to ensure that a child's head can't become trapped. Do not exceed this spacing.) On the side railing, the first baluster is spaced 3 in. from the end post (*drawing 5-U*), with the remaining balusters spaced 4 in. o.c.

After marking the baluster locations, I attach one of the lattice strips to the ends of the balusters with a couple of 3d galvanized box nails in each baluster. Then I flip the assembly over and nail the corresponding piece of lattice on the other ends of the balusters (*photo 5-40*). I attach the baluster assembly to the

5-40
After marking the baluster locations, I attach the lattice strips to the ends of the balusters with a couple of 3d galvanized box nails in each baluster.

5-41
I attach the baluster assembly to the porch rails with 3d galvanized box nails.

5-42
I assemble the window box with 1¼-in. galvanized bugle-head screws, predrilling and countersinking the holes to avoid splitting the wood. I set the end pieces in 3/4 in. from the ends of the front, back, and bottom.

rails with 3d galvanized box nails (*photo 5-41*). All that's left is to attach the railings to the posts by angling 2½-in. screws through the railing and into the posts.

Window Box

The window box is the last thing to build (*drawings 5-A and 5-V*). The house would probably look fine without it, but it's little touches like this one that make a playhouse really special.

I start by cutting out the parts from some 1 x 10 cedar (*drawing 5-V and Project Planner*). The front of the window box angles forward, so I need to rip a 15-degree bevel along the front edge of the bottom (*drawing 5-V*). I make this cut on the table saw, setting the rip fence so the bottom measures 4⁹⁄₁₆ in. wide from the long point of the bevel. Next I drill some 1/2-in.-dia. holes in the bottom for drainage, spacing the holes 6 in. o.c. (*drawing 5-V*).

The sides of the box are also cut at a 15-degree angle, which I make on the miter box. The front of the window box gets a 15-degree bevel on the top edge and is cut from a piece of 1 x 10. The back of the box is just square cuts, top and bottom.

I assemble the window box with 1¼-in. galvanized bugle-head screws, predrilling and countersinking the holes to avoid splitting the wood (*photo 5-42*). I set the end pieces in 3/4 in. from the ends of the front, back, and bottom. When the box is complete, I attach it underneath the front window with some 1¼-in. screws.

Painting the Playhouse

It's finally time to get the paintbrush going. I prime all the trim and siding with a latex primer. On the trim I use a dark green latex paint. On the siding I use a gold-colored latex stain. That's what I did. Of course, you can use any paint or stain color you like. Be sure to follow the manufacturer's directions.

When the paint is dry, I put in the windows. The only thing to do now is stand back and admire the result. You know, I wish I'd had a playhouse like this one when *I* was a kid!

6

dollhouse

project planner

Time: 4 days

Special hardware and tools:

Hot glue gun

Wood:

(1½) 60-in. by 60-in. sheet of 1/2-in. Baltic birch plywood
Cut according to plywood rough-cut diagrams, then lay out and cut according to drawings for dollhouse panels.

(1) 5-in. by 6-in. piece of 1/4-in. birch plywood
Cut according to drawing for sliding shop door.

(1) 2½-ft. 1 x 4 select pine
Rip and joint one piece 3/4 in. wide. Cut one piece 18½ in. long for beam. Use remaining piece for stair stringers (2 required).
Rip or plane remaining 30-in. length to 5/8-in. thickness, then rip 8 pieces 1/8 in. x 5/8 in., making a pass over jointer before ripping each piece. Cut to fit for eave trim, rake trim, and stair treads.

(1) 8-ft. 1 x 2 select pine
Cut one piece 42 in. long, rip or plane to 5/8 in. thickness, then dado according to plan to form 2 corners, rip in half, and cut to fit to make corner boards. Cut one piece 12 in. long and mill according to plan for door tracks (2 required). Cut one piece 12 in. long and one piece 18 in. long, then mill according to plan for roof support cleats. Rip remaining scrap into 1/4-in. by 1/2-in. strips for cleats to support stair platform (M) and plywood bin platform (X).

I WANTED TO BUILD a special dollhouse, one that could be enjoyed by boys as much as by girls and by adults as well as by children. I studied old dollhouses and looked at some new ones, just waiting and hoping for inspiration to strike. I thought long and hard, and here's the result: a true 1/16th scale model of (you guessed it) the New Yankee Workshop!

It's designed to be fun. The roof comes off so you can see into the workshop. Travel up the stairs at the end of the workshop and you'll find a sitting room on the second floor. The floor itself is removable so you can get down to the lower area, where I've set up a kitchen and a garage for the family car. It's a lot of fun to build and just as much fun to play with.

Before I get started, I'd like to talk about some important safety precautions. Making this dollhouse requires cutting some very small, thin parts on the table saw. The blade slot on a standard metal table insert is wide enough for narrow pieces to jam between the blade and the side of the slot — a dangerous situation that can cause accidents.

To work safely with small pieces, I replace the metal table insert with one that has a replaceable wooden strip. (My homemade wooden "zero clearance" insert, mentioned on page 15, would also work fine.) With the saw blade lowered as far as it will go, I hold the wooden insert down by positioning the rip fence over one edge (making sure the fence isn't right over the blade) and switch on the saw. Then I slowly raise the spinning blade up through the wooden insert to create a

6-A Major Anatomy and Dimensions

(1) 5-ft. 1 x 2 select pine
Cut 2 pieces 15 in. long.
Mill one piece according to plan for cleat to secure peak of second-story roof. Rip second piece into three 1/4-in. by 3/4-in. pieces, then cut to fit for cleats to support second floor. Mill remaining piece according to plan for cleat to hold large removable "south" roof (S) in place.

Scrap redwood or pine
Cut to fit for trim for sliding door.

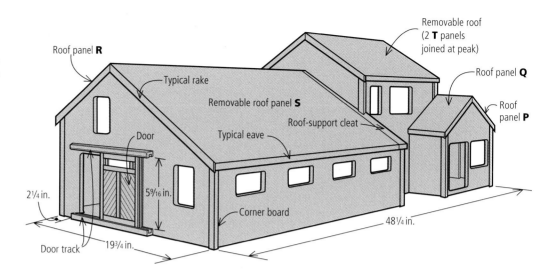

Roof panel **R**

Typical rake

Removable roof panel **S**

Roof-support cleat

Typical eave

Door

Corner board

2¼ in.

5⁹⁄₁₆ in.

19¾ in.

48¼ in.

Door track

Removable roof (2 **T** panels joined at peak)

Roof panel **Q**

Roof panel **P**

Cutting Diagrams: Plywood Rough Cuts

Half Sheet, 30 in. x 60 in.

Full Sheet, 60 in. x 60 in.

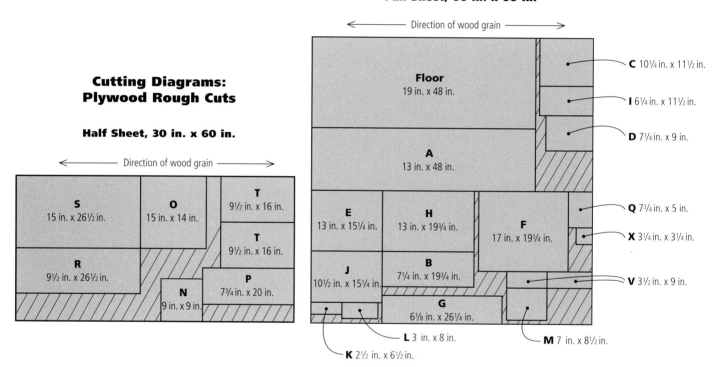

Direction of wood grain

Floor
19 in. x 48 in.

A
13 in. x 48 in.

E
13 in. x 15¼ in.

H
13 in. x 19¾ in.

F
17 in. x 19¼ in.

J
10½ in. x 15¼ in.

B
7¼ in. x 19¾ in.

G
6⅛ in. x 26¼ in.

C 10¼ in. x 11½ in.

I 6¼ in. x 11½ in.

D 7¼ in. x 9 in.

Q 7¾ in. x 5 in.

X 3¼ in. x 3¼ in.

V 3½ in. x 9 in.

L 3 in. x 8 in.

M 7 in. x 8½ in.

K 2½ in. x 6½ in.

Direction of wood grain

S
15 in. x 26½ in.

O
15 in. x 14 in.

T
9½ in. x 16 in.

T
9½ in. x 16 in.

R
9½ in. x 26½ in.

N
9 in. x 9 in.

P
7¾ in. x 20 in.

blade slot with zero clearance on either side (*photo 6-1*). This way, there's no slot for small pieces to fall into. Of course, I always use a push stick to keep my fingers well away from the blade.

Plywood Panels: Floors, Walls, Roofs, and Partitions

This project is made mostly from plywood, but not just any plywood will do. I need material that's good on both sides and has a solid core without any voids because occasionally an edge will show. I chose a type of birch plywood manufactured in Russia and known in this country as Baltic birch. It comes in metric

6-B FLOOR

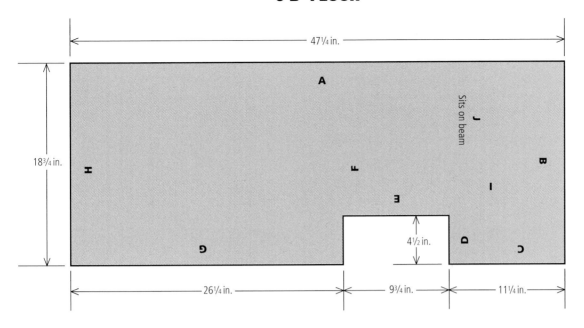

Removable Second Floor

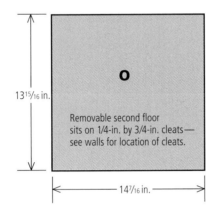

sizes, but a standard sheet measures 60 in. x 60 in. and just under 1/2 in. thick. I used 1½ sheets to build the dollhouse (see Project Planner).

To get started, I lay out the dollhouse panels on the plywood (see *Cutting Diagrams*). The cutting diagrams show rough sizes — slightly larger than the finished dimensions. I rough out the pieces with my circular saw and my table saw. When cutting large panels like this, I use my homemade panel cutter to make sure the panels are square. To keep track of all the parts, I label each piece with a letter on the edge so it's easy to identify later. These letters (shown in parentheses throughout this chapter) key the parts to the drawings.

Once the parts are roughed out, I'm ready to start with the floor — the only part I didn't code with a letter (*drawing 6-B*). I rip the 19-in. by 48-in. rough panel to its final 18¾-in. width. Then, using my panel cutter, I square one end, flip it around, and cut the other end to get a finished length of 47¼ inches. I use this procedure throughout the project to trim all rough panels to the finished dimensions.

I have to cut a 4½-in. by 9¾-in. notch in the floor (*drawing 6-B*). I clamp the floor piece on the workbench, lay out the area I want to remove, and make the 2

6-1

To work safely with small pieces, I replace the metal table insert with one that has a replaceable wooden strip. With the saw blade lowered as far as it will go, I hold the wooden insert down by positioning the rip fence over one edge (making sure the fence isn't right over the blade) and switch on the saw. Then I slowly raise the spinning blade up through the wood to create a blade slot with no room on either side for small pieces to fall into.

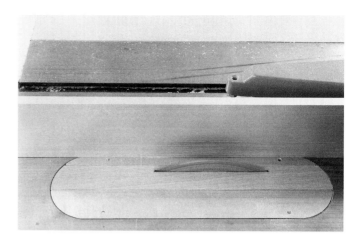

6-2

To cut a 4½-in. by 9¾-in. notch in the floor, I clamp the piece to the workbench, lay out the area I want to remove, and use a small circular saw and a square to make the two crosscuts.

6-3

To make the long cut along the grain of the plywood, I make a plunge cut with the circular saw.

crosscuts using a small circular saw and a square to help guide me (*photo 6-2*). To make the long cut along the grain of the plywood, I make a plunge cut with the circular saw (*photo 6-3*). To complete the cut, I finish up with a handsaw.

Next comes the "north" wall (A) (*drawing 6-C*). Its top edge gets a 30-degree bevel to meet the slope of the second-floor roof. To cut this bevel, I tilt the table-saw blade 30 degrees and adjust the rip fence to give me the correct width — 12²⁵⁄₃₂ in. to the long point of the bevel. I rip the full length of the wall.

After ripping the bevel, I move the rip fence 4⅛ in. closer to the blade to make a second beveled cut where the roof steps down over the shop (*drawing 6-C*). It's the same pitch as the second-floor roof, so I use the same blade setting. I rip in as far as I can and then crosscut as far as possible with the blade at 90 degrees, using the miter gauge to guide the piece. I finish the rest of the cut with a hand-saw.

On the east end of this north wall (A), I need to make a 30-degree cut for the shed roof over the garage. I make the angled cut with my circular saw and make the crosscut with my table saw. Here, too, I use a handsaw to cut all the way into the corner (*photo 6-4*).

6-C Walls

Note: Walls viewed from inside.

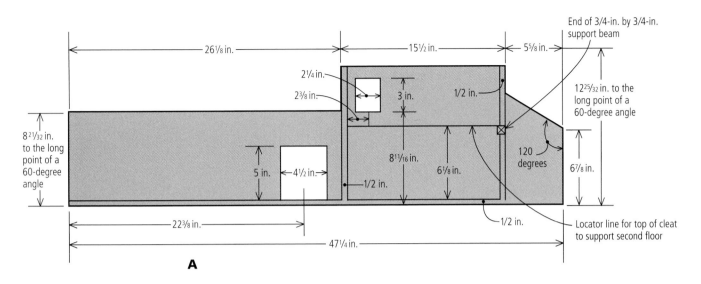

A

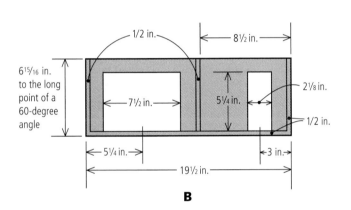

B

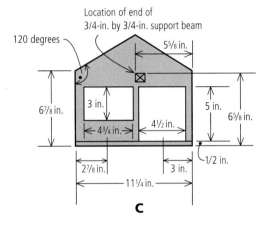

C

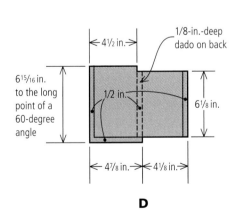

D

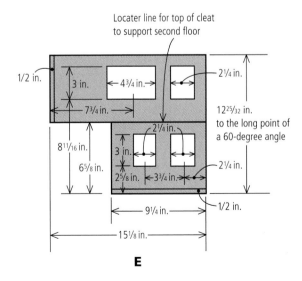

E

6-4
On the east end of the north wall (A), I need to make a 30-degree cut for the shed roof over the garage. After making the angled cut with my circular saw and the crosscut with my table saw, I use a handsaw to cut all the way into the corner.

6-5
I cut the roof pitch on the gable wall on the south side of the building (C) on the table saw with the miter gauge set at a 30-degree angle.

The next step is to make the gable wall on the south side of the building (C) (*drawing* 6-C). I square up the ends to a final width of 11¼ in. and cut the roof pitch on the table saw with the miter gauge set at a 30-degree angle (*photo* 6-5).

Now I'm going to make the short wall that extends from the gable end into the building to support the second floor (D) (*drawing* 6-C). The first cut I make is a 30-degree bevel cut along the top edge, to give me the pitch of the roof. Next I need to cut a 4⅛-in. by 1/2-in. notch at the bottom so the wall fits up over the floor. I make a stop rip cut on the table saw (*photo* 6-6) and use a handsaw to finish up.

After cutting the notch on the bottom of this gable side wall (D), I need to make a second notch on the top, beveled edge so the wall can fit under the second-story floor (*drawing* 6-C). After I rip as far as necessary on the table saw, I finish the cut off with a handsaw (*photo* 6-7).

The next piece is the two-story south wall of the building (E) (*drawing* 6-C). It, too, gets a 30-degree bevel on the top edge, and I cut out the 5⅞-in. by 6⅜-in. notch with my table saw and a handsaw.

The east garage wall (B) (*drawing* 6-C) gets a 30-degree bevel along the top edge. I rip this bevel on the table saw. Next, setting my rip fence 6¹⁵⁄₁₆ in. from the blade, I set the blade for a 90-degree cut and rip the bottom edge of the wall, guiding the beveled top edge of the wall against the fence. I trim the ends so the wall measures 19½ in. long.

The room divider partition (F), which separates the one-story section of the

6-D Walls

Note: Walls F, G, and H viewed from inside.

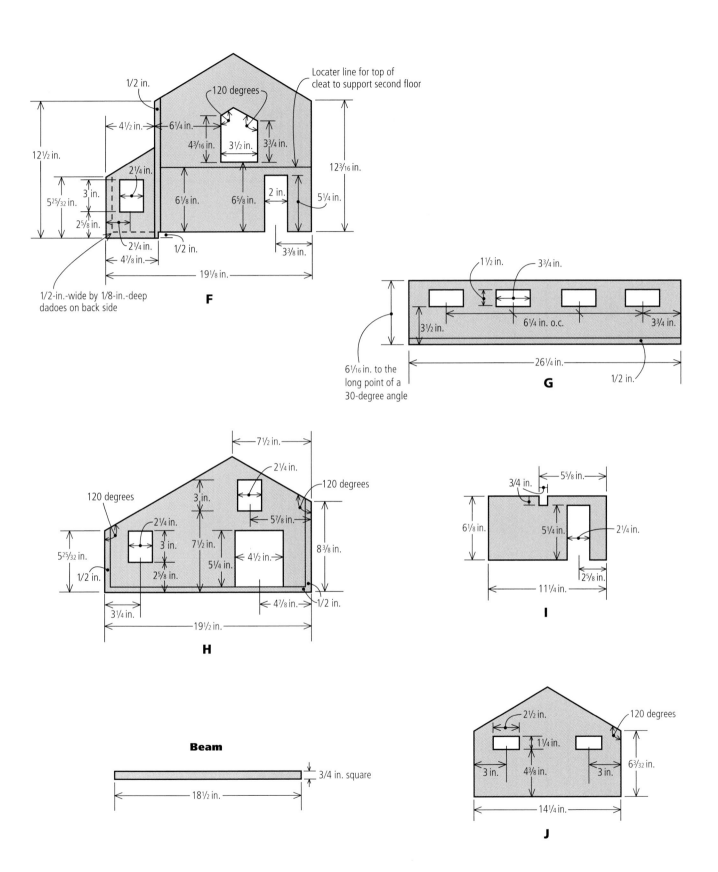

1/2 in.

120 degrees

Locater line for top of
cleat to support second floor

4 1/2 in.   6 1/4 in.

12 1/2 in.

4 3/16 in.   3 1/2 in.   3 3/4 in.

12 3/16 in.

2 1/4 in.

5 25/32 in.   3 in.

6 1/8 in.   6 5/8 in.   2 in.

5 1/4 in.

2 5/8 in.

2 1/4 in.   1/2 in.

3 3/8 in.

4 7/8 in.

19 1/8 in.

1/2-in.-wide by 1/8-in.-deep
dadoes on back side

F

1 1/2 in.   3 3/4 in.

3 1/2 in.

6 1/4 in. o.c.   3 3/4 in.

6 1/16 in. to the
long point of a
30-degree angle

26 1/4 in.   1/2 in.

G

7 1/2 in.

2 1/4 in.

120 degrees

120 degrees

2 1/4 in.   3 in.

3 in.

5 7/8 in.

7 1/2 in.

8 3/8 in.

5 25/32 in.

1/2 in.

3 in.   5 1/4 in.   4 1/2 in.

2 5/8 in.

3 1/4 in.   4 7/8 in.   1/2 in.

19 1/2 in.

H

3/4 in.   5 5/8 in.

6 1/8 in.

5 1/4 in.   2 1/4 in.

11 1/4 in.   2 5/8 in.

I

Beam

3/4 in. square

18 1/2 in.

2 1/2 in.

120 degrees

1 1/4 in.

3 in.   4 3/8 in.   3 in.

6 3/32 in.

14 1/4 in.

J

6-6

I need to cut a 4⅛-in. by 1/2-in. notch at the bottom of the short wall (D) that supports the second floor. I make a stop rip cut on the table saw and use a handsaw to finish up.

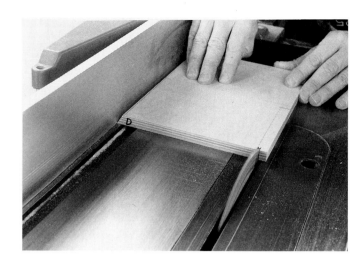

6-7

After cutting the notch on the bottom of the wall (D), I make a second notch on the top, beveled edge so the wall can fit under the second-story floor. After I rip as far as necessary on the table saw, I finish off with a handsaw.

6-8

I cut the beam notch in the short interior garage wall (I) on the table saw. I set the blade for a 3/4-in.-deep cut. Then I stand the wall on edge and use the miter gauge to nibble away the material.

building from the two-story section (*drawing 6-D*) requires several cuts. I cut the main-roof pitch on the table saw with the miter gauge set at 30 degrees. I cut the pitch of the low roof with the circular saw, make the vertical cut on the table saw, and use my handsaw to cut into the corner. I make the other cuts on the table saw, using a handsaw to cut into the corners.

The long one-story south wall (G) is a simple rectangle. The top edge gets a 30-degree bevel to accommodate the roof (*drawing 6-D*).

The short interior garage wall (I) is also a rectangle, with a 3/4-in. by 3/4-in. notch in the top for the beam that supports the second-story gable (*drawing 6-D*). I cut this notch on the table saw. Setting the blade for a 3/4-in.-deep cut, I

6-9
The exterior walls are joined to the floor with rabbet joints. On the table saw, I set my stack dado head to cut a groove as wide as the thickness of the plywood and cut a 1/8-in.-deep rabbet along the bottom edge of each first-floor exterior wall.

6-10
To cut the openings for the windows and doors, I make templates from 1/4-in. plywood with the various opening sizes I need. I clamp the appropriate template in place and make the openings with my plunge router and a 1/4-in.-dia. straight bit with a pilot bearing mounted above the cutter.

stand the wall on edge and use the miter gauge to nibble away the 3/4-in. notch (*photo 6-8*).

The last walls to make are the 2 gables at the west end (H) and east end (J) of the building (*drawings 6-A and 6-D*). I cut these parts to finished size on the table saw, using my miter gauge to make the angled cuts for the roof.

Rabbets and Dadoes

The exterior walls of the model are joined to the floor with rabbet joints. On the table saw, I set my stack dado head to cut a groove as wide as the thickness of the plywood (approximately 1/2 in.) and cut a 1/8-in.-deep rabbet along the bottom edge of each first-floor exterior wall piece (*photo 6-9*).

Using the same saw setup, I also mill a 1/8-in.-deep rabbet on one side of each corner where the exterior walls join.

I need to mill several dadoes in the walls with the same dado-head setup I used for the rabbets. I make one dado in the garage wall (B), 8½ in. from one end (*drawing 6-C*) to accommodate the short interior partition (I) (*drawing 6-D*). I mill one dado on the back of the short wall (D) on the south gable side wall (*drawing 6-C*) and a long dado on the partition wall (F) between the shop and the living space (*drawing 6-D*). The north wall (A) gets 2 dadoes (*drawing*

6-11
To assemble the walls, I brush glue in the rabbets and dadoes and secure the joints with some 1-in. brads. Here, I'm attaching the south gable wall (C).

6-12
I install the 18½-in.-long 3/4-in. by 3/4-in beam that supports the second-story gable wall, securing the beam with glue, a brad in the middle, and a couple of brads in each end.

6-13
The second-story gable end wall goes in next and rests on top of the beam.

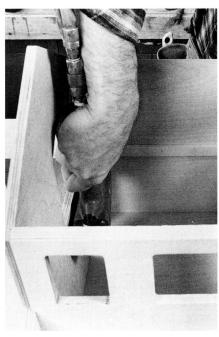

6-14
With the walls all assembled, I install 1/4-in. by 3/4-in. pine cleats on all 4 walls of the two-story living space to support the removable second floor (O). The top edge of the cleat is located 6⅛ in. above the floor.

6-C): one for the intersection of the partition (F) between the shop and the living space and one at the end for the second-story gable (J).

Now I can dry-fit the floor and walls together to make sure that everything fits.

Windows and Doors

Now I'm ready to lay out and cut the openings for the windows and doors. The easiest way is with a plunge router and a 1/4-in.-dia. straight bit and a pilot bearing mounted above the cutter.

I make templates from 1/4-in. plywood with the various opening sizes I need for my windows and doors. The router-bit bearing rides around the template cutout to make the opening in the dollhouse walls, so the openings in the templates must be larger all around than the finished window/door openings by the difference between the outside radius of the pilot bearing and the radius of the router bit. I lay out the openings on the template and cut them out with my jigsaw.

Now I clamp the appropriate template in place on the workpiece and rout the openings (*photo 6-10*). The second-floor doorway opening in the interior partition wall (F) gets 2 angled cuts at the top (*drawing 6-D*). I make these cuts with my jigsaw. When I've finished all the openings, I sand the surfaces smooth.

Up Go the Walls

Now I'm ready to assemble the walls. The procedure is to brush glue in the rabbets and dadoes and then secure the joints with some 1-in. brads.

I start by attaching the one-story south wall (G) to the floor. Next I install the long north wall (A). The interior partition wall (F) is the next one. The south gable wall (C) goes on next (*photo 6-11*). Now I add the west wall (H) and the east wall (B), then the south gable side wall (D) and the two-story south wall (E). Next comes the interior garage wall (I). At this point, I install the 18½-in.-long 3/4-in.-square beam that supports the second-story gable (*drawing 6-D and photo 6-12*), securing the beam with glue and brads. I put one in the middle and a couple in each end. The second-story east gable (J) goes in next and rests on top of the beam (*photo 6-13*).

With the walls all assembled, I install 1/4-in. by 3/4-in. pine cleats on all 4 walls of the two-story living space to support the removable second floor (O) (*photo 6-14*). The top edge of the cleat is located 6⅛ in. above the floor. I also install a 7¾-in.-long cleat on the shop side of the interior partition wall (F) with the end butted against the north wall. A second cleat, 6½ in. long, goes above the door opening on the inside of the north wall (A). Both cleats are 1/4 in. x 1/2 in. (*photo 6-15*). They support the stair platform (M) and are also located 6 in. above the floor.

Stairs and Plywood Bin

The stairs and the plywood bin have lots of little pieces, and I cut them all to the shapes shown in the plan (*drawings 6-E and 6-F*). On the inside of the 2 wall pieces for the plywood bin (V), I attach 1/4-in. by 5/8-in. cleats (*drawing 6-E*). The bin wall (V) closest to the stair platform gets 2 cleats — one on the outside to support the stair platform (M) and one on the inside to support the bin platform (X). The other bin wall (V) gets only the cleat to support the bin platform (X). The top edge of this cleat is 6 in. from the floor.

To start the assembly, I attach the stair-support panel (K) to the interior partition wall (F) with glue and 1-in. brads (*photo 6-15*). Next I attach the plywood bin walls (V) to the north wall (A) with glue and brads, nailing from the outside of the wall (*photo 6-16*). Now I can glue the plywood bin platform (X) between the bin walls and nail it in place.

The next thing to do is to attach the stair railing (L) to the edge of the stair platform (M) with glue and brads (bevels facing out) (*photo 6-17*) and install

6-E Stair, Platform, and Plywood Bin

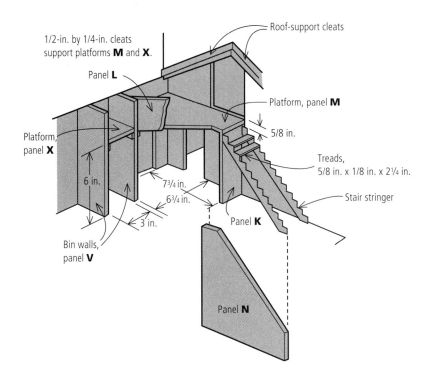

Roof-support cleats

1/2-in. by 1/4-in. cleats support platforms **M** and **X**.

Panel **L**

Platform, panel **M**

5/8 in.

Platform, panel **X**

6 in.

7³/₄ in.

6³/₄ in.

3 in.

Treads, 5/8 in. x 1/8 in. x 2¹/₄ in.

Stair stringer

Panel **K**

Bin walls, panel **V**

Panel **N**

6-15
To start the stair assembly, I attach the stair-support panel (K) to the interior partition wall (F) with glue and 1-in. brads. Note the 2 cleats to support the stair platform panel (M).

6-16
Next I attach the plywood bin walls (V) to the north wall (A) with glue and brads, nailing from the outside.

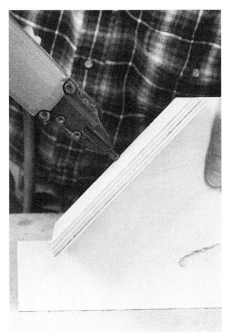

6-17
I attach the stair railing (L) to the edge of the stair platform (M) with glue and brads (bevels facing out).

6-F Stair, Platform, and Plywood Bin Panels

Note: Refer to stair, platform, and plywood bin detail for placement.

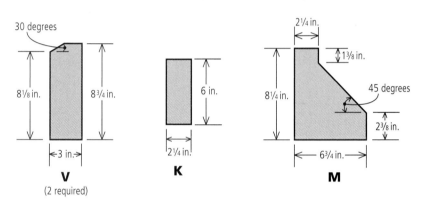

30 degrees

8⅛ in.

8¾ in.

←3 in.→

V
(2 required)

6 in.

2¼ in.

K

2¼ in.

1⅜ in.

8¼ in.

45 degrees

2⅜ in.

←6¾ in.→

M

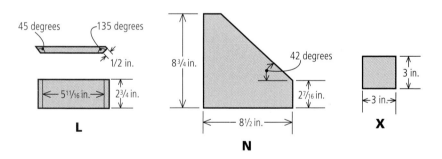

45 degrees

135 degrees

1/2 in.

←5¹¹⁄₁₆ in.→

2¾ in.

L

8¾ in.

42 degrees

2⁷⁄₁₆ in.

←8½ in.→

N

3 in.

←3 in.→

X

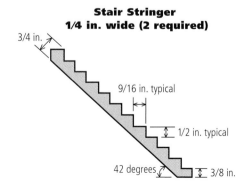

**Stair Stringer
1/4 in. wide (2 required)**

3/4 in.

9/16 in. typical

1/2 in. typical

42 degrees

3/8 in.

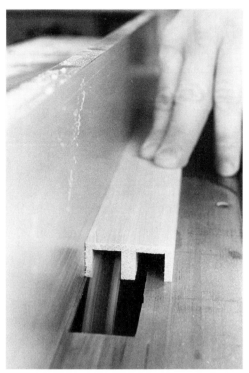

6-19
To make the corner boards, I set up my stack dado head to cut a 1/2-in.-wide groove and adjust the rip fence and blade height so that 1/8 in. of wood remains above and to the right of the cutter. I mill 2 grooves, flipping the workpiece end for end to make the second cut (shown here).

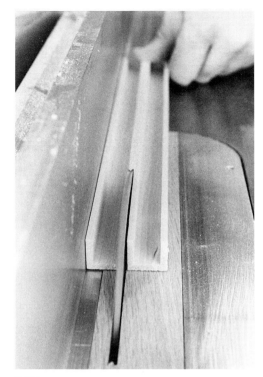

6-20
Next I switch to a regular blade and my "zero clearance" table-saw insert. I set the rip fence 5/8 in. from the blade. Holding the workpiece grooved side up, I rip a 5/8-in.-wide piece from each edge to make 2 long right-angled shapes from which I'll crosscut the corner boards.

this platform assembly on top of the cleats and stair-support panel (K) (*drawing 6-E*).

Now to build a miniature flight of stairs. I start by making the 2 stringers from a single piece of 3/4-in. pine (see Project Planner). With a square and a pencil, I lay out the treads and risers as shown (*drawing 6-F*). Then I cut them out on the band saw (*photo 6-18*). Next, on the table saw, I rip the piece to make two 1/4-in.-thick stringers.

To assemble the staircase, I glue and nail one stringer to the interior partition wall (F). The other stringer gets glued and nailed to the stair-rail panel (N) (*drawing 6-E*). This rail panel goes into place next, and then I'm ready to put on some treads.

I rip the stair treads from a 30-in. length of pine that I've planed to a 5/8-in. thickness (see Project Planner). From this piece I rip 1/8-in. by 5/8-in. strips on the table saw, making a pass on the jointer before each cut to give me a smooth surface for the tops of the treads. Using my miter box, I cut these thin strips into 2¼-in. lengths to make the treads. A dab of hot glue on the end of each tread holds it in place on the stringer.

Corner Boards

I want to make some corner boards to cover the exterior corners of the model

(*drawing 6-A*). To make them, I start with a 42-in. length of 1 x 2 pine (see Project Planner) and plane it to a 5/8-in. thickness.

On the table saw, I set up my stack dado head to cut a 1/2-in.-wide groove. Next I adjust the rip fence so it's 1/8 in. from the blade. I raise the dado head 1/2 in. above the table and mill a dado in a test piece of 5/8-in.-thick stock. There should be 1/8 in. of wood remaining above and to the right of the cutter. I adjust the table-saw setup if necessary and mill 2 grooves in the piece, flipping it end for end to make the second cut (*photo 6-19*).

Now I switch to a regular blade and my "zero clearance" table-saw insert. I set the rip fence 5/8 in. from the blade. Holding the workpiece grooved side up, I rip a 5/8-in.-wide piece from each edge to make 2 long right-angled shapes (*photo 6-20 and drawings 6-A and 6-J*).

I cut the corner boards to length on my miter box, angling the top ends to match the pitch of the roof. I glue the finished corner boards in place with a few dabs of hot glue.

The second-story floor (O) is a simple rectangle (*drawing 6-B*). As with all the other panels, I trim it to finished size with my panel cutter. It just drops into place on the cleats.

Raising the Roof

The roof goes on next. The east roof panel (P) has a 30-degree bevel along the top and bottom edges (*drawing 6-H*). After cutting the bevels, I glue and nail it in place on the model (*photo 6-21*).

The roof (Q) on the west side of the gable goes on next. This piece also has a 30-degree bevel on the top and bottom edges (*drawing 6-H*).

The shop roof comes next. This roof is a little more complicated because I have to make some roof-support cleats to hold up the end where it joins with the

6-G Roof-Support Cleats

For Large Removable Roof S

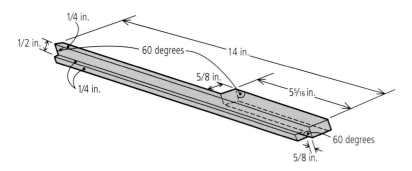

1/4 in.

1/2 in.

60 degrees

14 in.

1/4 in.

5/8 in.

5⁵/₁₆ in.

60 degrees

5/8 in.

For Roof with Skylights R

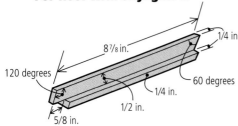

8⁷/₈ in.

1/4 in.

120 degrees

60 degrees

1/4 in.

1/2 in.

5/8 in.

6-H Roof Panels

Note: Refer to major anatomy for placement.

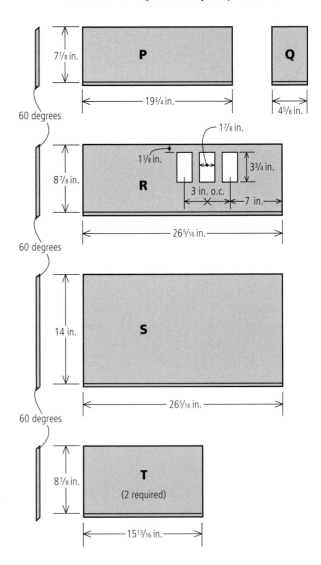

7¹/₈ in.

P

Q

19³/₄ in.

4⁵/₈ in.

60 degrees

1⁷/₈ in.

1¹/₈ in.

8⁷/₈ in.

R

3³/₄ in.

3 in. o.c.

7 in.

26⁵/₁₆ in.

60 degrees

14 in.

S

26⁵/₁₆ in.

60 degrees

8⁷/₈ in.

T

(2 required)

15¹³/₁₆ in.

6-I Cleat Details for Removable Roof Panel

Section Through Peak of Two-Story Roof

Note: 14 3/8-in.-long cleat — center under roof.

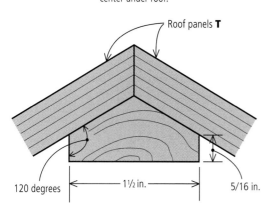

Roof panels **T**

120 degrees

1 1/2 in.

5/16 in.

Section Through Cleat to Hold Large Removable Roof

Note: 25 1/8 in. long — set end of cleat 1/4 in. from edge of roof panel that meets second-story section.

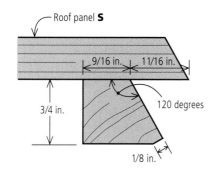

Roof panel **S**

9/16 in.   11/16 in.

3/4 in.

120 degrees

1/8 in.

6-J Roof Trim Details

Typical Rake Detail

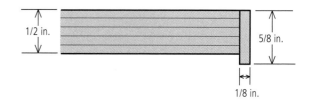

1/2 in.

5/8 in.

1/8 in.

Typical Eave Detail

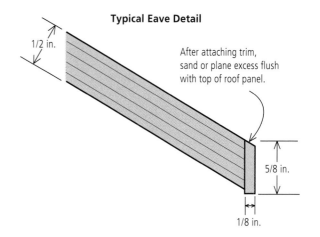

1/2 in.

After attaching trim, sand or plane excess flush with top of roof panel.

5/8 in.

1/8 in.

Section Through Corner Board

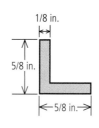

1/8 in.

5/8 in.

5/8 in.

interior partition wall (F). The cleat that supports the north half of the roof is pretty simple — a rabbeted piece of 3/4-in. pine, notched at one end to fit over the north wall (*drawing 6-G*). The cleat that supports the south half of the roof is more complex (*drawing 6-G*).

Here's how I make these 2 cleats. I start with two pieces of 1 x 2 pine — a 12-in. length and an 18-in. length (see Project Planner). With the "zero clearance" insert in my table saw, I set the blade just under 1/4 in. high and set the rip fence on the right-hand side of the blade exactly 1/4 in. from the blade. Now I hold the 12-in. workpiece on edge and make a rip cut on one edge of each piece.

Next I raise the blade to 1/2 in. high and adjust the rip fence so that I cut off 1/4 in. of material from the left edge of the piece (*photo 6-22*).

To complete the cleat for the north slope of the roof, I set the rip fence 1/2 in. from the blade and rip a cut, holding the rabbeted edge against the fence. I make a 30-degree angled cut at one end, and trim the other end to length, making a 5/8-in. notch so that the cleat fits over the north wall.

6-22
To make the second cut for the roof-support cleats, I raise the blade to 1/2 in. and adjust the rip fence so that I cut off 1/4 in. from the left edge of the piece. Note the "zero clearance" table-saw insert, which has no slot for small pieces to fall into.

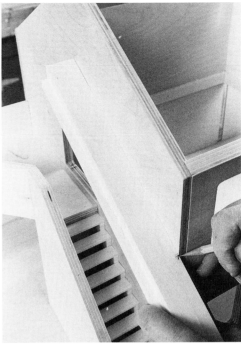

6-23
On the cleat for the south slope of the roof, I hold the cleat in position against roof-layout lines I've drawn on the interior partition wall (F) and mark where the cleat must be notched to fit around the wall.

6-24
To cut this notch, I first make a stopped rip cut on the table saw, then complete the notch with a backsaw, making the crosscut at 30 degrees to match the roof pitch.

6-25
I mill a 1/4-in. by 5/8-in. rabbet in the bottom of the north cleat so it will sit over the interior partition wall (F). I cut this rabbet on the table saw in 2 steps with a regular saw blade. First I set the rip fence 1/2 in. to the right of the blade. I raise the height to 1/4 in. and make the first rip cut (shown here). For the second cut, I raise the blade to a height of 5/8 in. and make a second rip cut to complete the rabbet.

The cleat for the south slope has a more complex shape because it has to fit around the corner of the wall. After milling a similar rabbet, I rip the piece on the table saw to a width of 1⅛ in., holding the rabbeted edge against the rip fence.

Next, on my miter box, I make a 30-degree cut at the top end of the cleat. Holding the cleat in position against roof-layout lines I've drawn on the interior partition wall (F), I mark where the cleat must be notched to fit around the wall (*photo 6-23*). To cut this notch, I first set the rip fence exactly 5/8 in. from the left side of the blade. Then I make a stopped rip cut, switching off the saw when I cut to the notch line. When the blade has stopped completely, I remove the piece and complete the notch cut with a backsaw, making the crosscut at 30 degrees to match the roof pitch (*photo 6-24*).

Now I put the cleat in position on the model so I can trim it to length. I mark where the end meets the face of the corner board and make a 30-degree cut on my miter box.

Next I have to mill a 1/4-in. by 5/8-in. rabbet in the bottom of the cleat so it will sit over the interior partition wall (F) and be flush with the face of the corner board. I cut this rabbet on the table saw in 2 steps with a regular saw blade. First I set the rip fence 1/2 in. to the right of the blade. I raise the height of the blade to 1/4 in. and make the first rip cut (*photo 6-25*). For the second cut, I raise the blade to a height of 5/8 in. and make a second rip cut to complete the rabbet.

The last step is to cut a notch where the cleat goes over the south shop wall (G). I do this by hand with a small dovetail saw. Now I can attach both roof cleats with glue and some 1-in. brads.

With the cleats in place, I'm ready to install the shop-roof panels (R and S). I square up the roof panels with my homemade panel cutters and rip 30-degree bevels on the top and bottom of each panel. I fasten the north side of the shop roof in place with glue and brads. The adjoining south side of the shop roof is designed to be lifted off. To keep it from sliding off the slope, I make a cleat from a piece of 1 x 2 pine (*drawing 6-I*). This 25⅜-in.-long cleat is beveled at a 30-degree angle and gets fastened to the bottom edge of the roof (S) with glue and nails as shown (*photo 6-26*).

To complete the shop roof, I rout 3 skylight openings in the north slope (R) (*drawing 6-H*). I use my plunge router, a template, and the same bit setup I used to rout the door and window openings.

The roof for the second story is much simpler. I mill 2 panels (T) with angled top and bottom edges and join them with a 1½-in. pine cleat (*drawing 6-I*). I secure the panels to the cleat with glue and nails (*photo 6-27*). The whole roof lifts off as one piece to allow access to the second-floor room.

Now I'm ready to trim out all the eaves with 1/8-in. by 5/8-in. strips of pine (*drawing 6-J*). I glue and nail on the strips and smooth up the edges with a block plane (*photo 6-28*). Now I can trim out the gable ends, just holding the 1/8-in. by 5/8-in. strips flush with the roof surface. I finish up by sanding the roof panels with my random-orbit sander.

Making the Door

The sliding door for the west wall of the shop is made from 1/4-in. plywood

Door

Note: All trim pieces on door are
3/8 in. wide x 1/8 in. thick —
trim both sides of door.

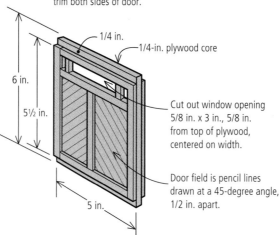

1/4 in.

1/4-in. plywood core

6 in.

5½ in.

Cut out window opening
5/8 in. x 3 in., 5/8 in.
from top of plywood,
centered on width.

Door field is pencil lines
drawn at a 45-degree angle,
1/2 in. apart.

5 in.

Section Through Door Track

Note: Track is 10½ in. long,
2 pieces required.

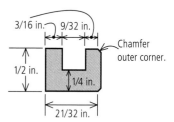

3/16 in. 9/32 in.

Chamfer
outer corner.

1/2 in.

1/4 in.

21/32 in.

6-26
The south side of the shop roof is designed to be lifted off. To keep it from sliding off the slope, I fasten a 25³⁄₈-in.-long cleat, beveled at a 30-degree angle, to the bottom edge of the roof (S) with glue and nails.

6-27
I secure the 2 second-story roof panels to a 1½-in. pine cleat with glue and nails.

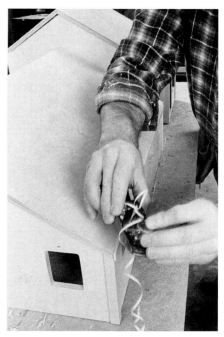

6-28
I trim out the eaves by gluing and nailing on 1/8-in. by 5/8-in. strips of pine and smooth up the edges with a block plane.

6-29

6-30

6-29
To simulate the frame of the full-size door, I trim it out with 1/8-in. by 3/8-in. strips of redwood, securing the strips with hot glue.

6-30
I make both door tracks from a single 12-in. length of 1 x 2 pine. I set my table-saw rip fence 3/16 in. from the blade, set the blade height to 1/4 in., and mill a groove in each edge of the workpiece. Then I make a second pass (shown here) with the opposite face against the fence to make a groove that measures 9/32 in. wide. A third pass down the middle will remove any remaining material.

(*drawing 6-K*) trimmed with 1/8-in. by 3/8-in. strips of redwood to simulate the frame of the full-size door. After cutting the 5-in. by 6-in. door to size, I lay out the window opening and cut it out with my jigsaw. The original shop door has a piece of leaded glass for the shop window. I'm just going to use a piece of clear plastic for the model and secure it with some hot glue. Now I can trim out both sides of the door with strips of redwood (*photo 6-29*).

The door slides on a couple of pine tracks (*drawing 6-K*). I make both tracks from a single 12-in. length of 1 x 2 pine. I set my table-saw rip fence 3/16 in. from the blade, set the blade height to 1/4 in., and mill a groove in each edge of the workpiece. Then I make a second pass with the opposite face against the fence to make a groove that measures 9/32 in. wide (*photo 6-30*). A little material still remains in the middle, so I slide my fence about 1/16 in. away from the blade and make one final cut down the middle to clean up the groove. I then rip a 1/2-in.-wide piece from each side of the 1 x 2. I chamfer the outer corners with a block plane and fasten the tracks to the west wall with glue and brads.

A little sanding here and there, and I'm finished with the woodworking part of the dollhouse. Painting the dollhouse is another story. I was lucky. I know an artist who painted shingles on the roof, shingles on the side walls, blue trim around the windows, doors, and clapboards on the west end. But that's not to say that you can't do it yourself. All it takes are some water-base paints, a steady brush hand, and endless amounts of patience.

cradle

project planner

Time: 3 days

Special hardware and tools:

Dovetailing jig with 1/2-in. box-joint template

Wood:

(1) 12-ft. 1 x 10 cherry
Cut 2 pieces 38 in. long and rip according to plan for lower sides. Cut one piece 38 in. long, joint and edge-glue to 38-in. long 1 x 4 (described below) to make a panel approximately 12½ in. x 38 in. for bottom. Cut 2 pieces 10 in. long and rip according to plan for hood sides.

(1) 4-ft. 1 x 10 cherry
Cut 2 pieces 16 in. long, joint and edge-glue to each other and to 16-in. long 1 x 2 (described below) to make a panel approximately 16 in. x 19½ in. for headboard. Cut one piece 14 in. long, joint and edge-glue to 14-in. 1 x 2 (described below) to make a panel approximately 10½ in. x 14 in. for footboard.

(1) 2-ft. 1 x 8 cherry
Resaw into 2 pieces approximately 5/16 in. thick, then plane to 1/4-in. thickness. Cut 3 pieces according to plan for hood.

(1) 4-ft. 1 x 6 cherry
Cut 2 pieces 24 in. long for rockers.

(1) 5-ft. 1 x 4 cherry
Cut one piece 38 in. long, joint and edge-glue to 38-in. 1 x 10 (described above) for bottom. Cut one piece 14 in. long for hood front crosspiece.

(1) 2½-ft. 1 x 2 cherry
Cut one piece 16 in. long, joint and edge-glue to

THESE DAYS, WHEN THE AVERAGE American family has only one or two children, most people don't think of a cradle as an essential piece of furniture. Yet it was in Colonial times. Large families were the rule in those days, and a cradle might hold ten or twelve infants in just one generation. One baby after another. Rocking around the clock!

From a Colonial mother's perspective, a cradle is a marvel of functional form. To understand why, picture a typical early-American home. Domestic life revolved around the huge kitchen fireplace on which the family depended for cooking and heat. The hood on a cradle kept out the cold drafts. The rockers extend beyond the sides of the cradle so a mother could rock it with her foot while she cooked, spun, or churned. Baby calmed down without disrupting the chores. Pretty efficient. And it's funny that in today's age of gadgets and modern devices, there's still nothing that soothes a baby more than being rocked to sleep in a cradle.

The handsome cradle shown here would become an heirloom in any family. It was inspired by an antique cradle I found in the Parsonage at Old Sturbridge Village in Sturbridge, Massachusetts. The original was made of pine, painted and grained to look like mahogany — a common practice in early nineteenth-century New England. The sides were made of a single wide board, and the corners were joined with simple nailed rabbet joints. The rockers, too, were just nailed to the bottom.

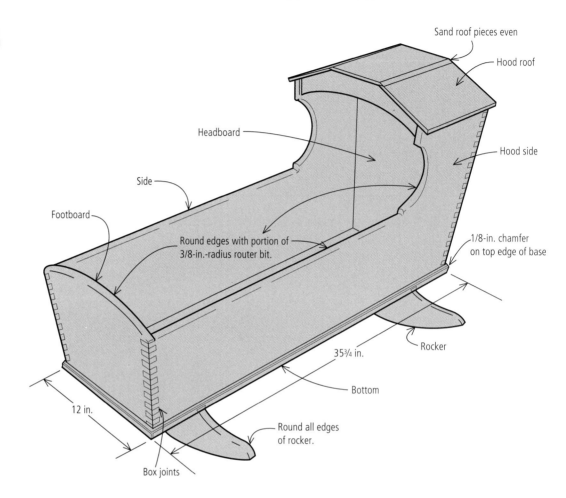

project planner

16-in. 1 x 10s (described above) for headboard. Joint remaining 14-in.-long piece and edge-glue to 14-in. 1 x 10 (described above) for footboard.

7-A Major Anatomy and Dimensions

Note: Attach headboard and footboard to base with two 1¼-in. screws in each.
Predrill elongated holes in bottom to allow for expansion and contraction.
Locate holes approximately 1 in. from sides.
Use one 1¼-in. screw at the midpoint of each side.

Sand roof pieces even

Hood roof

Headboard

Hood side

Side

Footboard

1/8-in. chamfer on top edge of base

Round edges with portion of 3/8-in.-radius router bit.

Rocker

35¾ in.

Bottom

12 in.

Round all edges of rocker.

Box joints

I chose to build my cradle from cherry instead of pine because cherry is a little more durable and looks better and better with age. I also changed a few other details. I joined the sides with what are known as box joints or finger joints. Box joints are much stronger than rabbet joints and look better, too. As for the rockers, I chose to join them to the base with sliding dovetail joints instead of with nails.

Making Panels

The first thing to do is to glue up 3 panels to make the headboard, the footboard, and the bottom of the cradle.

I cut to length the pieces of 3/4-in.-thick cherry for each panel (see Project Planner). The headboard panel requires 3 pieces. The footboard panel and the bottom panel are glued up from 2 pieces of wood each.

Then I joint all the edges, lay out the boards on my bench, and arrange them to get the best grain and color match within each panel. On the panel for the bottom, I'm more concerned with the edges looking good because that's the only part that will show in the finished cradle. The inside will be covered by bedding when the cradle's in use.

Glue alone is enough to hold these edge joints together, but biscuits make them that much stronger and also keep the boards from slipping out of alignment when I tighten the clamps. I want 2 #20 biscuits in each joint of the headboard and footboard panels and 3 in the joint of the bottom panel. With the boards placed edge to edge, I make a pencil mark to locate each biscuit slot, making sure to place the biscuits so I won't cut into one later when I cut out the parts. I cut the slots with my biscuit joiner, lining up its index mark with my pencil marks.

Now I'm ready to glue the panels together. I get my glue, biscuits, and clamps ready on the bench. Working on one panel at a time, I spread glue on the mating edges and put some in the biscuit slots as well. I pop the biscuits into their slots, assemble the boards, and put on the clamps. With any glue joint, the trick is to tighten the clamps just enough to bring the joint together — you don't want to squeeze all the glue out of the joint. Finally, I wipe off the excess glue with a damp sponge.

Sidepieces

The sides of my cradle are glued up from 2 pieces of 1 x 10 cherry. Each side has a long lower piece and a shorter piece above for the side of the hood (*drawing 7-B*). I don't want to glue these pieces together right now, because they'll be too awkward to handle during the next couple of steps.

What I want to do now is put a 6½-degree bevel along the bottom edges of the long pieces. The sides flare out 6½ degrees, and this bevel allows the bottom edges of the sidepieces to fit tightly against the bottom of the cradle.

First I joint the top edge of each lower sidepiece. Next I tilt my table-saw blade to a 6½-degree angle and set the rip fence to cut the board 8⁵⁄₁₆ in. wide, measuring from the short point of the bevel to the top edge. In other words, I measure along the *outer* face (*drawing 7-B*). Then I rip the bevel along the bottom edge.

The next thing to do is to cut these 2 long pieces to length. The headboard and footboard flare out 5 degrees, so I have to cut the ends at a 5-degree angle (*drawing 7-B*). With a pencil, I make little witness marks on the ends of the sidepieces to make sure that I angle the cuts in the right direction. Next, on my table saw, I set the miter gauge to 5 degrees and cut one end of each piece.

With one end cut, I mark each lower sidepiece for length — 36⅝ in. along the top edge — and crosscut the opposite end at 5 degrees (*drawing 7-B*).

Each hood sidepiece also gets a 5-degree crosscut along the back end. After jointing the bottom edge, I make the cut on the table saw. Then I measure 9¹⁄₁₆ in. along the bottom edge and cut the front end parallel to the back (*drawing 7-B*). To make this cut, I move the miter gauge to the slot on the other side of the blade without changing the angle setting. This gives me a parallel cut. Here, too, I make a witness mark on the wood to make sure that I angle the cut in the right direction. It's easy to make a mistake.

The top edge of the hood side gets beveled at 18½ degrees to match the angle of the roof (*drawings 7-A and 7-B*). I tilt the table-saw blade to 18½ degrees and position the rip fence to cut the hood side 8 in. wide, measured from the short

7-B Side

Note: Opposite side is a mirror image.
Box-joint layout is determined by cuts made in the headboard and footboard,
which are milled first. Bottom edges must align.

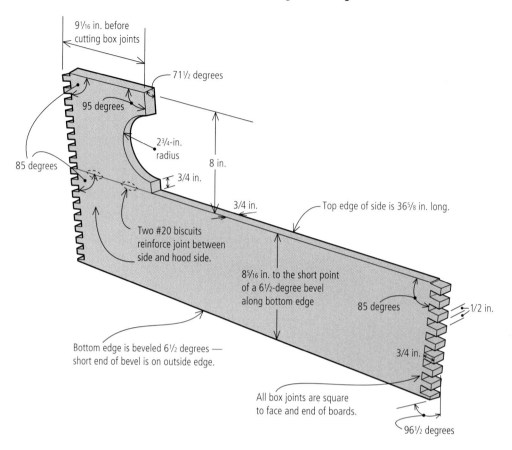

9¹⁄₁₆ in. before
cutting box joints

71½ degrees

95 degrees

2¾-in.
radius

8 in.

85 degrees

¾ in.

Two #20 biscuits
reinforce joint between
side and hood side.

¾ in.

Top edge of side is 36⅝ in. long.

8⁵⁄₁₆ in. to the short point
of a 6½-degree bevel
along bottom edge

85 degrees

½ in.

Bottom edge is beveled 6½ degrees —
short end of bevel is on outside edge.

¾ in.

All box joints are square
to face and end of boards.

96½ degrees

7-1
I make a poster-board
pattern to lay out the 2¾-
in.-radius cutout on the
hood sidepieces. I trace
the cutout onto the wood
and cut the curve on my
band saw.

7-2
I clean up the band-saw
marks on the hood sides
with my oscillating
spindle sander.

7-1

7-2

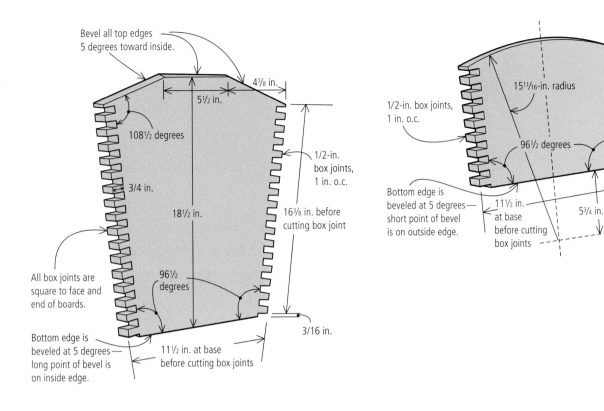

7-C Headboard
(viewed from inside)

Bevel all top edges 5 degrees toward inside.

4⅞ in.

5½ in.

108½ degrees

3/4 in.

18½ in.

1/2-in. box joints, 1 in. o.c.

16⅜ in. before cutting box joint

96½ degrees

All box joints are square to face and end of boards.

3/16 in.

Bottom edge is beveled at 5 degrees— long point of bevel is on inside edge.

11½ in. at base before cutting box joints

7-D Footboard
(viewed from outside)

15¹¹/₁₆-in. radius

1/2-in. box joints, 1 in. o.c.

96½ degrees

8½ in. before cutting box joints

Bottom edge is beveled at 5 degrees— short point of bevel is on outside edge.

11½ in. at base before cutting box joints

5¾ in.

1/4 in.

point of the bevel, or along the outer face (*drawing 7-B*). The bevel on the other hood side should be a mirror image of the one I just cut.

Next I make a poster-board pattern to lay out the 2¾-in.-radius cutout on the hood sidepieces (*photo 7-1*). I trace the cutout onto the wood and cut the curve on my band saw. I clean up the saw cuts with my oscillating spindle sander (*photo 7-2*).

Now I'm ready to join the sidepieces together. I mark and cut 2 biscuit slots in each joint before gluing and clamping the pieces together. Before I tighten the clamps, I slip little scrap-wood gluing blocks between the clamp jaws and the workpiece to keep the clamps from damaging the beveled edges.

Headboard and Footboard

The headboard and footboard flare out at a 5-degree angle. In order for the bottom edges to fit the bottom of the cradle properly, they have to be beveled to 5 degrees (*drawings 7-C and 7-D*). I make these rip cuts on the table saw, tilting the blade to 5 degrees.

Now I'm ready to cut the headboard to the correct height. The top edge, too, gets a 5-degree bevel, just as I did with the bottom edge. Measuring along the inside face of the headboard, I mark off 18½ inches to locate the short point of the bevel on the top edge (*drawing 7-C*). I adjust the table-saw rip fence to cut to this line and place the hood on the table saw with the inside facing up to make the cut.

7-3

I cut the angled sides of the headboard with my circular saw. I draw a pencil line to mark the 6½-degree angle, measure the distance between the edge of my circular saw's base and the blade, and clamp a straightedge that distance from the line. I guide the edge of the saw's base against the straightedge to make the cut.

Next I want to cut the sides of the headboard. The piece is just too big to maneuver easily on the table saw, so I'll make the cuts with my circular saw.

The sides must be cut at a 6½-degree angle (*drawing 7-C*). I draw a pencil line to mark the cut, then I clamp the board securely to my workbench. Next I measure the distance from the edge of my circular saw's base to the blade and clamp a straightedge that distance from the layout line (*photo 7-3*). I guide the edge of the saw's base against the straightedge to make a nice, straight cut. I have to reposition the straightedge to cut the opposite side.

The angled upper corners of the headboard must also be beveled to 5 degrees so the roof will fit (*drawing 7-C*). Once again, I use my circular saw and straightedge to make these cuts, but this time I have to tilt the saw blade 5 degrees.

The footboard is small enough to cut on the table saw with the miter gauge set to a 6½-degree angle. I cut one side to this angle, measure 11½ in. across the bottom edge, and make a mirror-image cut on the opposite side.

While my miter gauge is set to 6½ degrees, I need to cut a scrap-wood spacer, which I'll use later when I glue up the cradle. I cut one end of a piece of 1 x scrap about 3 in. wide to 6½ degrees. Then I measure 10 in. along the bottom edge and cut the other end to the same angle. I'll set this spacer aside for now.

The curve at the top of the footboard is a 15¹¹⁄₁₆-in.-radius arc (*drawing 7-D*). I make this cut on the band saw and clean up the edge with my oscillating spindle sander.

Box Joints

Now I'm ready to start milling the box joints. It's possible to cut box joints on the table saw, but I find it more convenient to use my dovetailing jig and a router. My jig has a variety of metal templates, including one for cutting 1/2-in. box joints.

I set up my router with a 5/8-in. o.d. guide collar and a 1/2-in. straight bit. Then, on the side edge of the headboard, I make a pencil mark 3/16 in. up from the inside bottom corner to mark the location of the bottom finger-joint notch (*drawing 7-C*). I position the headboard in my dovetailing jig, outside facing out, so that the router bit will cut on the pencil mark. I set the router bit for a 3/4-in.-deep cut and guide the collar around the template fingers to cut the joints. I flip the piece around (same face outward) to mill the box joints on the other edge.

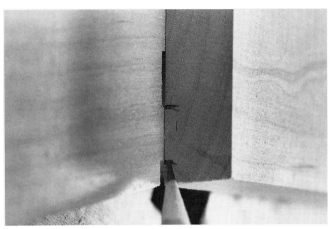

7-4
To lay out the finger joints in the sidepieces, I place the headboard on my bench, outside facing up. Now I take one of the sidepieces, also outside facing up, and place its back end on top of the completed finger joints in the headboard. I align the end of the sidepiece with the bottom of the 3/4-in. finger-joint notch in the headboard.

7-5
Next I align the bottom edges of the headboard and sidepiece, making pencil marks on the end of the sidepiece where it meets the bottom finger joint in the headboard. When I mill the finger joints in the sidepieces, I want to remove the material between these 2 marks.

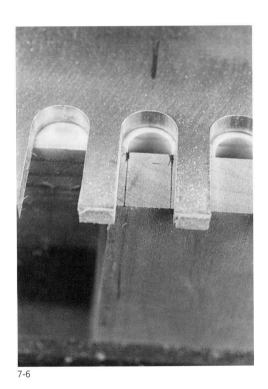

7-6

7-7

7-6
After marking the sidepiece, I slip it into the dovetailing jig with the outside face out. I align the pencil marks with the overcut area in the jig's wooden backer board so the router bit will remove the wood between the pencil marks.

7-7
Clamping the cradle is tricky because of the angles. Scrap-wood spacers at the hood and bottom of the cradle hold the cradle sides apart during clamping. Masking tape at the inside corners makes it easier to clean up excess glue.

    To lay out and mill the box joints on the footboard, I use the same procedure except that I make the pencil mark 1/4 in. up from the outside bottom corner to mark the location of the bottom finger-joint notch (*drawing 7-D*).

    In order to cut the finger joints in the sidepieces, I first have to do some layout so the joints line up. I place the headboard on my bench, outside facing up. Now I take one of the sidepieces, outside facing up, and place its back end on top of the finger joints in the headboard, aligning the end of the sidepiece with the bottom of the 3/16-in. finger-joint notch in the headboard (*photo 7-4*). Next I align the bottom edges of the headboard and sidepiece and make pencil marks on the

7-8

After removing the clamps and sanding the box joints smooth, I trim the bottom edges at the corners with a block plane so I'll have a flat surface for attaching the cradle bottom.

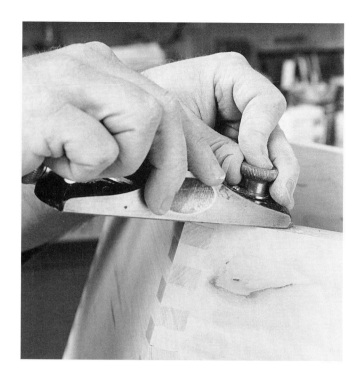

sidepiece where it meets the first (bottom) finger joint (*photo 7-5*). When I mill the finger joints in the sidepieces, I want to remove the material between these 2 marks.

Next I slip the sidepiece into the dovetailing jig with the outside face out. I align the pencil marks with the overcut area in the jig's wooden backer board (*photo 7-6*). Then I rout the joints. I repeat the entire procedure to mark and cut the other 3 corners of the cradle.

Now for a trial fit — just slip the pieces together. I'll glue the joints later. But before I do any assembly, I take the pieces apart and round over the edges at the top of the footboard and along the sides with a 3/8-in.-radius roundover bit in my router. I use only a portion of the bit, to ease the edges slightly. Then I finish-sand all the inside surfaces with my random-orbit sander. Sanding would be difficult to do after the cradle is glued up.

Now it's time for some assembly, but first I have to cut a piece of 1 x 2 scrap to use as a temporary spacer during glue-up. The ends of this piece are cut at a 6½-degree angle, and the finished spacer measures 13¹³⁄₁₆ in. from long point to long point. I also need the spacer I cut earlier that matches the shape of the footboard. Before I apply any glue, I place masking tape along the inside edges of every corner. The tape makes it a lot easier to clean up the glue later.

I brush glue onto the box joints on the headboard and onto the mating joints on the sidepieces. With the headboard flat on my bench, I slip the 2 sidepieces into place. Next I put the footboard in place to hold the sides apart (no glue yet) and insert the 13¹³⁄₁₆-in. scrap spacer between the 2 sidepieces as a temporary substitute for the hood crosspiece (*drawing 7-A*).

Clamping this assembly is tricky because of the angles. First I put one bar clamp across the bottom of the cradle at the headboard end and tap the headboard with my shot-filled mallet to close up the joints. I install a second clamp across the top of the headboard. A third clamp goes right in the middle. To pull

7-9
To rout the dovetail slots for the rockers in the bottom, I set up my router with a 3/4-in. dovetail bit set for a 3/8-in.-deep cut. On the bottom of the cradle, I measure 5 in. from each end and square a line across to mark the center of the dovetail slot. Next I clamp a straightedge parallel to this layout line exactly 3 in. further in — the distance from the center of the bit to the edge of the router base. I guide the router base along the straightedge to rout each slot in one pass.

the joint tighter, I install a clamp along each hood side, parallel to the lower side (*photo 7-7*).

Once the headboard is clamped in place, I insert the footboard-shaped spacer between the sides to hold them apart (*photo 7-7*) while I remove the footboard, glue it up, and clamp it (using the same method as for the headboard). Once the pieces are clamped, I remove the tape carefully before the glue dries.

When the glue has dried completely, I take off the clamps and sand all the box joints smooth and even. Then, with my low-angle block plane, I trim the bottom edges at the corners so I'll have a flat surface for attaching the cradle bottom (*photo 7-8*).

Completing the Bottom

The next step is to size the panel for the bottom of the cradle to 12 in. x 35¾ in. (*drawing 7-A*). I joint one edge of the panel and then rip and joint the opposite edge to give me a 12-in. width. Then, on my radial-arm saw, I crosscut the ends to length. Next I want to take out the slight unevenness at the joint, so I run the piece through my thickness planer, removing just enough wood to make it smooth. The top edge of the bottom gets a slight chamfer all around, which I make with my router and a chamfer bit.

The rockers fit into sliding dovetail joints in the bottom of the cradle (*drawing 7-E*). First I rout the dovetail slot in the bottom. I set up my router with a 3/4-in. dovetail bit set for a 3/8-in.-deep cut. Then, on the bottom of the cradle, I measure 5 in. from each end and square a line across to mark the center of each dovetail slot. Next I clamp a straightedge parallel to this layout line exactly 3 in. further in — the distance from the center of my router bit to the edge of the router base. I guide the router base along the straightedge to rout the slot in one pass (*photo 7-9*).

7-E Rocker Details

Rocker to Base

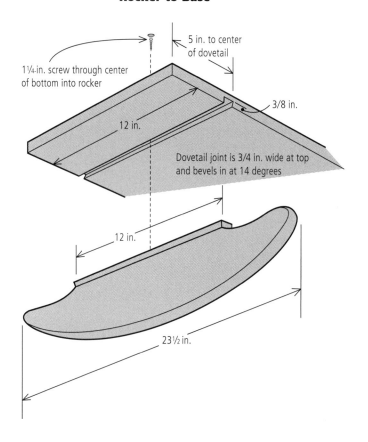

1¼-in. screw through center of bottom into rocker

5 in. to center of dovetail

3/8 in.

12 in.

Dovetail joint is 3/4 in. wide at top and bevels in at 14 degrees

12 in.

23½ in.

Pattern and section of rocker
(1 square = 1 square inch)

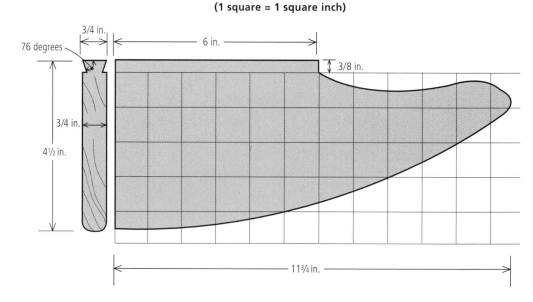

3/4 in.

76 degrees

6 in.

3/8 in.

3/4 in.

4½ in.

11¾ in.

7-10
I mill the rocker dovetails on my router table with the same 3/4-in. dovetail bit I used to cut the slot. I set the bit 3/8 in. above the table and adjust the router-table fence so that if I make a pass on each side of the workpiece, I end up with a dovetail that's a slip fit in the slot.

7-11
I secure each rocker with a single 8 x 1¼-in. screw dead center through the bottom of the cradle. This way, the bottom is free to expand and contract on either side of the screw without risk of cracking.

Making the Rockers

The first step in making the rockers is to mill dovetails along the top edges that will fit into the dovetail slots I just cut. I set up my router table with the same 3/4-in. dovetail bit I used to cut the slot and set it 3/8 in. above the table. I adjust the router-table fence so that if I make a pass on each side of the work-piece, I end up with a dovetail that's a slip fit in the slot (*photo 7-10*). I get this fit by trial and error, making cuts on scrap stock that's exactly the same thickness as the wood I'm using for the rockers.

After cutting the dovetails, I lay out the profile of the rockers with another posterboard pattern (*drawing 7-E*) and cut them out on the band saw. I clean up the edges on the drum sander and ease the edges with a 3/8-in.-radius roundover bit in my router. A touch of sandpaper to smooth the sides, and I tap the rockers home in their slots.

I secure each rocker with a single 8 x 1¼-in. screw dead center through the bottom of the cradle (*photo 7-11*). This way, the bottom is free to expand and contract on either side of the screw without risk of cracking. If I glued the rockers in their slots, the bottom would be sure to crack eventually because of wood movement.

7-12
To allow the cradle bottom to expand and contract across the grain without cracking, I want the screws in the headboard and footboard to be free to flex in their holes. To allow this, I elongate these 4 screw holes by rocking my drill bit back and forth. These slots are located on the top side of the cradle bottom.

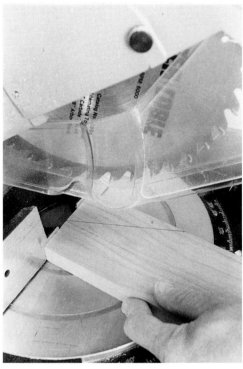

7-13
After cutting the ends of the hood crosspiece to 6½ degrees on my power miter box, I make the 2 cuts that follow the slope of the roof, holding the end of the crosspiece against the miter-box fence to make the cut.

Attaching the Bottom

Now I'm ready to install the bottom. With the cradle upside down on my bench, I place the bottom in position, hold it in place with a single clamp, and mark some holes so I can attach it with screws. I drill and countersink 6 holes — 2 in each end and one in each side.

The grain of the bottom runs at right angles to the grain in the headboard and footboard — a cross-grain situation that can cause stresses unless I make some provision for wood movement. To allow the bottom to expand and contract across the grain without cracking, I want the screws in the headboard and footboard to be free to flex in their holes. To allow this, I unclamp the bottom and elongate these 4 screw holes (parallel to the headboard and footboard) from above by rocking my drill bit back and forth (*photo 7-12*).

Front Crosspiece for Hood

The next piece I want to work on is the front crosspiece for the hood (*drawing 7-F*). It joins the sides of the cradle and supports the roof. On a 14-in. piece of 1 x 4 cherry (see Project Planner), I lay out the angles as shown in the drawing (*drawing 7-F*). First I cut the ends to 6½ degrees on my power miter box. Then I

7-F Hood Details

Front Crosspiece for Hood

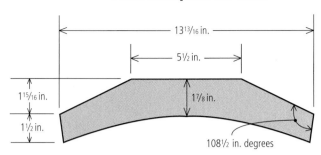

13^{13}/$_{16}$ in.

5½ in.

1^{15}/$_{16}$ in.

1^{7}/$_{8}$ in.

1½ in.

108½ in. degrees

Hood Panels

Note: Attach roof panels with 5/8-in. brads.
Panels overhang headboard by 1/4 in.

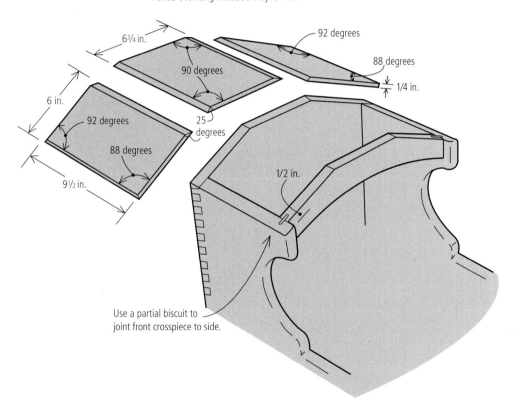

6¾ in.

92 degrees

88 degrees

1/4 in.

90 degrees

6 in.

92 degrees

25 degrees

88 degrees

1/2 in.

9½ in.

Use a partial biscuit to
joint front crosspiece to side.

make the 2 cuts that follow the slope of the roof, holding the end of the crosspiece against the miter-box fence to make the cut (*photo 7-13*). I saw out the
curved arch on the band saw, smooth up the cuts on the drum sander, and round
over the edges of the arch with a 3/8-in.-radius roundover bit.

The next job is to cut a biscuit slot at each end of the crosspiece and corresponding slots in the hood sides. Because the crosspiece is so narrow, I cut only
half a slot. I clamp the crosspiece on my workbench with a piece of scrap wood
clamped against the top edge of the crosspiece (*photo 7-14*). I use my biscuit

I cut half a biscuit slot in
each end of the hood
crosspiece by clamping it
on my workbench with a
piece of scrap wood
clamped against the top
edge. The biscuit joiner
cuts a slot in both the
crosspiece and the scrap
at the same time. When I
remove the scrap piece, I
have half a slot in the
crosspiece.

joiner to cut a slot in both the crosspiece and the scrap at the same time. When I remove the scrap piece, I have half a slot in the crosspiece. After cutting the slots, I glue and clamp the crosspiece in place and saw off the protruding ends of the biscuits with a backsaw.

Hood Roof

Installing the hood roof is the last bit of woodworking that remains to be done. For this I need some 1/4-in.-thick cherry — something you just can't buy at the lumberyard. But with a band saw and thickness planer, it's easy to cut thin stock yourself.

Starting with a 2-ft. piece of 1 x 8 cherry (see Project Planner), I true up one edge on the jointer. Then, on my band saw, I support the board vertically against the saw fence and rip the board straight down the middle into 2 thinner boards approximately 5/16 in. thick (*photo 7-15*). This procedure is known as "resawing" and the band saw's the best tool for the job.

Next I run these 2 thin boards through my planer to smooth up the saw marks and reduce the thickness to 1/4 in. Finally, I crosscut 3 pieces 11 in. long, from which I'll make the 3 roof boards (*drawing 7-F*).

The center roof board overlaps the 2 side roof boards and meets them at a very sharp angle (*drawing 7-F*). To cut this angle safely on my table saw, I've made a simple plywood jig that slides on the rip fence and makes it easy to hold work securely in a vertical position (*photo 7-16*). It is extremely dangerous to attempt this cut without a jig like this because the thin stock will get pulled down into the slot in the blade insert.

I start by beveling the 2 side roof boards. To make these angled rip cuts, I

7-15
I make the boards for the hood roof by "resawing" a piece of 1 x 8 cherry on the band saw. I support the board against the saw fence and rip the board straight down the middle into 2 thinner boards approximately 5/16 in. thick.

7-16
To safely cut the 25-degree bevels on the edges of the roof panels, I use a homemade jig that supports the board vertically. I move the rip fence to the left of the blade (the blade on my saw tilts to the right), tilt the saw blade 25 degrees, and position the rip fence so the blade will cut right up against the plywood face of the jig to rip a 25-degree bevel on one edge of each side roof board.

move the table-saw rip fence to the left of the blade (the blade on my saw tilts to the right), tilt the saw blade 25 degrees, and position the rip fence so the blade will cut right up against the plywood face of the jig (*photo 7-16*). I rip a 25-degree bevel on one edge of each side roof board.

Next I tilt the blade back to 90 degrees and position the rip fence 6 in. from the blade. I rip the side roof boards 6 in. wide, placing the beveled edge against the rip fence to make the cut. With the blade still at 90 degrees, I set my table-saw miter gauge to 88 degrees and make a 2-degree angled crosscut at one end of each piece. The 2 side roof boards must be mirror images of each other. I measure off 9½ in. along the edge and make a second angled cut at the opposite end (*drawing 7-F*). The finished side roof boards have a parallelogram shape and are 9½ in. long. Now I can nail these 2 side roof boards in place with some 5/8-in. brads. The ends of the boards overhang the headboard by 1/4 in.

Once the side roof boards are installed, I'm ready to complete and attach the

7-17
**I fasten the roof boards
with 5/8-in. brads.**

center roof board. I tilt the table-saw blade 25 degrees and bevel one edge using my jig. Then I place the center roof board in position on the cradle and mark the width (approximately 6¾ in.). I tilt the blade back up to 90 degrees again and rip along that line, leaving just the pencil mark on the wood. Next I tilt the saw back again to 25 degrees and rip a second 25-degree bevel, sawing to the pencil line. Then I cut the center roof board to a length of 9½ in. and nail it in place (*photo 7-17*). I clean up the joints with my block plane and sander. That about does it. A little final sanding, and this piece will be ready for the finishing room.

Finishing Up

A Danish oil finish is my favorite for cherry. It brings out the color, and the wood just looks richer with age. It's also an easy finish to repair if it ever gets nicked or scratched. You simply apply some more oil.

With a brush, I apply a liberal amount of the oil, allowing it to soak in for a minute before I wipe off the excess with a clean rag. I apply 3 coats, allowing each to dry overnight. Remember that oil-soaked rags are a fire hazard. They can ignite by themselves from spontaneous combustion. Always discard them outside.

That's all there is to it. I'll let the finish cure for at least a month before I place a baby in the cradle. Now, let's see, who do I know that's expecting?

8

trundle bed

Time: 5 days

Special hardware and tools:

(1) set of four 4-in. by 5/8-in. bed rail fasteners (item #28589)*

(8) 2¾-in. joint connector bolts (item #31856)*

(8) cross-dowels for joint connector bolts (item #31823)*

(4) soft twin wheel casters (item #24141)*

Note: Hardware available from The Woodworkers' Store, Medina, MN.

(24) 10 x 2½-in. flat-head steel wood screws

(16) 8 x 1¾-in. flat-head steel wood screws

(34) 8 x 1½-in. flat-head steel wood screws

(32) 6 x 1¼-in. flat-head steel wood screws

Wood:

(1) 12-ft. 8/4 x 8 poplar
Rip into 2 pieces 3¼ in. wide. From each piece cut two 42-in. lengths and two 28-in. lengths. Face-glue in pairs for head posts and foot posts.

(2) 14-ft. 8/4 x 6 poplar
Cut 2 pieces 77 in. long, rip and joint to 5 in. wide, and plane to 1½-in. thickness for side rails.

Cut 2 pieces 41 in. long, rip and joint to 5 in. wide, and plane to 1½-in. thickness for head rail and foot rail.

Plane remaining piece to 1½-in. thickness, then rip and joint 4 pieces 1⅛ in. wide. Cut 2 pieces 76⅞ in. long for side mattress support cleats for bed and 2 pieces 74¾ in. long for side mattress support cleats for trundle.

I F YOU HAVE A CHILD'S bedroom that's too small for twin beds, you might consider a trundle bed: a low bed that pulls out from under a regular-height bed and slides back underneath when it's not being used. Trundle beds are great space savers, and kids really love them for sleepovers. If you don't need the extra bed, the trundle makes a great place for storing toys or blankets. Just eliminate the mattress and you have a spacious storage area that rolls away out of sight.

I designed my trundle bed to fit a standard twin-size mattress. The upper bed takes a mattress and box spring, but the bottom bed needs only a mattress.

I built the bed mostly from poplar, a stable hardwood that's relatively inexpensive and paints up nicely. I used maple for the trundle guides and pine for the trundle slats that support the mattress (*drawing 8-A*). The headboard and sides of the trundle are made of 3/4-in. MDO board — a durable, high-quality plywood with a thin paper coating on each side. It's expensive, but it's an ideal material to paint.

Making the Posts

I get started by making the 4 bedposts (*drawing 8-A*). Each 3-in.-square post is glued up from 2 pieces of 8/4 poplar (see Project Planner).

From a 12-ft. length of 8/4 x 8 poplar, I rip 2 pieces 3¼ in. wide. From each of these 12-ft. lengths, I crosscut two 42-in.-long pieces for the head posts and two

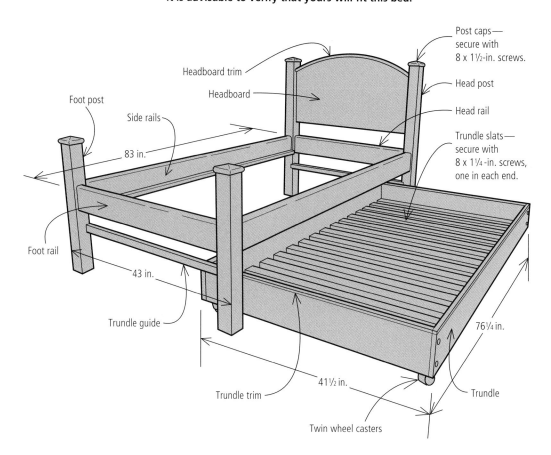
(1) 3½-ft. 8/4 x 3 poplar
Plane to 1½-in. thickness, then rip and joint 2 pieces 1⅛ in. wide. Trim to 37 in. long for end mattress support cleats for trundle.

(1) 1½-ft. 8/4 x 4 maple
Mill according to plan and then cut into 4 pieces 3½ in. square for post caps.

(2) 7-ft. 1 x 3 maple
Cut one piece 42 in. long. Rip and joint 42-in. piece and the remaining 7-ft.-long piece to 1⅞ in. wide. Mill according to plan for T trim pieces for top edge of trundle, getting 2 finished T pieces per length.

Plane remaining piece to 9/16-in. thickness, then rip and joint to 1⅜ in. wide for trim piece for top of headboard.

(1) 8 ft. 1 x 2 maple
Cut 2 pieces 39¼ in. long for trundle guides. Rip a 1/8-in. by 3/4-in. strip from each side of scrap and cut to fit according to plan to make trim pieces for ends of long side of trundle.

(4) 14-ft. 1 x 3 No. 1 common pine
Cut 16 pieces 40 in. long for trundle slats.

(1) 4-ft. by 8-ft. sheet of 3/4-in. MDO plywood
Cut 3 pieces 6 in. x 96 in., then cut into 2 pieces 76 in. long for trundle sides and 2 pieces 40 in. long for trundle ends.

Cut one piece 21 in. x 39 in. for headboard.

8-A Major Anatomy and Dimensions

Note: Since mattress and foundation sizes vary among manufacturers, it is advisable to verify that yours will fit this bed.

28-in.-long pieces for the foot posts. I joint one face of each piece flat and true on the jointer and face-glue the pieces in pairs — jointed faces together — to give me 4 blanks approximately 3¼ in. square.

When the glue is dry, I'm ready to size the post blanks. Here's the procedure. First I run the blanks through my jointer, taking just enough material off one face to flatten it. Then I mark that face with a pencil to make sure I don't plane it twice. Next I turn each piece over (planed face down) and keep running the opposite face through my thickness planer until I end up with a finished thickness of 3 in. (*photo 8-1*).

Now I go to work on the remaining 2 sides of the post (the sides with the glue lines). After jointing one side square to the faces I just planed, I go back to my planer, placing the just-jointed side face down and planing the opposite side to its final 3-in. thickness.

To square up the ends of the post, I turn to my power miter box. I cut one end, measure off the length I want (41½ in. for the head posts, 26 in. for the foot posts), and cut the opposite end.

Rail Mortises

Both the headboard and footboard have a crossrail that is attached to the posts with mortise-and-tenon joints (*drawings 8-A, 8-B, and 8-C*). Milling the

After flattening one face of each post blank on the jointer, I turn each piece over (planed face down) and use my thickness planer to make repeated cuts on the opposite face until I end up with a finished thickness of 3 in.

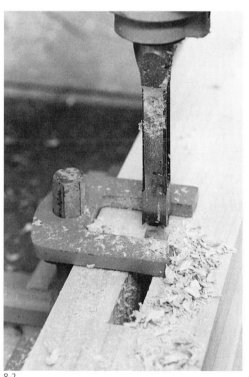

8-2

8-3

8-2 and 8-3
I mill the rail mortises on my hollow-chisel mortising machine with a 1/2-in. chisel. I cut along one edge of the mortise (*photo 8-2*), turn the piece around, and make a second pass along the opposite edge to cut the full 3/4-in. width of the mortise (*photo 8-3*).

mortises is the next job. There are several different ways to cut them. I could drill a series of holes and then chisel out the waste by hand. Or I could use a hollow-chisel mortising attachment on my drill press. A third option is to rout out the mortises with my plunge router. All work equally well.

But for this job, I'm going to use yet another mortising method — a hollow-chisel mortising machine. This single-purpose machine works just like the mortising attachment on my drill press but is more convenient than converting my drill press for mortising.

With a pencil and square, I lay out the 3/4-in.-wide by 4-in.-high rail mortises

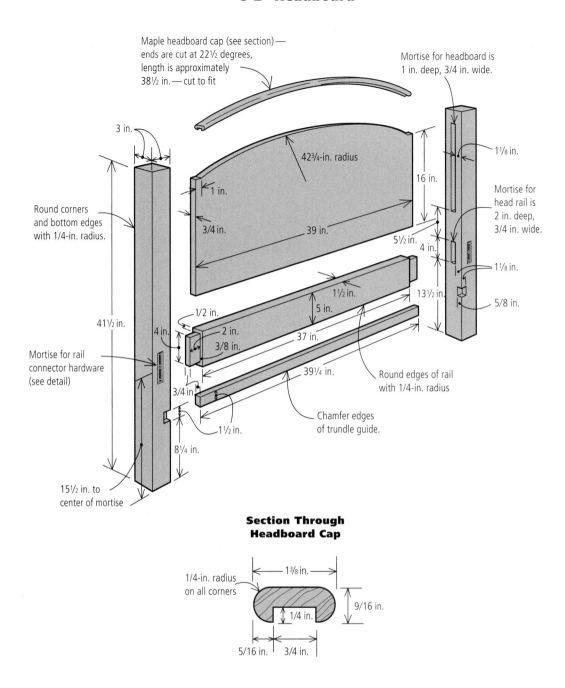

Maple headboard cap (see section)—
ends are cut at 22½ degrees,
length is approximately
38½ in.—cut to fit

Mortise for headboard is
1 in. deep, 3/4 in. wide.

3 in.

42¾-in. radius

16 in.

1⅛ in.

1 in.

Mortise for
head rail is
2 in. deep,
3/4 in. wide.

Round corners
and bottom edges
with 1/4-in. radius.

3/4 in.

39 in.

5½ in.

4 in.

1⅛ in.

13½ in.

5/8 in.

41½ in.

1½ in.

5 in.

1/2 in.

2 in.

37 in.

4 in.

3/8 in.

Mortise for rail
connector hardware
(see detail)

39¼ in.

Round edges of rail
with 1/4-in. radius

3/4 in.

Chamfer edges
of trundle guide.

1½ in.

8¼ in.

15½ in. to
center of mortise

**Section Through
Headboard Cap**

1⅜ in.

1/4-in. radius
on all corners

9/16 in.

1/4 in.

5/16 in.   3/4 in.

on the posts (*drawings 8-B and 8-C*). I install a 1/2-in.-wide mortising chisel (the widest one I own) and set it for a 2-in.-deep cut. Next I adjust the machine's fence so that the back edge of the chisel cuts on my layout line. I cut along one edge of the mortise (*photo 8-2*), turn the piece around, and make a second pass along the opposite edge to cut the full 3/4-in. width of the mortise (*photo 8-3*).

A shallower 3/4-in.-wide by 16-in.-high mortise is needed in each head post to receive the 3/4-in.-thick plywood headboard (*drawing 8-B*). For these mortises, I set the chisel for a 1-in.-deep cut (*photo 8-4*).

8-C Foot Posts and Rail

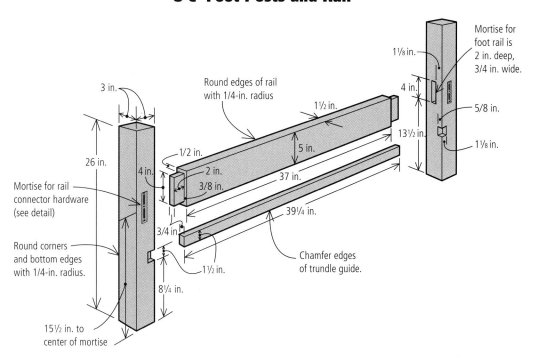

3 in.

Round edges of rail with 1/4-in. radius

1½ in.

Mortise for foot rail is 2 in. deep, 3/4 in. wide.

1⅛ in.

4 in.

5/8 in.

26 in.

1/2 in.

5 in.

13½ in.

4 in.

Mortise for rail connector hardware (see detail)

2 in.
3/8 in.

37 in.

1⅛ in.

Round corners and bottom edges with 1/4-in. radius.

3/4 in.

39¼ in.

Chamfer edges of trundle guide.

1½ in.

8¼ in.

15½ in. to center of mortise

8-4
A shallower mortise is needed in each head post to receive the 3/4-in.-thick plywood headboard. For these mortises, I set the chisel for a 1-in.-deep cut.

Headboard and Footboard

The head rail and foot rail come next. They have 2-in.-long tenons on each end, which fit into the mortises I milled in the posts (*drawing 8-B*).

After ripping, jointing, and planing the rails to size (see Project Planner) and trimming them to a length of 41 in., I'm ready to mill the tenons on the table saw.

The first thing to do is make what is called a shoulder cut along each face of

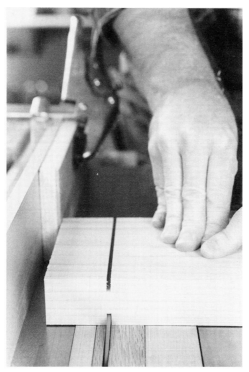 

8-5
To make the shoulder cuts for the rail tenons, I set up my table saw with a wooden gauge block clamped to the rip fence a couple of inches in front of the blade. I position the fence so the gauge block is 2 in. away from the left side of the blade and then make a 3/8-in.-deep cut on each side.

8-6
After making 1/2-in.-deep shoulder cuts on the top and bottom of the tenon, I complete the edge of the tenon by making repeated crosscuts to nibble away the material.

the rail. I set up my table saw with a wooden gauge block clamped to the rip fence a couple of inches in front of the blade. Since I want to cut a 2-in.-long tenon, I position the rip fence to the right of the blade so the gauge block is 2 in. away from the left side of the blade. I raise the blade 3/8 in. above the table — the depth of the mortise shoulder (*drawings 8-B and 8-C*).

To make the cut, I place a rail with one edge against the miter gauge and butt the right-hand end against the wooden gauge block. Using the miter gauge, I feed the rail forward into the blade to cut the shoulder. I turn the rail over and make an identical cut on the opposite face (*photo 8-5*). These cuts form the shoulders on the sides, or "cheeks," of the tenon. Using the same setup, I repeat this process on the other end of the rail.

The next cuts form the shoulders at the top and bottom of the tenon. Without moving the rip fence, I raise the blade to 1/2 in. Holding the rail on edge, I make a shoulder cut at one end. Then I complete the edge of the tenon by making repeated crosscuts to nibble away the material (*photo 8-6*). I repeat this process on the other tenons.

To complete the tenons, I cut the cheeks with my tenoning jig. First I raise the blade to a height of 2 in. I cut one side, then turn the rail around to cut the other side (*photo 8-7*). The finished tenon should be 3/4 in. thick and have a nice slip fit in the post mortises. I always test the fit on a scrap piece first and make any

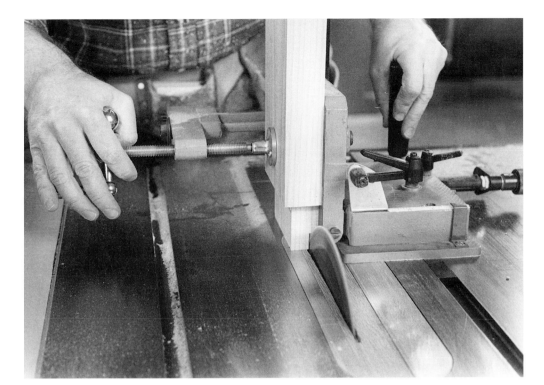

8-7
To complete the tenons, I cut the cheeks with my table-saw tenoning jig. I cut one side, then turn the rail around to cut the other side. To adjust the thickness of the tenon, I move the jig closer to or farther away from the blade as necessary.

necessary adjustments. To alter the thickness of the tenon, I move the jig closer to or farther away from the blade as necessary.

There are just a few more steps on the posts and rails. I ease the sharp edges of the rails with a 1/4-in.-radius roundover bit in my router table (*photo 8-8*). I also round over the bottom edges and corners of the posts but leave the top edges sharp. Then I sand the posts and rails with my random-orbit sander — it's difficult to sand once the parts are assembled.

The next piece to make is the headboard. On a 21-in. by 39-in. piece of 3/4-in. MDO plywood (see Project Planner), I lay out the curved top edge with a 42¾-in. radius, terminating the arc 1 in. from each end to form the "tenons" that will fit into the posts (*drawing 8-B*). I saw out the arch with my jigsaw.

To conceal the plywood edge at the top of the headboard, I bend a piece of maple around the curve (*drawing 8-B*). To make this headboard cap, I mill a 42-in.-long piece of maple to a 9/16-in. thickness and a 1⅜-in. width (see Project Planner). Next I round over all 4 edges using the same setup I used for rounding the edges of the posts and rails.

The next thing to do is mill a 3/4-in.-wide groove down the center of the piece to slip over the plywood (*drawing 8-B*). I install a stack dado head on my table saw and set it for a 3/4-in.-wide cut. I raise the blade 1/4 in. above the table and adjust the rip fence to center the groove in the workpiece. When the setup is right, I mill the 1/4-in.-deep groove in one pass (*photo 8-9*).

The ends of this maple headboard cap must be cut at an angle to fit properly against the posts when the headboard is assembled. I set my power miter box to a 22½-degree angle and cut one end of the maple strip. To determine the length, I bend the strip around the top of the headboard and mark the outer end. I place the maple strip on the top edge of the headboard, positioning the angled end on the 1-in. mark where the arch begins (*photo 8-10 and drawing 8-B*). Then I

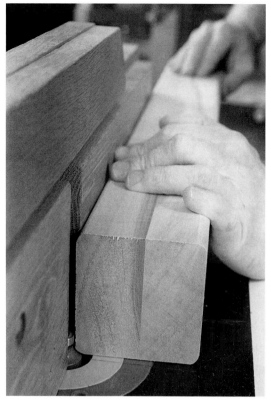

8-8
I ease the sharp edges of the posts and rails with a 1/4-in.-radius roundover bit in my router table.

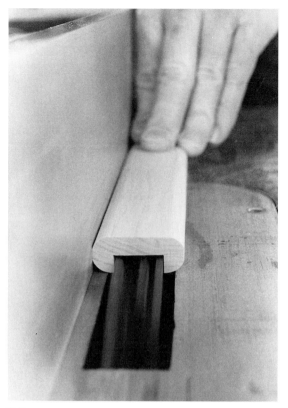

8-9
I mill a 1/4-in.-deep groove down the center of the headboard cap with a stack dado cutter set for a 3/4-in.-wide cut.

8-10
To determine the length of the maple headboard cap, I cut one end to a 22½-degree angle and place it on the top edge of the headboard, positioning the angled end on the 1-in. mark where the arch begins. Then I install a C clamp and a wedge at that end of the plywood to hold the strip in place as I bend the maple along the curve, making a pencil mark at the 1-in. mark on the opposite end of the headboard. I remove the strip and trim this end to a 22½-degree angle.

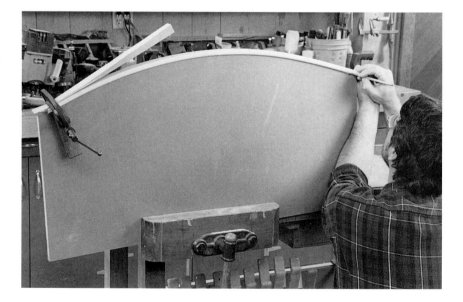

8-11

8-12

8-11 and 8-12
I glue and clamp the headboard assembly together and check for square by measuring across the diagonals. The assembly is square if the distances from corner to corner are the same.

install a C clamp and a wedge at that end of the plywood to hold the strip in place as I bend, using scrap blocks to protect the face of the plywood (*photo 8-10*). Then I bend the cap along the curve, making a pencil mark at the 1-in. mark on the opposite end of the headboard (*photo 8-10*). I remove the strip and trim this end to a 22½-degree angle.

Assembling the Headboard and Footboard

Now for a little assembly. First I want to install the maple headboard cap and clamp it in place. I position a C clamp at each end of the headboard to keep the ends of the strip from springing back. I brush glue in the groove of the maple strip, slip it under one C clamp, and align the end with the 1-in. "tenon" line on the headboard. Then I slip a wedge between the clamp and the maple strip to hold it in place. Next I bend the strip around the curve, clamping it in place with long bar clamps as I go. The opposite end must line up with the "tenon" line on the other side of the headboard.

Continuing with the assembly procedure, I brush glue in the headboard mortise of one of the posts and on one of the headboard "tenons." With the post lying mortise side up on my bench, I slip the headboard into the mortise, seating it with a few taps from my shot-filled mallet.

The head rail comes next. Some glue in the mortise, more glue on the tenon, and the tenon slides into the slot. Now I install the second head post (*photo*

8-11) and clamp the assembly with a few pipe clamps. It's important that the headboard assembly is square, so I check it by measuring diagonally across the corners (*photo 8-12*). If the distance is the same from corner to corner, the assembly is square. If not, I loosen the clamps and rack the assembly slightly until the diagonals are equal. I wipe off any excess glue with a damp cloth.

The footboard is a lot easier to put together — just one rail. I glue and clamp it together and set it aside to dry.

To complete the headboard, I make a couple of mortises in the lower portion of the posts to receive the ends of a maple trundle guide (*drawings 8-A and 8-B*). This guide allows the trundle to slide in and out without hitting the posts.

I set up my router with a 3/8-in.-dia. straight bit and a 5/8-in.-dia. guide collar. Next I make a simple jig to guide my router — just a piece of plywood with a notch cut in one edge. To determine the size of the notch, I simply subtract the radius of my router bit from the radius of the guide collar and add this dimension to the length (1⅛ in.) of the mortise I want to cut. For the width of the mortise (1½ in.), I add twice the difference between the radius of the router bit and the radius of the guide collar (1/8 in.). In other words, the notch in the jig measures 1¼ in. long and 1¾ in. wide. When I guide the collar around the notch, it cuts a mortise exactly the size I need — 1⅛ in. x 1½ in. x 5/8 in. deep (*drawing 8-B*). Each post gets a mortise. I cut identical mortises in the foot posts (*drawing 8-C*).

The router leaves rounded corners in the mortises, but instead of squaring up the corners as I often do with routed mortises, I find it easier in this case to round over the ends of the trundle guides on my stationary belt sander. Now I mill a 1/8-in. chamfer on the edges of the 1 x 2 maple trundle guides that face the trundle with a chamfering bit, sand the guides smooth, and glue them into their mortises.

Side Rails and Fasteners

The side rails are connected to the head- and footboard with special hardware known as bed rail fasteners (see Project Planner). These fasteners consist of 2 pieces that hook together. One piece, the one with hooks on it, gets mortised into the end of the rail (*drawing 8-D*); the other has slots to receive the hooks and gets mortised into the post (*drawing 8-E*). To attach the rail to the post, you just slip the fasteners together and drive the rail downward to lock the joint.

To install the bed rail fasteners, I first make a mortise in the end of the side rail for the hooked piece (*drawing 8-D*) with a 5/8-in. o.d. guide collar and a 3/8-in.-dia. straight bit set up in my router.

To guide the router, I make a simple jig from a piece of 1/4-in. plywood measuring approximately 3½ in. x 12 in. (*photo 8-13*). I lay out a rectangular opening in the center of the jig. The router collar rides around the inside of this opening to cut the mortise. The opening must be larger all around than the mortise to account for the offset between the guide collar and bit. To determine this offset, I subtract the radius of my router bit from the radius of the guide collar. I cut the opening on my mortising machine. (Verify the actual dimensions of your bed rail fasteners before making the jig.) Next I draw centerlines on the jig along the length and width of the opening. I'll use these centerlines to position the jig on the rail.

8-D Side Rail

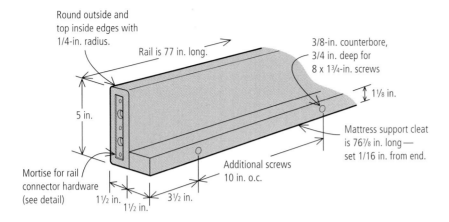

Round outside and top inside edges with 1/4-in. radius.

Rail is 77 in. long.

3/8-in. counterbore, 3/4 in. deep for 8 x 1¾-in. screws

1⅛ in.

5 in.

Mattress support cleat is 76⅞ in. long — set 1/16 in. from end.

Mortise for rail connector hardware (see detail)

Additional screws 10 in. o.c.

1½ in.

1½ in.

3½ in.

8-E Mortise Details for Rail Connectors

Note: Mortises are 1/8 in. deep. Hardware may vary — confirm dimensions before mortising.

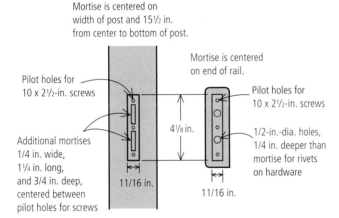

Mortise is centered on width of post and 15½ in. from center to bottom of post.

Mortise is centered on end of rail.

Pilot holes for 10 x 2½-in. screws

Pilot holes for 10 x 2½-in. screws

Additional mortises 1/4 in. wide, 1¼ in. long, and 3/4 in. deep, centered between pilot holes for screws

1/2-in.-dia. holes, 1/4 in. deeper than mortise for rivets on hardware

4⅛ in.

11/16 in.

11/16 in.

I draw centerlines on the end of each rail and attach the plywood jig to the end of a rail with a couple of screws (*photo 8-13*), using the centerlines to position the jig over the end of the rail. I set my router bit to cut a mortise as deep as the thickness of the bed rail fastener. Then I guide the router around the opening to cut the mortise. After removing the jig, I square up the corners of the mortise with a chisel (*photo 8-14*).

For the bed rail fastener to fit completely into the mortise, I need to remove some material to accommodate 2 rivets that project from the back of the fastener. I do so with a 1/2-in.-dia. brad-point drill, boring just deep enough so the hardware will fit flush in the mortise (*photo 8-15*). Only 3 more rail mortises to go, and I'm ready to install the fasteners with screws.

The next bit of business is to ease the sharp edges of the side rails with a 1/4-in.-radius roundover bit. I round only the 2 upper edges and the bottom outside edge. I leave the bottom inner edge square.

The final thing to do is install the 1⅛-in. by 1½-in. cleats that support the box spring and mattress (*drawing 8-D* and Project Planner). I drill pilot holes and

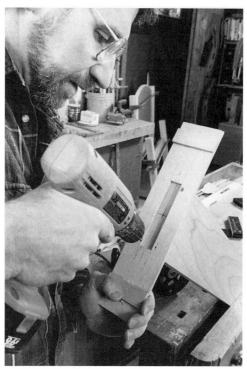

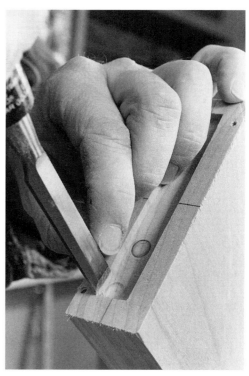

8-13
To guide the router for milling the
mortises for the bed rail fasteners, I make
a jig from 1/4-in. plywood with a
rectangular opening in the center. I attach
the plywood jig to the end of a rail with a
couple of screws, using centerlines drawn
on the jig and rail end to position the jig.

8-14
After routing the mortise and removing
the jig, I square up the corners of the
mortise with a chisel.

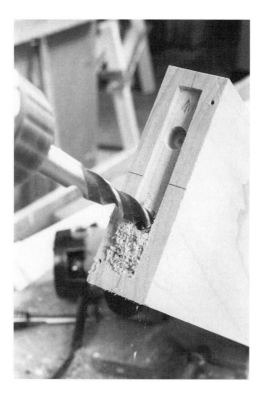

8-15
For the bed rail fastener to fit completely
into the mortise, I need to remove some
material to accommodate the 2 rivets that
project from the back of the fastener. I do
so with a 1/2-in.-dia. brad-point drill,
boring just deep enough for the hardware
to fit flush in the mortise.

8-16
I install the cleats that support the box spring and mattress with glue and 8 x 1¾-in. screws.

8-17
After routing mortises in each post for the slotted bed rail fasteners, I still need to remove a little more material underneath the slots to accommodate the hooks of the mating piece. That's a job for my hollow-chisel mortising machine, which I set up with a 1/4-in. bit.

3/8-in.-dia. counterbores 3/4 in. deep for the screw heads, spacing the holes 10 in. o.c. (*drawing 8-D*). Then I install the cleats with glue and 8 x 1¾-in. screws (*photo 8-16*). The ends of the cleats are set in 1/16 in. from the ends of the rails.

With the same plywood mortising jig I used for the rail ends, I rout a mortise in each post for the second piece of the hardware — the piece with the slots (*drawing 8-E*). After squaring up the mortise corners, I still need to remove a little more material underneath the slots to accommodate the hooks of the mating piece. That's a job for my mortising machine, which I set up with a 1/4-in. hollow-chisel bit (*photo 8-17*).

Post Caps

To make the 4 decorative caps for the tops of the bedposts, I start with a 1½-ft.-long piece of 8/4 maple exactly 3½ in. wide (see Project Planner). Next, on my table saw, I position the rip fence to the left of the blade (the blade on my saw tilts to the right) and tilt the saw blade to a 15-degree angle. I position the fence 1 in. from the blade (measured at the table) and raise the blade 2 in. Now I make a rip cut on one side. Next I flip the stock over and make a cut on the other side (*photo 8-18*).

On my power miter box, I crosscut this maple piece into 3½-in. lengths. This gives me 4 blocks, 3½ in. square with a bevel on 2 sides. I still have to bevel the

8-F Post Caps

Note: Round all corners and edges of cap before installing.

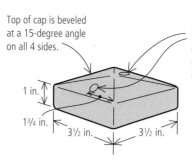

Top of cap is beveled at a 15-degree angle on all 4 sides.

Drill two 3/8-in. counterbores, 3/4 in. from edge, 1/2 in. deep, with 3/16-in. pilot holes for screws to secure caps — fill counterbores with plugs.

1 in.

1³/4 in.

3½ in.   3½ in.

8-18

To make the decorative bedpost caps, I position the rip fence to the left of the blade and tilt the saw blade to a 15-degree angle. I position the fence 1 in. from the blade (measured at the table), raise the blade 2 in., and make a rip cut on both sides.

8-19

After cutting the bedpost caps square, I still have to bevel the other 2 sides of each block. To do this safely on the table saw, I screw the blocks to a scrap of plywood so I can cut the bevels and keep my hands away from the blade. I cut one side, then rotate the block on the screw to cut the opposite side.

8-20

I install the bedpost caps with 8 x 1½-in. screws and put maple plugs in the holes.

other 2 sides of each block. To do this safely on the table saw, I screw the blocks to a scrap of plywood so I can cut the bevels and keep my hands away from the blade (*photo 8-19*). I cut one side, then rotate the block on the screw to cut the opposite side (*photo 8-19*).

Since the 1/4-in.-radius roundover bit is still in my router, I round the bottom corners of each block. I round all the other edges with my stationary belt sander and sand the blocks smooth. Next I need to drill a couple of holes for the screws that attach the blocks to the post (*drawing 8-F*). With a Forstner bit in my drill press, I drill two 3/8-in.-dia. counterbores in each cap, 3/4 in. from the edge.

8-G Corner Details—Trundle

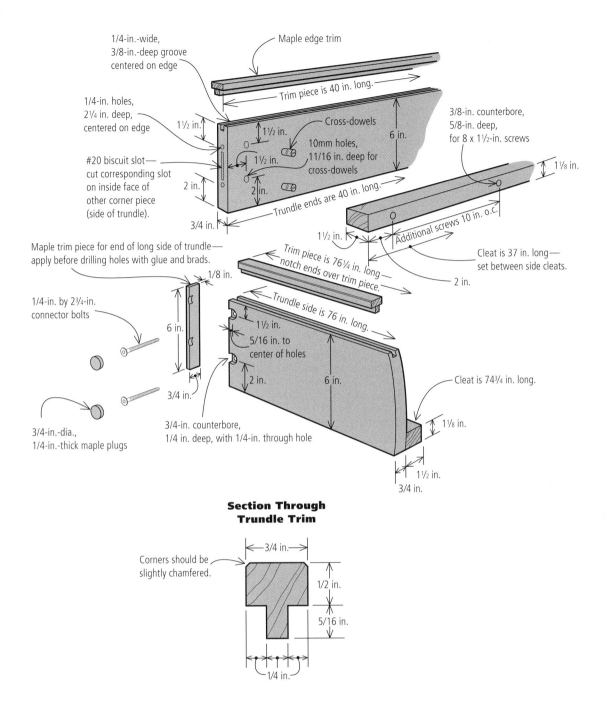

1/4-in.-wide, 3/8-in.-deep groove centered on edge

Maple edge trim

Trim piece is 40 in. long.

1/4-in. holes, 2¼ in. deep, centered on edge

1½ in.

1½ in.

Cross-dowels

10mm holes, 11/16 in. deep for cross-dowels

6 in.

3/8-in. counterbore, 5/8-in. deep, for 8 x 1½-in. screws

1⅛ in.

#20 biscuit slot— cut corresponding slot on inside face of other corner piece (side of trundle).

1½ in.

2 in.

2 in.

Trundle ends are 40 in. long.

3/4 in.

1½ in.

Additional screws 10 in. o.c.

Cleat is 37 in. long— set between side cleats.

2 in.

Maple trim piece for end of long side of trundle— apply before drilling holes with glue and brads.

1/8 in.

Trim piece is 76¼ in. long— notch ends over trim piece.

Trundle side is 76 in. long.

1/4-in. by 2¾-in. connector bolts

6 in.

1½ in.

5/16 in. to center of holes

3/4-in.-dia., 1/4-in.-thick maple plugs

3/4 in.

2 in.

6 in.

Cleat is 74¾ in. long.

1⅛ in.

3/4-in. counterbore, 1/4 in. deep, with 1/4-in. through hole

1½ in.

3/4 in.

Section Through Trundle Trim

Corners should be slightly chamfered.

3/4 in.

1/2 in.

5/16 in.

1/4 in.

These counterbores are 1/2 in. deep. Then I drill 3/16-in. pilot holes for the screws.

I install the caps with 8 x 1½-in. screws and plug the holes with maple plugs, which I cut with a 3/8-in.-dia. plug cutter (*photo 8-20*). Since I plan to use a clear finish on the caps, I try to line up the grain of the plugs with the grain of the caps so the plugs are barely noticeable. I then sand the plugs flush.

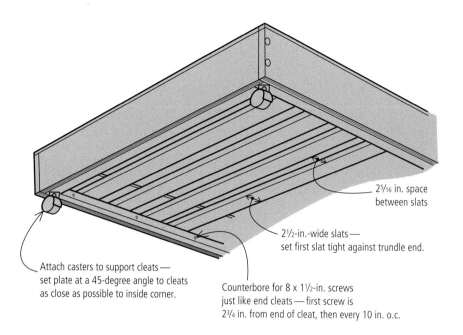

2⁵⁄₁₆ in. space
between slats

2¹⁄₂-in.-wide slats —
set first slat tight against trundle end.

Attach casters to support cleats —
set plate at a 45-degree angle to cleats
as close as possible to inside corner.

Counterbore for 8 x 1¹⁄₂-in. screws
just like end cleats — first screw is
2³⁄₄ in. from end of cleat, then every 10 in. o.c.

8-21
I cover the ends of the 2 long sidepieces with thin maple strips. I attach them with glue and a couple of brads.

8-22
I rout a groove in the top edge of the trundle sides and ends for the maple trim with a 1/4-in. slotting cutter. The pilot bearing limits the depth of cut to 3/8 in. On the long sides I stop the groove at the trim.

Making the Trundle

Now for the trundle that slides under the bed (*drawings 8-A, 8-G, and 8-H*). The sides and the ends of the trundle are made of 3/4-in. MDO plywood (see Project Planner). To join these pieces, I use a simple butt joint — but it has to be strong because the trundle will be pulled in and out all the time. To ensure adequate strength, I'm going to use a connector bolt — a piece of hardware often used by commercial furniture makers. Connector bolts have 2 components: a steel dowel pin that is recessed into the short end of the trundle and a bolt that goes through the trundle side and threads into the dowel pin (*drawing 8-G*). This makes a very strong joint.

To conceal the top edges of the plywood I'm going to install a T molding made of maple (*drawing 8-G*). This molding fits into a 1/4-in. by 3/8-in. groove milled in the plywood. On the ends of the plywood, I don't want to make a groove, because it would weaken the butt joint where the connector bolts go. So on the ends, I'm going to install a 1/8-in.-thick strip of maple (*drawing 8-G*).

After cutting out the sides and the ends of the trundle, I get started by milling the thin maple strips that cover the ends of the 2 long sides (see Project Planner). First I joint the edges of the wood. Then, with my "zero clearance" table-saw insert in place, I set the rip fence to cut a 1/8-in. by 3/4-in. strip to the left of the saw blade. I crosscut the strips to length and attach them with glue and a couple of brads (*photo 8-21*). When the glue dries, I use my random-orbit sander to sand the edges flush with the plywood.

Next I mill the 1/4-in.-wide by 3/8-in.-deep groove in the top edge of the trundle sides and ends (*drawing 8-G*) with a 1/4-in.-slotting cutter in my router. The pilot bearing on the bit limits the depth of cut to 3/8 in. On the 2 (short) ends of the bed, the groove runs the full length of the plywood. But on the (long) sides, I stop the groove at the maple trim (*photo 8-22*).

Installing Connector Bolts

Now I'm ready to drill the holes for the connector bolts. The first thing I want to do is make 3/4-in.-dia. counterbores in the sides of the trundle to recess the heads of the bolts (*drawing 8-G*). To mark the centers, I measure in 7/16 in. from the end and square a line across the plywood. On this line I lay out one center 2 in. up from the bottom edge and another 1½ in. down from the top (*drawing 8-G*). With a 3/4-in.-dia. Forstner bit in my drill press, I counterbore 1/4 in. deep for each connector bolt (*photo 8-23*). Since I have to drill 8 of these holes, I clamp a straightedge across my drill-press table so the bit falls on my 7/16-in. layout line (*photo 8-23*). When I butt the end of the rail against the straightedge, the bit falls right on the centerline. This saves time and ensures that the holes are all located exactly 7/16 in. from the end.

Next I switch to a 1/4-in.-dia. drill and bore through the centers of the counterbores, using the straightedge as a stop to position the bit on center (*photo 8-24*). The connector bolts will go through these holes.

Now I'll switch bits once again and drill the holes in the trundle ends for the cross-dowels of the connector bolts (*drawing 8-G*). For these holes I use a 10mm-dia. drill and I reposition the straightedge to center the holes 1½ in. from the end of the plywood. I drill these holes 11/16 in. deep (*photo 8-25*).

To further strengthen the joint and align it, I'm going to install a biscuit in each joint (*drawing 8-G*). I cut one slot in each joint with my biscuit joiner.

Now I'm ready for some assembly. I apply glue to the joints and glue a biscuit in each slot. Then I assemble the trundle sides and ends and clamp them together.

The next step is to drill 1/4-in. holes through the connector bolt holes clear through to the dowel holes. I drill these holes with my handheld drill and use a square as a guide to make sure the drill goes straight (*photo 8-26*). The drill should break through to the dowel holes and go at least 3/4 in. into the opposite side.

8-23

With a 3/4-in.-dia. Forstner bit in my drill press, I counterbore 1/4 in. deep for each connector bolt hole. To save time and ensure that all 8 holes are exactly 7/16 in. from the end, I clamp a straightedge across my drill-press table so that when I butt the end of the rail against the straightedge, the bit falls right on my layout line.

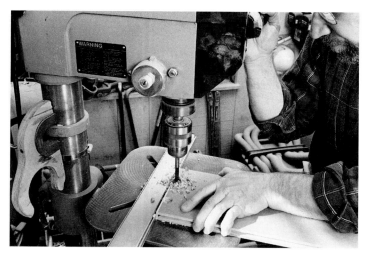

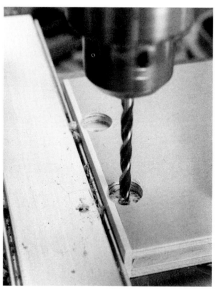

8-24

I switch to a 1/4-in.-dia. drill and bore through the centers of the counterbores, using the straightedge as a stop to position the bit on center.

8-25

I switch bits once again and drill the holes in the trundle ends for the cross-dowels of the connector bolts. For these holes, I use a 10mm-dia. drill and reposition the straightedge to center the holes 1½ in. from the end of the plywood. I drill these holes 11/16 in. deep.

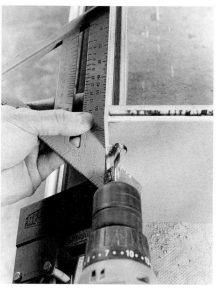

8-26

The next step is to drill 1/4-in. holes within the connector bolt holes clear through to the dowel holes. I use a square as a guide to make sure the drill goes straight. The drill should break through to the dowel holes and go at least 3/4 in. into the opposite side.

8-27

To install the connector bolts, I thread the bolt into the cross-dowel and tighten it with an Allen wrench.

8-28
I attach the cleats that support the trundle mattress with 8 x 1½-in. screws.

Now to install the connector bolts. First the cross-dowel goes into its hole. With a screwdriver, I turn the slot in the end of the cross-dowel in the direction of the bolt. Then I thread the bolt into the dowel and tighten it with an Allen wrench (*photo 8-27*). I install the other 7 connector bolts and tighten them all.

Mattress Support System

The support system for the trundle mattress consists of 1 x 3 pine slats spaced about 2½ in. apart. These slats are supported by 1⅛-in. by 1½-in. slat supports, or cleats, fastened to the sides and ends (*drawings 8-A, 8-G, and 8-H*). The cleats also give me a place to attach the swivel casters on which the trundle rolls.

After cutting the cleats to size and length (see Project Planner and *drawing 8-G*), I drill pilot holes and 3/8-in.-dia. counterbores 5/8 in. deep for the screw heads, spacing the holes 10 in. o.c. (*drawings 8-G and 8-H*). Now I can attach the cleats with 8 x 1½-in. screws (*photo 8-28*).

The casters go on next. I set the plate of the caster at a 45-degree angle as close to the inside corner of the cleats as possible (*drawing 8-H and photo 8-29*). I want to make sure that the casters don't stick out beyond the sides of the bed when they swivel, or they'll hit the bedpost when I pull out the trundle.

Now for the slats. I crosscut 16 pieces 40 in. long and fasten them to the cleats with 6 x 1¼-in. screws. The first slat goes in tight against the trundle end, and I space the others 2⁵⁄₁₆ in. apart (*photo 8-30*). A scrap piece of wood makes a convenient spacer.

The next thing to make is the T-shaped trim to conceal the plywood edges (*drawing 8-G*). I cut some lengths of 1 x 3 maple (see Project Planner) and set up my table saw with a dado head set for a 3/4-in.-wide dado. The idea is to make

8-29
I set the plate of the caster at a 45-degree angle as close to the inside corner of the cleats as possible. I want to make sure that the casters don't stick out beyond the sides of the bed when they swivel, or they'll hit the bedpost.

8-30
I fasten the slats to the cleats with 6 x 1¼-in. screws. The first slat goes in tight against the trundle end, and I space the others 2⁵⁄₁₆ in. apart using a piece of scrap wood as a spacer.

8-29

8-30

two Ts from each length of wood. I set the rip fence 1/2 in. from the blade and mill a 3/4-in.-wide groove in each side. Then I flip the piece end for end and make a second pass on each side, this time with the opposite side of the workpiece against the fence (*photo 8-31*). Finally, I replace the dado head with a regular saw blade. I set my rip fence 7/8 in. from the blade and rip 2 T-shaped pieces (*photo 8-32*).

Now I trim the T molding to length and dry-fit it into the grooves in the trundle bed sides. I sand all the edges smooth and flush with the sides. I'll glue the T molding in place later, after I paint the bed, since I want the maple to have a natural finish.

I still need to make some maple plugs to cover the heads of the connector bolts (*drawing 8-G*). With a 3/4-in.-dia. plug cutter in my drill press, I cut 8 plugs from a piece of 1 x maple (*photo 8-33*). I drill only 3/8 in. through the wood. To separate the plugs from the board, I set the rip fence of my table saw 1/2 in. from the left side of the blade so that the 1/4-in.-thick plugs fall to the left of the blade, and rip the board to separate the plugs (*photo 8-34*). I'll glue these plugs into their holes later after the base has been painted.

Putting on Paint

All the maple parts of the bed will get a clear, polyurethane finish. I'll paint all the poplar and MDO board surfaces.

First I brush a coat of water-base sanding sealer on all the maple. Next I brush a coat of latex enamel primer on all the surfaces I want to paint.

When the sealer and primer are completely dry, I sand all the surfaces with some 220-grit sandpaper. I vacuum off the dust and run a tack cloth over the wood to remove any dust that the vacuuming missed. I apply a coat of water-base polyurethane to the maple parts and brush some nice "apple green" latex enamel on the poplar and plywood.

8-31
I make 2 pieces of the T-shaped trundle trim from each length of wood. I set the rip fence 1/2 in. from the blade and mill a 3/4-in.-wide groove in each side. Then I flip the piece end for end and make a second pass on each side, this time with the opposite side of the workpiece against the fence.

8-32
Finally, I replace the dado head with a regular saw blade. I set my rip fence 7/8 in. from the blade and rip 2 T-shaped pieces.

8-33
I make maple plugs to cover the heads of the connector bolts with a 3/4-in.-dia. plug cutter in my drill press. I drill only 3/8 in. through the wood.

8-34
To separate the plugs from the board, I set the rip fence of my table saw 1/2 in. from the left side of the blade so that the 1/4-in.-thick plugs fall to the left of the blade, and rip the board to separate the plugs.

When the finish is dry, I glue in the T molding around the top of the trundle. I also install the maple plugs that cover the connector bolts. I simply glue these into their holes. I like the plugs to stand proud of the surface a little bit — a nice decorative touch. Now all I need is a couple of mattresses, and this nice little bed is ready for use.

9

storage units

project planner

Time: 6 days

Special hardware and tools:

(3 sets) Blum 18-in. epoxy drawer slides (brown)

(2 pair) Blum 95-degree, snap-closing, full-overlay hinges

35mm-dia. bit to drill mortise for hinges

(12) brass pin-style shelf supports with rubber shelf cushions

(8) 3-in. polished brass wire pull

1/4-in. self-centering bit (item #22567 from The Woodworkers' Store, Medina, MN)

(18) 6 x 1-in. screws

Wood:

(2) 48-in. by 96-in. 3/4-in. piece of red-oak-veneered plywood

(1) 48-in. by 48-in. 3/4-in. piece of red-oak-veneered plywood

Cut sheets according to plywood cutting diagrams for sides, tops, shelves, doors, and drawer fronts.

(1) 18-in. by 36-in. 3/4-in. piece of cabinet-grade plywood

Trim to 17¼ in. x 35 in. for bottom of drawer base cabinet.

(1) 60-in. by 60-in. piece of 1/2-in. Baltic birch plywood

Rip 6 pieces 7 in. wide, then cut one piece 17⅞ in. long from each for drawer sides (6 required).

Trim 3 of the remaining 7-in.-wide pieces to 33½ in. for drawer-box fronts (3 required).

Rip remaining 7-in.-wide pieces to 6½-in.-width and trim to 33 in. for drawer backs (3 required).

(1) 48-in. by 96-in. piece of 1/4 in.-red-oak-veneered plywood

ANY PARENT CAN TELL YOU that chaos is the natural state of a young child's room. There's never enough storage space to house the toys, books, clothes, and treasures that make up a young one's cherished possessions. This handsome storage unit is a parent's dream come true. Two units — a 3-drawer bureau with a bookcase on top, and a spacious 2-door storage cabinet — provide plenty of room. It's furniture your children can grow with, too, being as useful for college students as it is for preschoolers.

The storage unit is made from high-quality red-oak-veneered plywood. I used A-A grade ply, which means that both sides have a premium-quality face veneer. Plywood makes sense for any project that requires a lot of wide panels. It's easier and faster than gluing up oak boards and more dimensionally stable than solid-wood panels.

Cutting Out Parts

The cutting diagram provides the finished dimensions for all the plywood parts of the storage units (*see Cutting Diagram*). No matter how careful I am when I rip long pieces, sometimes I get a slight variation on the edge. To avoid this problem, I rip the pieces slightly wider than I need and then trim them to final width later, when the pieces are shorter and easier to handle.

Wrestling large sheets of plywood over the table saw is not easy when you're

9-A Major Anatomy and Dimensions

Crosscut one piece 66 in., then rip to 35³⁄₁₆ in. wide. Crosscut this 35³⁄₁₆-in.-wide piece into one piece 38⅜ in. long for back of book- case and one piece 26⅜ in. long for back of base cabinet.

(1) 60-in. by 60-in. piece of ¼-in. Baltic birch plywood
Crosscut one piece 33 in. long, then rip into 3 pieces 17³⁄₁₆ in. wide for drawer bottoms. Crosscut remaining piece 26⅜ in. wide and rip to 35³⁄₁₆ in. long for back of drawer unit.

(1) 8-ft. 5/4 x 8 red oak
Plane to 1 in., then rip and joint 4 pieces 1¼ in. wide. From each strip cut one piece 38 in. long and one piece 20 in. long for edging for tops of base cabi- nets. Trim 3 of the remaining pieces to 34¼ in. for edging for adjustable shelves.

(1) 6-ft. 1 x 5 red oak
Rip and joint 3¾ in. wide, then cut 2 pieces 35 in. long for base trim.

(1) 14-ft. 1 x 4 red oak
For edge trim for base cabinet sides, doors, and drawers, cut one piece each: 20 in., 28 in., and 30 in. Cut 2 pieces 38 in. Rip and joint all pieces into 4 pieces ½ in. wide x ¾ in. thick. Cut 2 of the 38-in. strips into 6 pieces 10 in. long.

(1) 8-ft. 1 x 4 red oak
Rip and joint 2 pieces 1½ in. wide, then cut one piece 56 in. long and one piece 36 in. long from each for book- case stiles and rails.

(1) 12-ft. 1 x 3 red oak
Cut 4 pieces 35 in. long for base unit rails.

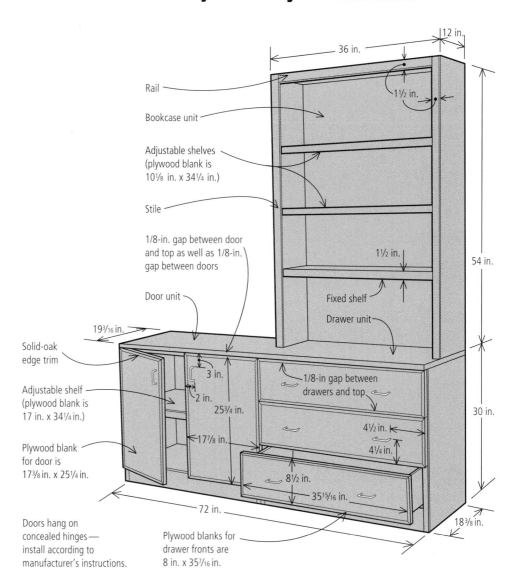

Rail

Bookcase unit

Adjustable shelves (plywood blank is 10⅛ in. x 34¼ in.)

Stile

1/8-in. gap between door and top as well as 1/8-in. gap between doors

Door unit

Solid-oak edge trim

Adjustable shelf (plywood blank is 17 in. x 34¼ in.)

Plywood blank for door is 17⅜ in. x 25¼ in.

Doors hang on concealed hinges — install according to manufacturer's instructions.

Plywood blanks for drawer fronts are 8 in. x 35⁷⁄₁₆ in.

12 in.

36 in.

1½ in.

1½ in.

54 in.

Fixed shelf

Drawer unit

19³⁄₁₆ in.

3 in.

2 in.

25¾ in.

17⅞ in.

8½ in.

35¹⁵⁄₁₆ in.

72 in.

1/8-in gap between drawers and top

4½ in.

4¼ in.

30 in.

18⅜ in.

Drawers are supported by drawer slides — install according to manufacturer's instructions.

working alone in the shop. I've come up with a couple of tricks that help. First I position my workbench so it's less than 8 ft. from the saw. This way, I can rest one end of the plywood on the bench and one end on the saw table as I get into position. I also need some support on the outfeed end of the saw. In addition to my outfeed table, I set up 2 rollers to support the plywood as it comes off the saw.

Chipping and tearout can be a problem when sawing veneered plywood — especially when cutting across the grain of the face veneer. To avoid tearout and the ragged edge that results, I use a very sharp 60-tooth carbide blade.

The first piece I want to cut is a 96-in.-long strip wide enough to make the 2 sides and the top of one of the base cabinets. The finished sides will be 18⅛ in. wide, so I set my rip fence for an 18¼-in.-wide cut. With the back end of the ply- wood sheet supported on my workbench, I switch on the saw and carefully start

9-Cutting Diagrams
3/4-in. Oak Plywood

Note: All dimensions given are exact sizes.

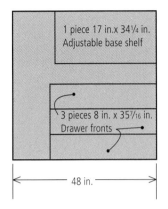

1 piece 17 in. x 34¼ in.
Adjustable base shelf

3 pieces 8 in. x 35⁷/₁₆ in.
Drawer fronts

48 in.

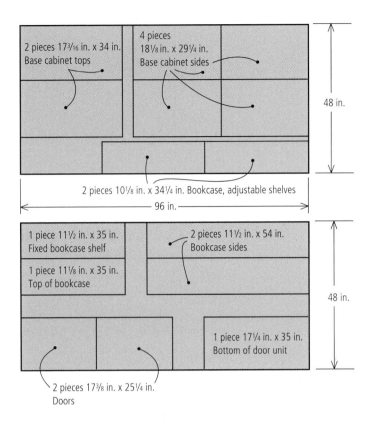

2 pieces 17³/₁₆ in. x 34 in.
Base cabinet tops

4 pieces
18⅛ in. x 29¼ in.
Base cabinet sides

48 in.

2 pieces 10⅛ in. x 34¼ in. Bookcase, adjustable shelves

96 in.

1 piece 11½ in. x 35 in.
Fixed bookcase shelf

1 piece 11⅛ in. x 35 in.
Top of bookcase

2 pieces 11½ in. x 54 in.
Bookcase sides

48 in.

1 piece 17¼ in. x 35 in.
Bottom of door unit

2 pieces 17³/₈ in. x 25¼ in.
Doors

9-1
Cutting large sheets of plywood is not easy when you're working alone. To begin with, I stand on the left side of the sheet to make it easier to keep the edge against the rip fence. About halfway through the cut I move to the back end of the sheet to complete the cut.

9-B Base Cabinet Side

Note: 4 required, 2 as shown,
2 as mirror image.

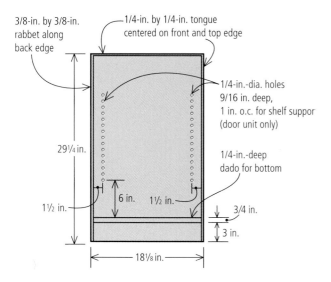

3/8-in. by 3/8-in.
rabbet along
back edge

1/4-in. by 1/4-in. tongue
centered on front and top edge

1/4-in.-dia. holes
9/16 in. deep,
1 in. o.c. for shelf suppor
(door unit only)

1/4-in.-deep
dado for bottom

29¼ in.

1½ in.

6 in.   1½ in.

3/4 in.

3 in.

18⅛ in.

9-2
There's no better tool for squaring up panels than my homemade panel cutter.

9-3
To mill the dadoes in the cabinet sides, I set the rip fence 3 in. from the stack dado head and guide the end of the piece against the fence.

the cut. To begin with, I stand on the left side of the sheet to make it easier to keep the edge against the rip fence. About halfway through the cut I move to the back end of the sheet to complete the cut (*photo 9-1*). Next, from the same sheet, I rip a second 18¼-in.-wide piece to make the sides and top of the other base cabinet.

The next thing I do is to crosscut these long pieces into shorter lengths for the cabinet sides and tops (*see Cutting Diagram*). There's no easy way to do this on the table saw, and the boards are too wide to cut on my radial-arm saw. A small circular saw is the best tool for making these cuts. With a framing square and a pencil, I mark and then cut the pieces about 1/4 in. to 1/2 in. longer than the fin-

9-C Top of Base Cabinets
(2 required)

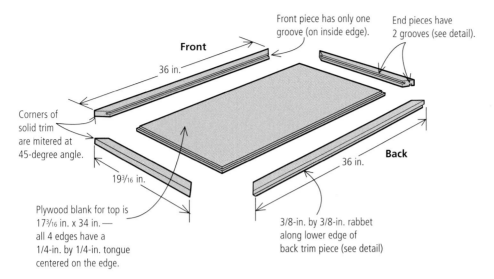

Front piece has only one groove (on inside edge).

End pieces have 2 grooves (see detail).

Front

36 in.

Corners of solid trim are mitered at 45-degree angle.

19³/₁₆ in.

Back

36 in.

Plywood blank for top is 17³/₁₆ in. x 34 in. — all 4 edges have a 1/4-in. by 1/4-in. tongue centered on the edge.

3/8-in. by 3/8-in. rabbet along lower edge of back trim piece (see detail)

Details

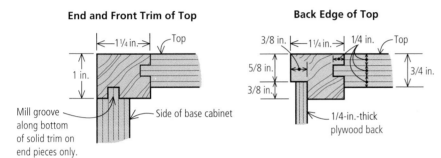

End and Front Trim of Top

1¼ in.

Top

1 in.

Mill groove along bottom of solid trim on end pieces only.

Side of base cabinet

Back Edge of Top

3/8 in.

1¼ in.

1/4 in.

Top

5/8 in.

3/8 in.

3/4 in.

1/4-in.-thick plywood back

ished length. It doesn't matter if there are small veneer chips from the circular-saw blade — I'm going to square up each piece later on the table saw.

Now that the pieces are smaller, they're easier to handle and I can rip them more accurately on the table saw. The first step is to rip about 1/16 in. off each piece to give me a straight, true edge. Next, holding this straight edge against the fence, I rip each piece to finished width — 18⅛ in. for the cabinet sides and 17³/₁₆ in. for the cabinet tops (*see Cutting Diagram and drawings 9-B and 9-C*).

With the 2 long sides of each piece parallel, I'm ready to square up the ends. There's no better tool for this job than my homemade panel cutter. First I square up one end. Then I measure for length — 29¼ in. for the cabinet sides and 34 in. for the cabinet top — and square up the other end (*photo 9-2*). Using the same procedure, I cut out the rest of the parts of the storage units from the other 48-in. by 96-in. piece and the 48-in.-square piece of plywood (*see Cutting Diagram*).

Dadoes and Rabbets

Once all the plywood pieces are cut to size, I'm ready to mill some 1/4-in.-deep by 3/4-in.-wide dadoes. The bottoms of the 2 base cabinets fit into dadoes

9-D Base Cabinet Details

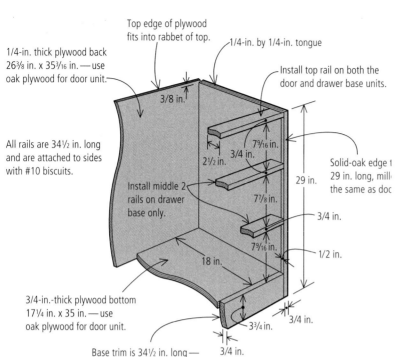

Top edge of plywood fits into rabbet of top.

1/4-in. by 1/4-in. tongue

1/4-in. thick plywood back 26³⁄₈ in. x 35³⁄₁₆ in. — use oak plywood for door unit.

Install top rail on both the door and drawer base units.

3/8 in.

7⁹⁄₁₆ in.

All rails are 34½ in. long and are attached to sides with #10 biscuits.

3/4 in.

2½ in.

29 in.

Solid-oak edge t 29 in. long, mill the same as doo

Install middle 2 rails on drawer base only.

7⁷⁄₈ in.

3/4 in.

7⁹⁄₁₆ in.

1/2 in.

18 in.

3/4-in.-thick plywood bottom 17¼ in. x 35 in. — use oak plywood for door unit.

3¾ in.

3/4 in.

3/4 in.

Base trim is 34½ in. long — attach to bottom and sides with #20 biscuits.

9-E Bookcase Side

Note: One as shown, one mirror image.

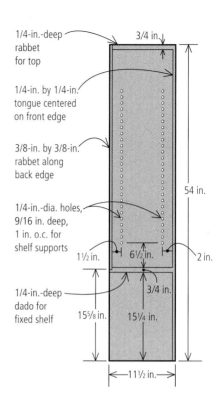

1/4-in.-deep rabbet for top

3/4 in.

1/4-in. by 1/4-in. tongue centered on front edge

3/8-in. by 3/8-in. rabbet along back edge

54 in.

1/4-in.-dia. holes, 9/16 in. deep, 1 in. o.c. for shelf supports

1½ in.

6½ in.

2 in.

1/4-in.-deep dado for fixed shelf

3/4 in.

15⅝ in.

15¼ in.

11½ in.

---

in the cabinet sides (*drawings 9-B and 9-D*), and the fixed shelf of the bookcase unit is dadoed into the sides of the bookcase (*drawing 9-E and 9-F*).

I set up my stack dado head on the table saw and adjust the height for a 1/4-in.-deep cut. To mill the dadoes in the cabinet sides, I set the rip fence 3 in. from the blade and guide the end of the piece against the fence (*drawing 9-B and photo 9-3*). For the dadoes in the sides of the bookcase, I set the rip fence 15¼ in. from the blade (*drawing 9-E*).

While I still have the stack dado head set up on the table saw, I mill a 1/4-in. by 3/4-in. rabbet at the top ends of the bookcase sides to receive the top (*drawing 9-E and photo 9-4*). For this step, I attach a wooden auxilliary fence that I can position right up against the blade without damaging the rip fence.

Each base cabinet has a 1/4-in.-plywood back that fits into 3/8-in. by 3/8-in. rabbets milled in the back edges of the cabinet sides (*drawings 9-B and 9-D*). The next thing to do is mill these rabbets on the table saw with my stack dado head. I reduce the width of the cutter to 1/2 in. and raise it from 1/4 in. to 3/8 in. high. I reset the fence so that I'm removing 3/8 in. of material.

The bookcase, too, has a plywood back that extends from the fixed shelf to the top (*drawing 9-F*). I mill a 3/8-in. by 3/8-in. rabbet along the top rear edge of this fixed shelf. This keeps the bottom edge of the plywood back from showing below the shelf.

Using the same setup, I mill 3/8-in. by 3/8-in. rabbets in the bookcase sides as well, but I need to stop them at the fixed shelf so they won't show below the shelf (*drawing 9-F*). Here's how I make these stopped rabbets. On the side of my wooden rip fence, I make 2 pencil marks — one at the leading edge of the dado

9-F Bookcase Details

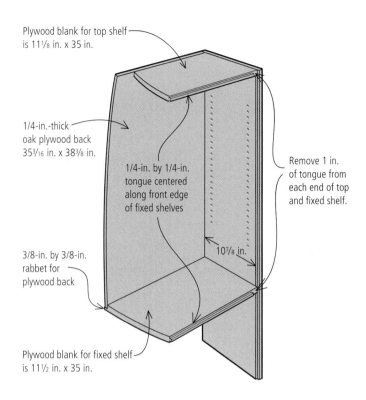

Plywood blank for top shelf is 11⅛ in. x 35 in.

1/4-in.-thick oak plywood back 35³/₁₆ in. x 38⅜ in.

1/4-in. by 1/4-in. tongue centered along front edge of fixed shelves

Remove 1 in. of tongue from each end of top and fixed shelf.

10⅞ in.

3/8-in. by 3/8-in. rabbet for plywood back

Plywood blank for fixed shelf is 11½ in. x 35 in.

Details

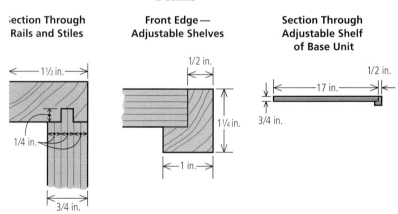

Section Through Rails and Stiles

1½ in.

1/4 in.

3/4 in.

Front Edge — Adjustable Shelves

1/2 in.

1¼ in.

1 in.

Section Through Adjustable Shelf of Base Unit

1/2 in.

17 in.

3/4 in.

9-4

While I still have the stack dado head set up on the table saw, I mill a 1/4-in. by 3/4-in. rabbet at the top ends of the bookcase sides to receive the fixed top shelf. I attach a wooden auxiliary fence to my rip fence so I can position it right up against the blade without damage.

To mill the stopped rabbets in the bookcase sides, I make 2 pencil marks on my wooden rip fence — one at the leading edge of the dado head and one at the trailing edge. I then make a pencil mark on the outer face of the bookcase side where I want the rabbet to stop. For the left-hand side, I position the pencil mark on the plywood over the pencil mark on the outfeed side of the dado head and, with the saw running, carefully lower the plywood onto the spinning blade to start the cut. When the plywood is flat on the table, I feed it through to complete the cut.

head and one at the trailing edge. Next, on the outer face of each bookcase side, I make a pencil mark where I want the rabbet to stop — where it meets with the rabbet I milled in the shelf.

To mill the rabbet on the right-hand bookcase side, I cut from the top toward the bottom. When the pencil mark on the plywood aligns with the first indicator mark on the fence, I switch off the saw and wait for the blade to completely stop before removing the workpiece.

The left-hand bookcase side is a mirror image of the right, so I have to start the rabbet at the bottom and cut toward the top. With the saw running, I position the pencil mark on the plywood over the pencil mark on the outfeed side of the dado head and carefully lower the plywood onto the spinning blade to start the cut (*photo 9-5*). When the plywood is flat on the table, I feed it through to complete the cut.

Tongue-and-Groove Edge Trim

Wherever the edge of the plywood might show (for instance, around the front of a drawer or the top of a cabinet), I conceal it with pieces of solid-oak edging (*drawing 9-A*). The strongest way to attach these trim pieces is with a tongue-and-groove joint — a 1/4-in. tongue on the plywood and a matching groove in the oak trim.

To make the tongues, I set my stack dado head to cut a 1/4-in.-wide rabbet 1/4 in. deep. I test the setup with a piece of scrap plywood, cutting a rabbet along the top and bottom of one edge to form a 1/4-in.-wide tongue in the middle (*photo 9-6*). The height of the cutter determines the width of the tongue, so I adjust the height as necessary until the tongue is exactly 1/4 in. wide. When the setup is right, I mill tongues on the following parts: the drawer fronts, the cabi-

9-6
To make the tongues, I set my stack dado head to cut a 1/4-in.-wide rabbet 1/4 in. deep and then cut such a rabbet along the top and bottom of one edge to form a 1/4-in.-wide tongue in the middle.

net doors, the front edges of the cabinet sides, the 2 cabinet tops as well as the sides, top, and fixed shelf of the bookcase (*drawings 9-A, 9-B, 9-C, 9-D, 9-E, 9-F, 9-G, and 9-H*).

I also need to mill tongues on the top edges of the base cabinet sides (*drawing 9-B*). Because this is a cross-grain cut, the veneer is likely to chip unless I take some precautions. Before milling these tongues, I first score the veneer with a sharp utility knife to sever the fibers cleanly. To guide the knife, I use a scrap piece on which I've milled a tongue. I hold the knife against the tongue and slide the scrap and the knife along the edge of the plywood to score the veneer (*photo 9-7*). After scoring, I mill the tongues on the table saw.

Once I've finished all the tongues, I'm ready to mill the oak for the edge trim (see Project Planner). The edging for the cabinet tops and shelves is 1 in. thick and 1¼ in. wide (*drawings 9-A, 9-C, and 9-F*). The edging for the cabinet doors, drawers, and sides is 3/4 in. thick and 1/2 in. wide (*drawings 9-A, 9-D, 9-G, and 9-H*). I also mill oak for the face frame of the bookcase and the edging of the adjustable shelves. The face-frame pieces are 3/4 in. thick and 1½ in. wide (*drawing 9-F*). The shelf edging is 1 in. thick and 1¼ in. wide (*drawing 9-F*).

With the trim pieces all cut to size and slightly longer than their finished length, I'm ready to mill the 1/4-in. by 1/4-in. grooves. With my dado head set for a 1/4-in.-wide cut, I start with the door and drawer trim. The grooves in these pieces must be perfectly centered (*drawing 9-H*). I make a cut in a test piece, then flip it end for end and start to make a second pass on the opposite edge. If the blade removes any material on this second pass, the groove isn't centered. I adjust the fence as necessary and then mill the grooves in all the door and drawer trim (*photo 9-8*).

The grooves in the thicker edge-trim pieces for the base cabinet tops and the face frame of the bookcase are not centered (*drawings 9-C and 9-F*). Without

9-G Drawer
(3 required)

**Note: Before building drawers,
be sure drawer slides require 1/2-in. side clearance.**

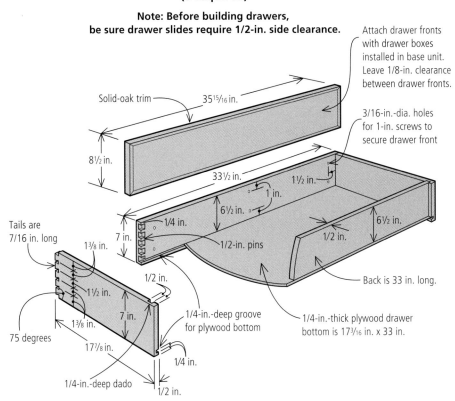

Attach drawer fronts
with drawer boxes
installed in base unit.
Leave 1/8-in. clearance
between drawer fronts.

Solid-oak trim

35^{15}/$_{16}$ in.

3/16-in.-dia. holes
for 1-in. screws to
secure drawer front

8^{1}/$_{2}$ in.

33^{1}/$_{2}$ in.

1^{1}/$_{2}$ in.

1 in.

6^{1}/$_{2}$ in.

Tails are
7/16 in. long

1^{3}/$_{8}$ in.

1/4 in.

7 in.

6^{1}/$_{2}$ in.

1/2 in.

1/2-in. pins

1^{1}/$_{2}$ in.

1/2 in.

1/4-in.-deep groove
for plywood bottom

Back is 33 in. long.

1^{3}/$_{8}$ in.

7 in.

75 degrees

17^{7}/$_{8}$ in.

1/4 in.

1/4-in.-thick plywood drawer
bottom is 17^{3}/$_{16}$ in. x 33 in.

1/4-in.-deep dado

1/2 in.

9-H Edge Detail—
Door and Drawers

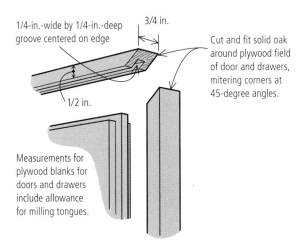

1/4-in.-wide by 1/4-in.-deep
groove centered on edge

3/4 in.

Cut and fit solid oak
around plywood field
of door and drawers,
mitering corners at
45-degree angles.

1/2 in.

Measurements for
plywood blanks for
doors and drawers
include allowance
for milling tongues.

changing my table-saw setup, I mill a 1/4-in.-wide groove 1/4 in. from the upper edge of the cabinet-top trim pieces and from one edge of the face-frame pieces. Note that the 2 end pieces of the cabinet-top trim get grooves near the outside bottom edge. The back edge piece gets only one groove and a rabbet, which I'll mill later (*drawing 9-C*).

Now I'm ready to cut the oak trim that frames the plywood top of each base cabinet. I set my power miter box for a 45-degree cut and miter one end of each

9-7
Before milling the tongues on the top edges of the base cabinet sides, I first score the veneer with a sharp utility knife to sever the fibers cleanly. To guide the knife, I use a scrap piece on which I've milled a tongue. I hold the knife against the tongue and slide the scrap and the knife along the edge of the plywood. This score keeps the veneer from chipping when I mill the tongues.

9-8
I mill 1/4-in. by 1/4-in. grooves in the trim pieces with my dado head. The grooves in these trim pieces must be perfectly centered.

trim piece. I slip each trim piece onto the tongue to mark the length. Then I miter the other end. Now I can dry-fit the trim around the top panel and clamp it in place to check the fit. I trim the miters as necessary for a perfect fit and then glue and clamp the pieces in place (*photo 9-9*). No mechanical fasteners needed here — glue alone is strong enough. While one panel is drying, I clamp up the second one.

After removing the clamps, I'm ready to mill a 3/8-in.-square rabbet on the back edge of each top frame to receive the plywood back of the cabinet (*drawing 9-C*). Because these are "blind" rabbets (that is, the ends don't show), I mill them with a router and a 3/8-in. rabbeting bit instead of the table saw, stopping before the end so the rabbet doesn't show (*photo 9-10*). After routing the rabbets, I square up the corners with a chisel.

Now I'm ready to assemble the drawer base cabinet. With one of the side-pieces face up on my workbench, I put glue in the lower dado and put the plywood bottom in place. I secure it with 2 long clamps, hold it square to the side with a framing square, and attach it with 4d finish nails, toenailing from both sides of the shelf for a strong joint (*photo 9-11*). I repeat this procedure to install the other side.

The top goes on next. I apply some glue in the grooves of the end trim pieces

9-9
I dry-fit the trim around the top panel and clamp it in place to check the fit. I trim the miters as necessary for a perfect fit and then glue and clamp the pieces in place.

9-10
I mill a 3/8-in.-square "blind" rabbet along the back edge of each cabinet-top frame with a router and a 3/8-in. rabbeting bit, stopping before the end so the rabbet doesn't show.

9-11
With one of the sidepieces of the base drawer cabinet face up on my workbench, I put glue in the lower dado and put the plywood bottom in place. I secure it with 2 long clamps, hold it square to the side with a framing square, and attach it with 4d finish nails, toenailing from both sides of the shelf.

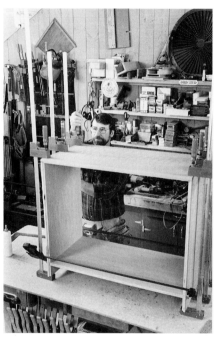

9-12
The top of the drawer cabinet goes over the tongues, and I clamp it in place.

9-13
The front edges of the cabinet sides get covered with oak trim strips, which I glue and clamp in place.

9-14
It's difficult to hold the biscuit jointer steady on the line when cutting slots for the top rail and drawer dividers. I find it helpful to clamp a scrap of wood right on the line so the biscuit jointer has a place to sit.

9-15
I mill a "modified" slot on the ends of the top rail and drawer dividers, extending the slot so it comes through the edge. This allows me to slip it over the biscuits in the ends of the cabinet base.

9-16
The toekick board is joined to the front edge of the plywood bottom with 4 biscuits. I mill slots for them and also make "modified" slots in both the cabinet sides and the ends of the toekick board. This way I can just slip a biscuit up from the bottom when the trim is in place.

and to the mating tongues on the cabinet sides. The top goes on over the tongues, and I clamp it in place (*photo 9-12*). No fasteners needed here. Now I can put on the 1/4-in. plywood back and secure it in place with some 1-in. brads.

The front edges of the cabinet sides get covered with oak trim strips, which I glue and clamp in place (*photo 9-13*).

While the glue on the drawer base cabinet is drying, I assemble the door base cabinet in just the same way. Both the door and the drawer cabinets get a 3¾-in.-wide by 34½-in.-long base trim, or toekick board (*drawing 9-D*), and a 2½-in.-wide by 34½-in.-long rail under the top (*drawing 9-D*). The drawer cabinet also gets 2 additional 2½-in.-wide by 34-in.-long pieces to separate the drawers (*drawing 9-D*). All these pieces are joined to the sides with #10 biscuits.

On the cabinet sides, I draw a line to mark the location of each piece. It's difficult to hold the biscuit jointer steady on the line. I find it helpful to clamp a scrap of wood right on the line so the biscuit jointer has a place to sit (*photo 9-14*). I mill biscuit slots in the sides for the top rail and 2 drawer dividers. On the ends of each piece, I mill a "modified" slot, extending it through the edge (*photo 9-15*). This allows me to slip it over the biscuits. With biscuits in place (but no glue), I dry-fit the assembly to check the fit. When everything looks good, I glue the biscuits in the cabinet sides and tap the top rail and drawer dividers into place.

The toekick board is joined to the front edge of the plywood bottom with 4 #20 biscuits (*drawing 9-D*). I mill these slots and also make "modified" slots in both the cabinet sides and the ends of the trim board. This way I can just slip a biscuit up from the bottom when the toekick board is in place (*photo 9-16*), glue it into place, and clamp it up. Both cabinets get the same treatment.

9-17
Here I'm installing the 1/4-in. plywood back.

9-18

9-19

9-18 and 9-19
In order for the vertical pieces of 1¼-in.-wide oak trim to fit properly on the bookcase, I need to remove a little bit of the tongue on the top and fixed shelf. I place the trim in position and make a pencil mark on the shelf tongues (*photo 9-18*). Next I make a cut on these lines with a backsaw and then cut out the material with a chisel (*photo 9-19*).

9-20
I find it easiest to glue up all 3 drawer fronts at once. That way I use fewer clamps.

9-21
I turn the drawer upside down on the bench and check for square by measuring across the diagonals. When the diagonals are equal, I tack the bottom to the drawer back with some brads.

Building the Bookcase

While the base cabinets are drying, I start building the bookcase. I've already milled all the tongues, dadoes, and rabbets, so now I'm ready for a little assembly. But first I finish-sand the surfaces of the plywood bookcase parts. With one side of the bookcase lying flat on the bench, I glue the fixed shelf into its dado and toenail it in place from both sides with some 4d nails. The top of the bookcase is the next piece to install. The other side goes on next, followed by the 1/4-in. plywood back (*photo 9-17*).

With the bookcase face up on my bench, I'm ready to install the oak trim that covers the plywood edges. In order for the vertical pieces of 1¼-in.-wide oak to fit properly, I need to remove a little bit of the tongue on the top and on the fixed shelf. I place the trim in position and make a pencil mark on the shelf tongues (*photo 9-18*). I make a cut on these lines with a backsaw and then chisel out that bit of the tongue (*photo 9-19*). Now I can glue on the vertical trim pieces. With the vertical pieces in place, I can measure, cut, and install the horizontal trim on the top and the bottom shelf.

Making the Drawers

The drawers are simply boxes made of 1/2-in. plywood joined with half-blind dovetails at the front and dado joints at the rear (*drawing 9-G*). The drawer front is attached to the box with 6 x 1-in. screws. The drawer bottoms are made from 1/4-in. plywood, and I think the drawer looks better if the grain on the plywood runs across the width of the drawer rather than from front to back.

The drawer fronts are made just like the cabinet tops — plywood panels surrounded by a solid-oak frame joined with tongue-and-groove joints. I miter and install the oak trim pieces just as I did with the top and clamp them in place. I find it easiest to glue up all 3 drawer fronts at once. That way I use fewer clamps (*photo 9-20*).

To make the drawer boxes, I rip all the drawer stock to width and trim the

9-22

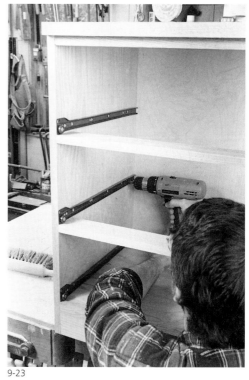

9-23

ends to the lengths shown in the drawing (see Project Planner). Next, on the table saw, I mill 1/4-in. by 1/4-in. grooves on the sidepieces and the bottom edges of the drawer-box front to accept the plywood drawer bottom (*drawing 9-G*). The next step is to mill a 1/4-in.-deep by 1/2-in.-wide dado at the back end of each sidepiece to house the back of the drawer box (*drawing 9-G*).

I use my router dovetailing jig to cut the half-blind dovetails. I set up my jig and router to give me 1/2-in.-wide pins spaced 1⅜ in. o.c. and 7/16-in.-long tails (*drawing 9-G*). Every manufacturer's dovetailing jig works differently, so I won't go into detail about how I set up my jig but I rout the tails in the sidepieces first and the matching pins in the drawer-box fronts next.

With the dovetails complete, I give the drawer parts a good finish sanding on all surfaces, inside and out. Now I glue up the dovetails and tap the joints together. Next I'm ready for the back. I put a little glue in the dadoes and secure the back with some 1-in. brads in each end. Next, with the drawer on the bench, I slip in the bottom piece of plywood. I turn the drawer upside down on the bench and check for square by measuring across the diagonals (*photo 9-21*). When the measurements are equal, I tack the bottom to the drawer back with some brads. I clean up the dovetails with my random-orbit sander.

The drawers ride on drawer slides (see Project Planner). One part of the slide is attached to the drawer (*photo 9-22*); the other part is attached to the inside of the base cabinet (*photo 9-23*). I install each part of the drawer slide with screws.

Next, on the drill press, I drill 4 holes in the drawer fronts to attach the wire drawer pulls. I space the holes as shown in the plan (*drawing 9-A*).

Now I'm ready to install the drawer fronts on the drawer boxes. I find it easier to do this with the drawer boxes installed in the case. I place all 3 drawer boxes on their drawer slides. Holding a 1/8-in.-thick wooden spacer against the underside of the top, I hold the top drawer front against the spacer and align it

9-24

9-25

9-24
To install the drawer fronts, I place the drawer boxes on their drawer slides. Then I temporarily attach each drawer front to the drawer box with 2 screws through the holes for the drawer handles. I use a 1/8-in.-thick wooden spacer to give me an even 1/8-in. gap between drawer fronts.

9-25
For the front rows of shelf-support holes, I position the jig against the front edge of the cabinet so the holes are 2 in. from the front edge and drill 1/4-in. holes with a self-centering bit.

from side to side. Then I temporarily attach it to the drawer box with 2 screws through the holes I drilled for the drawer handles. I repeat this procedure for the other 2 drawers, using the 1/8-in. spacer to give me an even 1/8-in. gap between drawers (*photo 9-24*). Now I remove the drawers and permanently attach the drawer fronts with 6 x 1-in. screws from the inside of the drawer.

Adjustable Shelves

The 2 adjustable shelves of the bookcase, and the shelf inside the door cabinet are made of 3/4-in. oak plywood with a piece of solid-oak trim along the front edge (*drawings 9-A and 9-F*). After milling the 1-in. by 1¼-in. by 34¼-in. oak edging to size (see Project Planner), I set up the dado head in my table saw for a 3/4-in.-wide rabbet. I mill a 1/2-in. by 3/4-in. rabbet in each piece of edging and glue and nail it to the front edge of the shelves with 4d finish nails. This edging is not only decorative, it also adds rigidity to keep the shelves from sagging.

The shelves rest on metal shelf supports that fit into 1/4-in.-dia. holes drilled 1 in. o.c. in the plywood sides (*drawing 9-B*). It's impossible to space these accurately without some type of jig. I make a simple homemade jig from a piece of pegboard to drill the holes. The holes in the pegboard are already spaced just the right distance apart.

Here's how I make the jig. I cut a strip of pegboard about 16 in. long and about 4 in. wide. Measuring from the center line of one row of holes, I rip one edge 1½ in. from the centerline and the opposite edge 2 in. from center. This way I can drill holes 1½ in. or 2 in. away from an edge. I use a 3/8-in. Forstner bit to counterbore the center row of pegboard holes slightly so that the tip of a self-centering bit fits into the recess.

To use the jig, I place it flat against the cabinet side with one edge against the

9-26
To install the hinges, I drill a 35mm flat-bottomed hole in the door for each hinge with a special 35mm bit.

9-27
I insert one part of the hinge in the hole and attach it with screws. I attach the mating part of the hinge inside the cabinet and install the door.

back of the cabinet to space the holes 1½ or 2 in. away from the back as shown in the plan (*drawings 9-B, 9-E, and 9-F*). Then I drill one hole 9/16 in. deep with my self-centering bit. I insert a 1/4-in.-dia. dowel through the jig hole into the hole I just drilled. This holds the jig in place as I drill through the other holes in the jig. When I run out of holes, I simply reposition the dowel and jig and keep on drilling. For the front rows of holes, I position the jig against the front edge of the cabinet so the holes are 2 in. from its front edge (*photo 9-25*).

Cabinet Doors

The cabinet doors are made just like the drawer fronts — tongue-and-grooved plywood panels with mitered oak edging all around (*drawing 9-A*). The cabinet doors swing on concealed, overlay hinges sometimes referred to as European-style hinges. These hinges are great because they can be adjusted easily to provide a nice even gap around the doors.

To install them, I drill a 35mm flat-bottomed hole in the door for each hinge (*photo 9-26*) with a special 35mm bit that's available from most mail-order catalogs that sell European hinges. I insert one part of the hinge in the hole and attach it with screws. I attach the mating part of the hinge inside the cabinet and install the door (*photo 9-27*), following the instructions that come with the hinges to level and adjust the doors.

Finishing Up

Before I get started with the finish, I have a couple of hours of sanding to do. It's times like this when I'm thankful for my random-orbit sander. Since it doesn't leave scratches when I sand across the grain, it really speeds the task of sanding the mitered panels and the face frame of the bookcase. I remove the dust with a vacuum and tack cloth, and I'm ready to finish.

The challenge I face in coming up with a finish for this storage unit is to end up with something so tough and durable that even a student can't destroy it. I start with a coat of sanding sealer. After that's dry, I give it a light sanding with 220-grit paper and at least 2 coats of a tough gloss polyurethane. Now that's a piece of furniture any child (or parent) will be proud to own.

index

Page numbers in italics refer to photographs; those in boldface refer to the drawings.

W

the new yankee workshop project index

All of the projects in the five *New Yankee Workshop* books are listed below:

(CL): *Classics from the New Yankee Workshop*
(KS): *The New Yankee Workshop Kids' Stuff*
(MS): *Mostly Shaker from the New Yankee Workshop*

(NY): *The New Yankee Workshop*
(OP): *The New Yankee Workshop Outdoor Projects*